Cambridge Studies in Social Anthropology

General Editor: Jack Goody

56

THE MAKING OF GREAT MEN

For other titles in this series turn to page 253

This book is published as part of the joint publishing agreement established in 1977 between the Fondation de la Maison des Sciences de l'Homme and the Press Syndicate of the University of Cambridge. Titles published under this arrangement may appear in any European language or, in the case of volumes of collected essays, in several languages.

New books will appear either as individual titles or in one of the series which the Maison des Sciences de l'Homme and the Cambridge University Press have jointly agreed to publish. All books published jointly by the Maison des Sciences del l'Homme and the Cambridge University Press will be distributed by the Press throughout the world.

Cet ouvrage est publié dans le cadre de l'accord de co-édition passé en 1977 entre la Fondation de la Maison des Sciences de l'Homme et le Press Syndicate de l'Université de Cambridge. Toutes les langues européennes sont admises pour les titres couverts par cet accord, et les ouvrages collectifs peuvent paraître en plusieurs langues.

Les ouvrages paraissent soit isolément, soit dans l'une des séries que la Maison des Sciences de l'Homme et Cambridge University Press ont convenu de publier ensemble. La distribution dans le monde entier des titres ainsi publiés conjointement par les deux établissements est assurée par Cambridge University Press.

The making of great men

Male domination and power among the New Guinea Baruya

MAURICE GODELIER

Translated by Rupert Swyer

The right of the
University of Cambridge
to print and sell
all manner of books
was granted by
Henry VIII in 1534.
The University has printed
and published continuously
since 1584.

CAMBRIDGE UNIVERSITY PRESS
Cambridge
New York   New Rochelle   Melbourne   Sydney

and

EDITIONS DE LA MAISON DES SCIENCES DE L'HOMME
Paris

Published by the Press Syndicate of the University of Cambridge
The Pitt Building, Trumpington Street, Cambridge CB2 1RP
32 East 57th Street, New York, NY 10022, USA
10 Stamford Road, Oakleigh, Melbourne 3166, Australia
and
Editions de la Maison des Sciences de l'Homme
54 Boulevard Raspail, 75270 Paris, Cedex 06

Originally published in French as *La production des grands hommes*
by Librairie Arthème Fayard, Paris, 1982 and © 1982

First published in English by the Maison des Sciences de l'Homme and
Cambridge University Press, 1986 as *The Making of Great Men: Male
Domination and Power among the New Guinea Baruya*.
English translation © Maison des Sciences de l'Homme and Cambridge University
Press 1986
Reprinted 1987

Printed in the United States of America

Library of Congress Cataloging in Publication Data
Godelier, Maurice.
The making of great men.
(Cambridge studies in social anthropology ; 56)
Translation of: La production des grands hommes.
Bibliography: p.
Includes index.
1. Baruya (Papuan people) – Social life and customs.
I. Title.   II. Series: Cambridge studies in social
anthropology ; no. 56.
DU740.42.G6213   1986   306'.0899912   85–5711

British Library Cataloging in Publication applied for

ISBN 0 521 25917 7 hard covers
       0 521 31212 4 paperback
France only:
       2 7351 0136 3 hard covers
       2 7351 0137 8 paperback

To my parents.

To Warineu, Kandavatche, Djirinac, and Ambiaraiwe, who guided me with patience and intelligence back into the world of their youth, before the arrival of white men.

To the masters of the rituals, Inamwe the great shaman, Tchouonoondaye whose task it was to separate the boys from the world of women, Ypmeie of the Baruya clan who turned them into warriors and men.

To all the Baruya and particularly to Koummaineu, friend and companion for so many years.

Contents

Preface   *page* ix

1 Introduction to Baruya society   1

Part One
   Social hierarchies in Baruya society   7

2 Women's subordinate position   9
   The signs of male domination: bodies, space, gestures   10
   The place of men and women in their various activities   11
   Magic in the production processes   16
   The subordination of women in the production of relations
   of kinship   19
   One woman equals one woman   23
   A last look at the principle of female equivalence   28

3 The institution and legitimization of male superiority:
   initiations and the separation of the sexes   31
   The male life cycle   31
   The woman's life cycle   40
   Are the women's initiations genuine initiations?   46
   The Baruya vision of the process of the reproduction of life;
   the significance of bodily substances   51
   Female powers and the ambivalence of woman   63

Part Two
   The production of great men: powers inherited,
   powers merited   77

4 Male hierarchies   79

vii

Contents

Hereditary status and interlineage hierarchies:
the *kwaimatnie*-owners 81
Warriors, shamans, cassowary hunters: status for the taking 96

5 The discovery of great men 100
The *aoulatta:* the great warrior 103
The *koulaka:* the shaman 112
The *kayareumala:* the cassowary hunter 126
The *tsaimaye:* the salt maker 130

6 General view of Baruya social hierarchies 136

7 The nature of man/woman relations among the Baruya:
violence and consent, resistance and repression 141
Forms of female resistance and rebellion 149
Male violence and repression 151

8 Great men societies, big men societies: two alternative
logics of society 162
The paradigm of the big man 163

Part Three
Recent transformations of Baruya society 189

9 The colonial order and independence 191

Conclusion 225

10 The ventriloquist's dummy 227

Bibliography 239
Index 245

Twelve unnumbered pages of photographs appear between pp. 188 and 189.

viii

Preface

This book is about power, primarily that of one sex over another: the power of men among the Baruya, a mountain tribe in the interior of New Guinea, that immense island north of Australia better known to the French as Papua.

Until 1960, the Baruya were self-governing and their society was one of those that our own calls primitive, because it lacked those two pillars of "civilization," namely, classes and the state. In 1960, Australia decided that the time had come for it to civilize the Baruya, and it extended the power of its state over them. To bring them peace, it undertook to "pacify" them and, having pacified them, it set about governing them.

Before 1951, the Baruya had never seen a white person; yet without being aware of it, they had already become materially, economically dependent upon them. This dependence had begun a decade earlier. On a visit to a tribe with which they regularly bartered their salt for stone implements, they first laid eyes on fine steel axes and machetes, probably made in Sheffield or Solingen. Nobody had been able to explain who had manufactured these marvels, but they enthusiastically adopted them. Without giving the matter another thought, they flung their stone and bamboo tools, with which their ancestors used to clear forest, into that selfsame forest, or abandoned them in their gardens. Therefore, as with many tribes living in "inaccessible" regions, their material subordination to the world of the white man predated their political and ideological subordination, and this material subordination has never ceased to grow, even though their country has been independent since 1975.

By 1951, however, they had already been made aware of the presence of the white man. One day they had looked up into the sky, terrified, as two huge birds tore out of the sky, spitting fire at each other, then chased each other over the horizon to the east. This must have been an episode in the Battle of the Pacific, toward the end of World War II. A little later, the Baruya learned from a distant tribe, to which they had traveled in order to obtain steel axes, that inside the belly of these firebirds lived beings of human aspect, but with a different skin.

The Baruya governed themselves with neither ruling class nor state until 1960, although inequalities existed. One part of society, the men, governed the other, the women; it was not that they ruled society without the women, but against them. So the classless Baruya join the long list of societies that already attest inequality between the sexes. The subordination, oppression, even exploitation of women are social facts, whose origins lie not in the emergence of classes but predate them and are different in nature; male domination consolidated and renewed itself in a thousand different ways with the myriad forms of exploitation of man by man in a society that preceded our own. Needless to say, there is no good reason why things in classless societies should happen everywhere, or even in general, as they have among the Baruya. At any event, there is good reason to study a classless society whose mechanisms and ideas condition and legitimize in other forms the male domination that exists in our own society.

The Baruya social order, however, does not reduce itself to the equality of all men among themselves relative to the women. For the same mechanisms that establish this equality work simultaneously, and just as much, to produce certain men who stand out from the rest and rise above them. Some do so by virtue of their exceptional skill in activities that everybody is supposed to perform, such as war and agriculture; others become "great" by virtue of their special ability to perform functions useful to all but accessible to only a few, those who display the requisite gifts (shamanism) or who inherit the exclusive right to perform them (e.g., initiation rites). Needless to say, it is one thing to become "great" through inheritance of a function that makes one great because of one's lineage and ancestors, and quite another to become so through personal worthiness, a distinction that nobody can gain through inheritance alone. But whether inherited or merited, certain positions of power do exist in Baruya society, and these form a social hierarchy distinct from men's general dominance over women. It is a complex hierarchy, which rests upon, amplifies, and has its roots in this dominance, although it is not coterminous with it. The making of "great men" is therefore the vital complement and capstone of male domination: the central argument of this book.

This is not to say that the Baruya are utterly lacking in women who are widely regarded as "greater" than the others, and, the men confidentially admit, greater even than many of themselves. What is unthinkable is the idea that any woman could be as great as the great men, the great warriors, or the great shamans. The only sphere in which superiority might have been possible – shamanism, the only area in which the two sexes cooperate and compete in a common activity that is useful to society as a whole – is so conceived and organized that the female shamans are excluded on principle from the most arduous and glorious magical struggles, namely, those aimed at enemy tribes; and above all, it is not in the power of any female shaman to initiate others.

Two types of inequality thus combine to create order in the social life of the Baruya: inequalities between men and women on the one hand, and among men themselves on the other. The term *inequality* implies powers and privileges for certain members of the tribe. One striking feature of Baruya social organization, however, is the absence of direct links between power and wealth. Wealth does not give its owner power, and power does not bring with it wealth. The contrast between this society and ours is obvious; the contrast is more striking with all those New Guinea societies ruled by "big men," those important men who have risen above their fellows primarily thanks to their impressive ability to produce and/or accumulate wealth in terms of pigs, shells, and so forth, and to distribute it with calculated generosity, each thus gathering around him a group of loyal retainers, under obligation to help him aggrandize his name while hoping to share in his glory and largesse, by supporting him with their goods and services.

The problem is whether or not there is some deep-seated reason preventing wealth and power from combining in the Baruya's social structure. I believe that there is such a reason, and that it lies mainly in the principle that governs the social aspect of the reproduction of life, that is, relations of kinship in their society. In contrast to many other societies in Melanesia and elsewhere, only a woman is worth another woman, and cannot be exchanged for pigs or other forms of material wealth when two groups wish to ally and ensure their reproduction. The entire development of certain forms of power and wealth is ruled out by the governing principle of relations of kinship. Perhaps this instance may give us some insight, by way of contrast and through its negative aspects, into some of the conditions that have led to the formation of classes and the breakup of community societies elsewhere.

The last feature that we have chosen to study, in which the Baruya transcend their particularity, is the role that sexuality plays in their thought and theories, acting as a kind of cosmic foundation of women's subordinate position, and of even the oppression that they endure.

In their view, every aspect of male domination, whether (to resort to our own categories) economic, political, or symbolic, can be explained by sexuality and by the different position that each sex occupies in the process of the reproduction of life. To be sure, similar attitudes can be found in our own culture, among those who regard the subordination and oppression of women as "natural." But I must point out straightaway that the concept of nature as it exists in our society is unknown to the Baruya; they do not place men on the side of culture and women on that of nature, but rather the contrary.

However, as in our own culture, sexuality – the differences of form, substance, and bodily function, the anatomical and physiological differences that arise from the different functions of the sexes in the process of the reproduction of life – supplies a steady stream of material from which are fashioned the messages and explanations that serve to interpret and justify the social inequalities between men and women. It is as if sexuality were constantly being solicited to occupy every nook and cranny of society, to act as a language to express, and as a reason to legitimize, facts of a (mainly) different order. Although one is right in thinking that the existence and diversity of male domination in many societies stem not from a single cause but from many, and that they rest upon more than one basis, one does wonder what it is that pushes sexuality and human sexual differences to the forefront of social consciousness, of conscious thought and language, making them bear witness to and justify inequalities that are of an essentially different order.

For in what society is sexuality not ubiquitous, carrying its load of fantasies wherever it goes? Yet it may be, as our analysis of the Baruya suggests, that sexuality only breeds fantasies when asked to do so, when forced to fabricate messages and hold forth on facts whose origins lie elsewhere and transcend it, when sexuality starts to serve as sign and meaning for things that in fact bear no relation to it. Over and beyond the twists and turns of desire of the other and the self, the visible dominance of sexuality seems to be a kind of dissembled confession of its invisible subordination to other relations between men and women within the overall logic underlying the workings of each society. Indeed, one sometimes wonders whether psychoanalysis – which in our culture claims to be the rigorous study of sexuality and desire – really does perceive all the extraneous elements in sexuality. Yet without listening, and without an attempt to decipher the signals thus heard, its theoretical discourse is liable to produce nothing more than mythology, as convincing, and as unconvincing, as the Baruya myths.

The three main themes of this book will be the machinery of male domination, the production of great men, and the ideological justifications of this social order. I could have written a different book about the Baruya, several even, and I intend to do so. I owe it to the Baruya in the first place, to those who have encouraged me, and lastly to myself. If I have chosen to devote this first book to the relations between men and women and male domination, rather than to a study of relations of kinship or land tenure, it is because the former involves the major social contradiction in their system to my way of thinking. Furthermore, it is no longer possible to ignore male domination in our own society, or to remain indifferent to the real struggles of those men and women who wish to put an end to it. Like many others, I long believed that it was first necessary to fight for the abolition of class relations, and that all the rest – oppression between the sexes, races, nations – would unravel or be resolved once these class relations had been abolished. It was a scientifically false vision of classes, races, and the sexes, a politically conservative

xii

vision which, in the name of revolution, justified us in turning a blind eye to and doing nothing about all these other forms of domination and oppression; they could and should await their turn. Needless to say, analysis of a single case, the Baruya or any other, is not in itself sufficient to build an explanation of the forms and reasons for male domination in the history of humanity. Many empirical studies are necessary. But these will only acquire their full importance after we have become better able to state the problems and formulate the relevant questions. Such progress might be achieved by leaps and bounds on the occasion of one or another of these studies.

My choice of theme and ideological background also stems from my desire to write for a wider public than that of my fellow anthropologists. It is a risky undertaking, liable to end up as neither fish nor fowl, too technical for some yet insufficiently precise for others. I must therefore rely on the indulgence of all.

One may easily imagine, on reading these pages, just how much time and confidence it must have taken on the part of the Baruya to introduce me to their way of thinking and allow me to see (as they themselves expressed it) not only the leaves, branches, and the trunk, but also some of the most secretly buried roots of their thought. I must ask the reader who may sometimes be tempted, according to the lights of his or her own philosophy or mood, to regard the secrets confided to me by the Baruya as derisory, grotesque, or even obscene, to remember that for them they are an essential part of their identity, a vital, sacred force inherited from the past, on which they depend in order to withstand all those voluntary or involuntary pressures that our world brings to bear upon them, often enough in perfectly good faith, but more often still deliberately. An anthropologist cannot side with those who, deliberately or unaware, despite and/or destroy the society that they wish to know and make known. Knowledge is not a game without consequences. Every society has secrets that it protects and that protect it. To hand them carelessly over to the public without debate or precaution would not merely be treacherous or irresponsible, but would actually pervert the work of scientific investigation into a force of aggression and domination.

The Baruya did not tell me everything, and I promised them not to divulge all they told me. What I have withheld, the reader will have guessed, relates to the men's efforts, strenuously hidden from the women, to produce great men without women's intervention. It is indeed one of the contradictions of social science; for to keep silent is to side with the men against the women, whereas to put these things down in writing is already tantamount to weakening the power of those men who agreed to pass on to a stranger, a friend and a man like themselves, what they still wish to conceal from their womenfolk. Such contradictions are inevitable; we can neither ignore them nor abolish them, and they must be allowed to pursue their course. The anthropologist cannot avoid speaking out and acting, both in the societies that he

xiii

studies and in his own. But he should never act and speak for others in the society that welcomes him as a guest, just as in his own society he cannot allow others to speak and act in his place. To these opposing demands there is no simple solution.

Understandably it took a good deal of time and money and material resources to learn these things. France is a long way from New Guinea, and the Baruya do not live near the capital of their country, Port Moresby. I should like to take this opportunity of thanking those public and private institutions that have helped me to complete my work: the Centre National de Recherche Scientifique, Paris, to begin with, which generously granted the bulk of the funding necessary for my frequent visits to the field since my first visit in 1967; the Wenner-Gren Foundation, which on two occasions facilitated otherwise impossible undertakings; and, lastly, the Maison des Sciences de l'Homme in Paris, which has ever been ready to lend a hand in sorting out otherwise inextricable situations. And, in the name of the Baruya, I should like to thank the Fyssen and Polignac foundations for having generously responded to the tribe's appeal, conveyed through me, and helped me to purchase its first truck, after it had completed construction of the mountain road which for the first time linked it directly to the rest of the world.

In 1975, I invited a young anthropologist, Jean-Luc Lory, to join me in the field to help me complete my study on kinship and land tenure. He subsequently developed a keen interest in shamanism and discovered certain important facts from which I in turn have benefited. Then, in 1979, Pierre Lemonnier, a specialist in the study of technologies, joined the team for a more extensive and more detailed study of the material conditions of the Baruya, which I had already started to explore. Today, both are engaged in the huge task of comparing the social structures of all the Anga tribes on the basis of what we know of the Baruya, and I expect their findings to recast my own outlook.

I must say that this book, however imperfect it may be, would never have reached its present form and balance without Marie-Elisabeth Handman, its first reader, who devoted much of her time to tidying up the style and harmonizing its internal proportions.

Needless to say, though, research is more than just a question of material or inellectual matters. In a country such as New Guinea, however much things may have changed since 1967, one still needs a guide, a place to sleep, a timely helping hand, and the list of all those who helped me when I was in need is too long for inclusion here: Europeans and New Guineans, missionaries and civil servants, doctors and carpenters. I should like also to thank the government of Papua New Guinea which has smoothed the path of my research program since independence.

Lastly, I address my concluding remarks to the Baruya, to those dozens, hundreds even among them, who at some time or other gave me a fragment of the substance of this book, or deployed their ingenuity to alleviate some of the hardships of life in the bush, to which a white man will never become wholly accustomed.

1

Introduction to Baruya society

This chapter is merely intended to sketch in the outlines of Baruya society. Later chapters analyze the essential aspects of their social organization in greater detail: the division of labor, property, relations of kinship, male and female initiation, and warfare; in all cases from the standpoint of relations between men and women.

In September 1979, the Baruya numbered 2,159 individuals spread among 17 scattered villages and hamlets, at an altitude of between 1,600 and 2,300 meters along two high valleys, Wonenara and Marawaka, in a chain of mountains, the Kratke Range, whose tallest peak is Mount Piora (3,720 meters). This region was the last in the Eastern Highlands province of New Guinea to pass under the control of the Australian colonial administration, in June 1960. It was first explored in 1951 by a young officer, James Sinclair who, having heard talk of a tribe, the Batia, renowned for the salt that it made and traded with its neighbors, had mounted an expedition to seek them out. These Batia were none other than the Baruya. Yet it was not until 1960 that the Australian administration decided to set up a reconnaissance and control post at Wonenara. In 1965, the region was declared pacified and open to free movement for white men.

By their language, material culture, and social organization, the Baruya belong to a distinct collection of tribes or local groups long referred to by certain of their neighbors by a term of insult, which has become widespread since its adoption by the Australian administration. This term, *Kukakuka*, is not employed by the Baruya themselves. In their language, *Kuka* means "to steal," "thief." Today, linguists, missionaries, and anthropologists are striving to have this offensive term struck from official documents and parlance, and propose to replace it by that of *Anga,* which in all the languages of this vast ethnic grouping signifies "house." It may not be altogether satisfactory to call all these groups Anga, but it is surely better than calling them "thieves."

Linguistically, the Anga groups as a whole are unrelated to the Melanesian

1

Figure 1. Territory and languages of the Anga tribes

languages spoken by the coastal tribes of Papua and New Guinea, but it may one day be possible to link them to the phylum of non-Austronesian languages spoken in the interior of New Guinea. This matter will be for the linguists to decide; for the time being they lack the necessary evidence to conclude one way or another. Whatever the final word on the origins and groupings, we do know today, thanks to the work of Richard Lloyd, that the Anga populations speak some eleven languages among them. [Figure 1] According to glottochronology, these took more than a thousand years to differentiate among themselves, starting from a common root-language; certain of them, however, such as Langamar, diverge considerably from the others. The striking thing about the distribution of these languages is the wide disparity in the number of speakers. The most widely spoken are the Kapau and Menye languages, the first spoken by 30,000, the second by at least 12,000 people, whereas the least-spoken, Kawacha, probably has fewer than 50 speakers today. The Baruya rank fourth, well behind Kapau and Menye, with

5,248 speakers who include the Baruya themselves and seven small tribes who are their more or less immediate neighbors.

The extent of difference in the number of people speaking these languages reflects an event that helps to explain the history of the Baruya themselves, namely, the impressive expansion of the Kapau and Menye groups to the detriment of their neighbors, some of whom have disappeared entirely. In all, over 70,000 individuals probably speak these eleven languages and share a culture. For the most part they live in the northern part of a vast, extremely rugged expanse of territory stretching from the Vailala River in the west to the Bulolo River to the east, and from the Watut River in the north to a point some miles from Karema on the Gulf of Papua coast in the south. We still do not know how many local groups occupy this huge tract of land, for some of them, east of the Vailala River, live in a remote, almost inaccessible region and have never properly been studied. All these groups, however, are reputed to live in a state of perpetual warfare, and their raids used to sow fear and even panic. Some of them, in the Wau and Bulolo area, actually killed the first Europeans to enter their territory in search of gold, and subsequently put up armed resistance to expeditions sent by the Australian administration to pacify them and obtain their submission.

These facts shed light on the history of the Baruya and agree with many features of their oral traditions and those of their neighbors. The Baruya claim descent from a group of refugees called Baruyandalie. They split off from the Yoyue tribe when their native village, a place called Bravegareubaramandeuc, situated three days' walk from Marawaka, not far from Menyamya, was burned and some inhabitants, the Baragaye, were massacred by others with the help of an enemy tribe, the Tapache. These Tapache were themselves pushed by other groups: the Mouontdalie – evidence that there was a general expansion of the Menye (Menyamya) and Kapau (south of Menyamya). The Baruya refugees did the same themselves later on, when they seized the territory of the Andje who had given them hospitality, and forced them to flee farther, and in their turn to drive out yet other groups. Thus by degrees Anga groups expanded toward the northwest through the process of war and uprooting of populations which periodically gave birth to new local groups or tribes, resulting from new combinations of ancient, but now splintered, groups; in order to commemorate their emergence, these groups gave themselves new names.

According to our estimates, the flight of Baragaye refugees to Marawaka must have taken place around the end of the eighteenth century. Their descendants gradually swelled in numbers until they decided to grab the territory of the local groups that had given them shelter. They achieved their goal with the complicity of one of these groups, the Ndelie, who belonged to the Andje tribe and who also betrayed their own folk. A new tribe thus arose; it took the name of one of the clans of the victorious refugees, the Baruya clan,

3

and absorbed certain lineages of the vanquished local groups, generally lineages or segments of lineages to which the refugees had given women. Finally, in the early twentieth century, the Baruya gradually penetrated the neighboring valley of Wonenara, driving out its inhabitants. These also belonged to the Anga linguistic group and they now constitute, together with the Baruya, the northwestern frontier groups of the Anga. Beyond stretch the territories of the Aziana, Awa, Tairora, Fore, and other tribes whose languages and cultures are profoundly different. Anthropologists such as K. E. Read, J. B. Watson, L. L. Langness, R. Salisbury, and others consider them to be variants of a mode of social organization specific to the Eastern Highlands.

The social organization of the Baruya may briefly be described as an acephalous tribe consisting of fifteen clans, eight of which descend from the Menyamya refugees and seven of which were absorbed from local groups. The clans are divided into lineages, which are themselves segmented. Residence is patrilocal, and it seems that originally each lineage dwelt together in a separate place. But continual vendettas, the possibility and (on occasion) the urgent need to go live with one's affines (relatives by marriage) or with one's maternal kinsmen, have led to coexistence and interdigitation around a central core of segments of lineages belonging to different clans.

The Baruya live at the foot of slopes covered with vast tracts of primary forest (tropical rain forests) and secondary forest. The latter consists of the vegetation that grows in the taro gardens, which are generally cultivated at an altitude of between 1,800 and 2,300 meters and are left fallow for periods of between fifteen and twenty-five years. Below 2,000 meters, the forest increasingly gives way to grassy savanna, most of which results from over-intensive cultivation scorched by the populations whom the Baruya ousted after their arrival. Before the advent of steel tools the savanna, choked by tall tough grass (*Imperata cylindrica*) was left untouched. In those days, the Baruya had nothing but bamboo swords and stakes to cut the grass and uproot clumps and stumps. Today, with their shovels and machetes, they can reclaim this once unproductive land. Furthermore, now that the tribal wars which formerly made it essential to perch villages on top of steep, almost inaccessible hills have ceased, there is a general trend to locate villages and gardens below in the warmer zones. The region lies 3° from the equator. Rainfall is heavy and seasonal variations fairly sharp. Temperatures vary considerably between night and day owing to the altitude. The midday temperature of 30° centigrade often falls to 8° or 9° centigrade at night. Horticulture is the main economic activity, supplemented by pig breeding and a sizable output of vegetable salt. Salt is filtered and crystallized into bars weighing approximately three to four pounds, and used to serve as a means of exchange or currency. Until around 1940, the Baruya used several different types of adzes fitted with polished stone blades to hack away the forest or manufacture their weapons and implements. They used bone chisels, bamboo knives, and string bags woven from vegetable fibers. However, as we have seen, in the decade preceding the arrival of the first white man the steel ax and machete made their appearance among the Baruya, trickling through the channels of intertribal trade in the opposite direction to their salt bars. Without any outside encouragement or pressure, the Baruya then considerably stepped up their production of salt in order to substitute these new means of production for their traditional stone tools. However, this substitution was not completed by 1951 when Jim Sinclair's patrol set foot on their territory.

Their essential crop is the sweet potato, which is cultivated relatively intensively in the deforested areas surrounding the villages and in the secondary forests. The taro comes quite a long way behind in terms of diet, but is a plant of the first importance from the ceremonial and social standpoints. It is grown in the primary forest on newly cleared land or in irrigated gardens. Their techniques of draining waterlogged land and of irrigation by means of channels, and even by means of conduits made of bamboo or hollowed pandanus trunks laid end to end, and of light terracing following the relief of the land, temporarily halting soil erosion on steep slopes, are evidence that the Baruya are familiar with intensive forms of agriculture, even if they tend to prefer slash-and-burn horticulture and scratching the soil with a digging stick. Hunting and gathering play a minimal role in subsistence, but have great ceremonial importance.

Ownership of the land is collective in the sense that all the descendants of a common ancestor are joint owners of the land cleared by that ancestor. Everywhere cordyline bushes planted by the first men to clear the land stake out the boundaries of their property. Land-use patterns are flexible, however. Anyone can easily obtain permission from his maternal kin or his wife's brothers to use a parcel of their land for a garden on the understanding that he will render them the same service if asked. Women retain the right to use their ancestor's land through their lifetime, but they do not inherit it and, consequently, cannot hand it on to their children.

The social division of labor governs the material activities of the Baruya, that is, hunting, gathering, horticulture, pig breeding, salt production, the manufacture of weapons, implements, clothing, adornments, house building, and so on, indicating with great precision what each person can and must do according to sex and age. We shall analyze this division of labor later. Each Baruya is capable of doing, more or less successfully, all that is expected of him or her, but certain individuals, especially in activities with an artistic content, such as the manufacture of adornments, stand out from the rest by their taste and skill. Among men, this is so in the wickerwork headpieces into which they stick their feathers, and for the women, in the making of string bags and fiber bracelets which they dye and hand out among themselves and to the men.

5

One activity not covered by the simple sexual division of labor but that really does amount to a specialized handicraft, is the production of salt from the ashes of a plant cultivated for this purpose. The most complex operations, namely, evaporation and crystallization, are performed by men who have learned the technical and magical secrets involved from one of their relatives or neighbors.

These tasks are performed either individually or collectively, depending on their difficulty, on their degree of urgency, and on the material means of production available to the Baruya. For instance, all the men in a village cooperate to clear the primary forest in the appropriate season for planting taro, and the women join forces to go and gather and carry the straw needed to thatch houses. As we shall see, this cooperation involves a network of social relations, primarily those of kinship (more those of affinity than of consanguinity), followed by those of neighborhood and coresidence.

PART ONE

Social hierarchies in Baruya society

2

Women's subordinate position

When I first visited the Baruya, in 1967, walking from village to village by day and sleeping at night in the men's house, which stands at the top of each village and where the initiates live, what struck me immediately were the signs that there existed a dual hierarchy: between men and women on the one hand, and between those men who were admiringly pointed out to me as great warriors, *aoulatta,* and the rest.

Signs of women's subordination to men were plentiful, but the most spectacular was the scene I witnessed over and over again along the trail each time a man passed by or overtook a woman or group of women. The women would stop at once, turn their heads, and if one of their hands was free, quickly draw a flap of their bark cloak across their faces. The man would walk on without a glance at them, and the women would resume their journey.

Sometimes though a handful of young initiates would stop short at the sight of a group of women rounding a corner, and plunge into the undergrowth on either side of the trail to hide. If this spot offered no hiding place, they would freeze where they were, turn their backs to the trail, hiding their faces beneath their cloaks just as the women did when men passed by. At that time, all men, young and old, still went about armed with their bow, steel ax, and machete, and the men's houses were chock full of boys and young men who frequently spent part of their day practicing their archery skills and comparing their performances.

I also discovered that the Australian administration was interested in finding out the exact number and names of the great warriors, whom it referred to in its census figures as fight leaders and suspected of possessing powers capable of working either for or against it. Indeed, it had already appointed some of them *luluai* or *tultul,* that is, appointed to represent the Baruya in dealings with the central authorities. In other words, some of the war chiefs had become pseudo-headmen of the village.

Social hierarchies in Baruya society

In 1981, women still frequently stopped to let men pass, but few, apart from the old women, still hid their faces. The great warriors were old or dead. Men rarely went about carrying their bow. Many children, including some girls, went to school each day, and the young men spent more time on the coastal rubber or copra plantations than on archery. Still, many years spent with the Baruya since 1967 have merely confirmed my initial impressions, while enabling me to discover other, more complex though less visible hierarchies, whose architecture I shall be describing below.

The signs of male domination: bodies, space, gestures

There are abundant outward signs of men's dominance over women. First among these are the bodily adornments, the fact that among the Baruya the men are the fair sex. On their brow they wear a red headband, the color of the Sun, of whom the Baruya claim to be the sons. They decorate their heads with different feathers depending on their stage of initiation and function; an eagle's feather, for example, signifies a shaman. The loincloth [*pulpul* in pidgin] takes the form of an enormous sporran covered by numerous reed belts. The women are much dowdier in appearance, and they are forbidden to wear or to touch the men's headfeathers.

Formerly, Baruya territory was crisscrossed by parallel paths, the women's paths lying below the men's ones. The villages themselves were divided into three zones, and this division still persists. Dominating the village were one or more men's houses, surrounded by a palisade marking off the area strictly forbidden to women. The men's house is where the boys live after having been taken away from their mothers for purposes of initiation at around the age of nine or ten. They remain here until around twenty or twenty-one, when they will marry. Married men return to sleep in the men's house whenever their wives give birth or menstruate. Right at the bottom of the village, in a coppice or patch of undergrowth, the women give birth to their children beneath shelters of leaves and branches, which they burn after use. This spot is strictly forbidden to men, and whenever anyone suggests that they try to set foot here they refuse to do so, displaying their disgust by a series of shouts, strident laughter, and foot-stamping that in our culture would be taken as a sign of hysteria.

A men's house is a vast edifice, the largest in the village, sturdy, built to last, with a bouquet to indicate its function to visitors. The menstrual huts built by the women, on the other hand, consist of branches cut and bent over to form a lean-to, onto which clumps of grass are thrown. That is sufficient for a few days. Women bury the placenta and stillborn babes or those they do not wish to keep in the nearby undergrowth.

Between these high and low places in the villages lies a bisexual area, containing houses in which families live together, the family consisting of

10

husband, his wife or wives, his unmarried daughters and uninitiated sons. But the moment one enters a house, one finds that the segregation of the sexes is reproduced once again. The interior is divided by an imaginary line passing through the middle of the hearth, which stands in the center of the circular floor. The wife and her children live and sleep in the semicircle closest to the door. On the other side, beyond the hearth, lies the husband's area, and this is where all men entering the house are supposed to take up their position. A woman must avoid entering the male part of the house, and in no case may she walk across the hearth, as her vagina would be liable to open over the fire, which serves to cook food destined for the man's mouth. The hearth itself is built by the men from the husband's lineage, his father and brothers, who kindle the first fire there, like the Sun, in Baruya mythology, which gave to men the primordial fire. It is men too, the husband's coinitiates, who build the newlyweds' home and top off the roof with four or five pointed sticks known as *nilamaye,* "Sun flowers," placing the building beneath the protection of the Sun, which is the father of all the Baruya.

But we need to look beyond these outward signs, adornments, bodily attitudes, areas, and gestures permitted or forbidden, and to analyze the place accorded by the norms of Baruya society to men or women in the various activities that produce their material and social existence.

The place of men and women in their various activities

Access to the means of production and to the means of destruction

Land tenure of either farm or hunting land, which is the primary condition of existence, is in the hands of the men, who transmit it from one to the other.[1] Wives, their sisters, or their daughters have no part in this. Women do, however, retain lifetime use-rights over the lands of their ancestors, but as I have already pointed out, they never inherit them.

The manufacture of weapons and implements is an exclusively male activity, just as the manufacture of salt and the task of going to trade it for stone blades or the black palm wood with which they used to make their tools and bows were reserved for the men.

Even the digging stick, the women's essential tool for planting and harvesting, is not made by the women themselves. A father will make it for his daughter, a husband for his wife, and give it to her. As men, they naturally possess the necessary tools, that is, polished stone adzes or, today, steel axes. But this male monopoly over the manufacture of the means of production

[1] Maurice Godelier, "Land Tenure among the Baruya of New Guinea," *Journal of Papua and New Guinea Society* (November–December 1969): 1–15; in collaboration with C. D. Ollier and D. P. Drover, "Soil Knowledge amongst the Baruya of Wonenara, New Guinea," *Oceania* 42 (1) (September 1971): 33–41.

makes the women both materially and socially dependent on the men. Obviously, women would be perfectly capable of going and cutting a branch of hardwood and sharpening it into a point if they were socially permitted to do so. Indeed, all the women now use machetes given to them by their husbands or fathers to cut firewood, but they do not use them to make their own digging sticks.

Women are thus excluded from land ownership, the manufacture and control of tools, hence of the material means of production. Nor do they have the right to own or use weapons such as clubs, shields, or bows and arrows, since war and hunting are men's business. They are also thus excluded from the control and use of means of destruction, in other words, the material means of armed violence. Finally, they are excluded from the production of salt, which even yesterday was the Baruya's principal means of trade – the production and trade in salt with neighboring tribes being absolutely vital to procurement of the material conditions of existence not produced by themselves (including bodily adornments, which in Baruya society are necessary to signify and materialize the status of each individual according to sex, age, and function). The importance of these exchanges for all Baruya, whatever their sex, age, or function, for which the men enjoy exclusive responsibility, is an additional factor of domination over women. Furthermore, men gained prestige from the very real dangers that they ran when going to exchange salt with neighboring tribes, for they were sometimes killed and eaten on the way.

The Baruya, however, were incapable of assuring their own material reproduction alone. An essential part of their physical and social reproduction depended on the existence of a full-blown regional economy, that is, on a division of labor between more or less neighboring tribes, and on a network of trade routes along which each tribe's specialized products could pass from hand to hand, according to commonly accepted procedures.

Needless to say, as in any trade network based on an "international" division of labor, some of the groups in this regional "economy" were practically in a position to procure other people's products without producing anything in return, exploiting their position as middlemen. In general though, each local group specialized in the production or gathering of one or two products, while benefiting from its position as middleman between its neighbors.

The notion that "primitive" tribes were self-sufficient is not applicable to these inland societies in New Guinea, whose subsistence was dependent on horticulture, itself in turn dependent on forest clearance by means of stone tools. For only very few tribes found the types of rock necessary to the manufacture of their implements and their weapons on their own territory. This material necessity forced tribes into a trading network, and in turn imposed certain forms and limitations on political relations and warfare between the tribes. No group could afford to be at war, at any rate not for long, with all its neighbors at once. But since the most important of all material

Women's subordinate position

conditions of production was possession of a territory with varied resources, no group could avoid arming itself and fighting to defend its territory if it came under attack, or to extend it at its neighbors' expense if its resources began to run out. This description indeed characterizes the state of the Baruya's relations with their neighbors. Their ancestors had concluded a kind of everlasting peace agreement with the Youndouye by one day making a hole in a tree trunk in the forest and solemnly exchanging salt for bark cloaks and arrows through the opening. Since that time, the Youndouye have been the Baruya's main partners in the Wonenara Valley. Relations with the Andje, who live on the other frontier, are totally different. It was the Andje who had formerly given shelter to the Baruyan refugees, and it was they who had then driven the latter from their territory. Warfare between the two tribes has never entirely died down. On the other hand, the Baruya were periodically at war or at peace, depending on circumstances, with the other neighboring tribes, that is, the Wantakia, the Usarumpia, and the Yuwarrounatche (see figure 9).

Sex differentiation in the labor processes

Hunting is reserved for men because they own the territory, weapons, and dogs and are familiar with the habits of their game and with trapping techniques. Gathering berries, mushrooms, ferns, ants' eggs, and the like is the women's job. The women sometimes kill rats or fish with their stick or catch field mice with their hands, as children do. But only the women catch frogs and tadpoles, with a kind of net trap that they make themselves. The men could do this job, but do not do so because the social and symbolic significance of tadpole fishing would not allow it. The reason lies in the Baruya belief that the first men were born of the metamorphosis of tadpoles, which were discovered by women. Women therefore existed before men, and made miniature bows, arrows, and clothes which they left at the water's edge. After their departure, the tadpoles came out of the water, took possession of these objects, donned the clothes, and changed into men.

Remaining are several areas of material life, horticulture, stockbreeding, house building, the manufacture of tools, clothes, bags, in a word, all the different kinds of domestic crafts practiced by the Baruya. Here is not the place for an exhaustive list of all the tasks implied by the various labor processes.

What we can say is that, in gardening, men do most of the forest clearance. They fell the trees, lop off the branches of those that they leave standing in the middle of cultivated parcels as reserves of deadwood, split tree trunks into planks in order to build fences to protect their gardens from trampling by wild and domestic pigs. In the savanna gardens, they uproot huge clumps of *pitpit* [pidgin for the reedlike grass *Saccharum*, here *S. edule*] by means of stakes (nowadays spades). They dig irrigation and drainage channels in

13

their taro gardens. They also build small terraces in the irrigated taro patches. Lastly, they clear patches of forest to plant pandanus trees and gather their fruit, which ripens up to fifteen meters above the ground. In the villages, near their houses, they plant clumps of bamboo and betel or areca trees.

The women, meanwhile, clear away the undergrowth, after the trees have been felled to make way for a garden in the forest. They burn branches lopped by the men, plant and weed the garden, gather and carry tubers and vegetables, which they then cook. They raise pigs, which they feed with part of what they gather in their gardens. They cultivate reeds, using them to make *pulpuls* (loincloths) for themselves and members of their families. They also make the fiber-string bags which they and the men carry. They gather the straw used to thatch houses, but it is the men who fashion the frame, floor, and hearth and who thatch the roof. Women generally carry children, food, kindling wood, the stakes used to fence the gardens once the men have split them and left them lying around in the forest. Whenever the men go off into the mountains on a big hunt, which may last several weeks, the women regularly bring them food, either cooked or ready for cooking.

Finally, theirs is the exclusive task of bringing up children and preparing food for the family. Each evening, they send their initiate sons a bag of food, which a younger brother or sister carries as far as the barrier leading to the men's house.

Comparing the tasks reserved for men with those reserved for women, we find that the women's tasks:

a. require less physical strength, or to be more precise, do not entail a great deal of physical effort in a short space of time (as does felling a tree);
b. involve fewer risks of accident (many men are killed climbing the trees to pollard them, gather their fruit, or winkle out opossums, the principal game);
c. require less mutual help or cooperation among individuals – the women work alone much more than the men, carrying out generally more monotonous, routine tasks (gathering sweet potatoes, feeding the pigs, cooking, gathering deadwood).

Indeed, it is to these differences that Baruya men refer when describing women's tasks as inferior to theirs and unworthy of them, even while willingly acknowledging that they are indispensable and supplement their own work. Needless to say, Baruya women could – even if taking a little longer than the men – fell trees with an ax, dig ditches, shoot with a bow and arrow, but socially they do not have the right to do so or to learn the appropriate techniques. It needs to be pointed out that nothing in their education gives them, if not the resolve, at least the urge to do so. So the division of labor among the Baruya cannot account for men's social dominance, since it presupposes it. This is a theoretical remark valid for all societies, and it shows just how erroneous it is to try to deduce, as some have done, relations of production from the social division of labor.

Any social division of labor is in fact the outcome of the relation of two

14

types of factor: on the one hand, the forces of production (the material and intellectual means at a society's disposal in order to act on nature) and, on the other, relations between social groups and the material conditions of their existence, that is, as much with the surrounding nature as with the means available to them to act upon it.

Distributing the fruits of labor

The means of subsistence, agricultural produce, *pulpul,* and bark cloaks are apportioned equally between men and women.

As regards the tools necessary to perform her tasks, for example, knives, machetes, kitchen utensils, and digging sticks, a woman usually has all she needs, made or bought for her by her father or husband. Once something has been given her, it is hers to keep. Woe to the man who tries to take back from one of his wives a tool that he has given to her in order to give it to another one! A fearful row would ensue, ending in violence.

Matters differ when it comes to sharing game, pig meat, and money. At a girl's first menstruation, or when a married woman gives birth, the men are obliged to go into the forest to hunt and to present her with a large quantity of game. She consumes part of it herself, distributing the rest to the women to whom she has obligations of kinship or friendship. But the men often go off to hunt for themselves, discreetly eating their catch in the forest or back in the men's house. The women know this, and during the female initiations older women exhort the younger not to nag their menfolk about it.

With pig meat the situation is rather different, since the women enjoy real and rather substantial rights over a product that is largely the result of their work. There are two ways for a family to slaughter a pig. Either it kills one in order to eat the meat itself, in which case it gives part of it to close relatives of husband and wife, or else it joins forces with other families who kill one or two of their own pigs at the same time. In the second case the cutting up and cooking are treated as a ceremony and are performed by the men. In both cases, it is the men who kill the animal and cut it up, but when the cooking is done collectively a series of little rituals is performed around the oven dug in the ground in order to eliminate the pollution that men and women who have had sexual relations might introduce into the meat. Above all, when the oven is opened, the first part removed (the forelegs) is sent to the men's house in the village, where the initiates and married men assemble to eat it. This levy and this collective consumption clearly signal the domination of the male sex and reassert the men's collective control over a product that is mainly the result of the women's work.

However, in the case of both family and collective slaughter, the women are on hand when the meat is shared, although it is their husbands or brothers who do the distributing. The women say to whom they want meat given and, generally, the husband respects his wife's wishes, for to do otherwise would be to risk a violent argument as well as the displeasure of the men or women to whom she wanted to make a gift (and who would be sure to hear of it). What is more, a woman can easily have her revenge by neglecting her pigs or her gardens. So the difference between the men's and women's situation as regards game and pig meat is clear. The men unaided catch their game and dispose of it at their discretion; in the case of pig meat, the women do have genuine rights over it, but always in the last resort under the men's control. Nor do the signs of male dominance end when the oven is opened and the first share of meat takes place, for the women receive what the Baruya regard as the offal, namely, the intestines and the tongue, which is given to them on the grounds that pigs eat excrement, human or otherwise, lying around in the bush or in the villages, whereas the men share the liver, which they regard as the seat of life, the seat of the animal's strength, and which they often cook among themselves in the bamboo groves.

Where money is concerned, we first need to distinguish what a woman can earn herself by selling sweet potatoes to the missionaries, civil servants, or to an anthropologist. This money she may keep and do with as she wishes. But the women expect their husband or their brother to share with them part of the money earned working in the plantations, or by selling coffee or chilis to the government agricultural officers, or to the representatives of private companies who occasionally visit the area to buy these products. No man shirks this obligation; when he has several wives, he may to be sure favor one, but he is bound, unless he wants to make his domestic life a misery, to share his money fairly, equally among all his wives, or to give them comparable gifts. It goes without saying, moreover, that a man back from the plantations must give presents to his relatives, brothers, sisters, parents-in-law, brothers-in-law, some of his coinitiates, to his initiate sponsor, and so on. His little nest egg will not last more than two or three months.

I have described how men's and women's place in the production process and the distribution of their products appeared to me. This presentation still lacks something, namely, the place of magical practices. The Baruya believe them indispensable to the success of farming, hunting, salt making, and all other activities, such as warfare, house building, cooking pig meat, not to mention childbirth, healing the sick, and so on.

Magic in the production processes

When clearing virgin forest, the men select a giant tree from among those standing on the parcel to be cultivated, and they decorate its trunk with magic plants, cowrie necklaces, and black feathers taken from a bird of paradise, the same as those worn by the young third-state initiates, the *tchouwanie*. Two men then attack the tree with axes, while all those taking part in the clearance wait, holding sticks decorated with magic leaves. When the giant begins to shudder and topple, they shout at the top of their voices, hurling their sticks toward the crashing tree, in the hopes of chasing the angry tree spirit toward their enemies' territory, where it will wreak revenge by killing anyone it catches felling other trees in the forest. So the Baruya are never really at peace with their enemies, for even after the official cessation of hostilities between warriors, war continues by means of the firing of these invisible yet murderous spirit-missiles.

Once the ground has been tidied up in a garden, the fence erected, and a certain number of plots marked out inside the compound and shared among kinfolk or neighbors, the man who took the initiative of clearing the forest performs a brief magical ceremony in the middle of the garden, on one of the patches earmarked for cultivation by his wife.[2] This magic, which helps sweet potatoes, taros, and other plants to grow, is handed down to him from his ancestors, and he will pass it on to his sons. It is worth pointing out, by the way, that a man always asks his wife's opinion when he is about to divide his garden into plots and to invite certain other women to cultivate it. He must first think of his wife, his sisters, sisters-in-law, his mother, his mother-in-law, his daughters, and so forth. His wife begins by choosing the plot or plots that she plans to cultivate, and then decides with her husband how many other women, and which ones, are to share the rest of the garden. In fact, husband and wife (wives) know perfectly well to whom they are under obligations of mutual help, and apart from cases of open conflict between brothers-in-law, a husband never denies use of a plot in the garden he has cleared to the women belonging to his wife's lineage or to married women belonging to this lineage, particularly since he has usually been helped by their husbands, his brothers-in-law. Some time later, each of the women in receipt of a parcel will in turn come to plant magic plants, mainly flowers, in the middle and around the edges of her parcel, muttering formulas inherited from her mother, and which she will ultimately teach her daughters.

We shall not go into the details of this agricultural magic, but it should be pointed out that there is some inequality among the clans in this field, and that some are reputed to possess far more effective magical powers than others. It is a well-known fact among the Baruya, for instance, that the Andavakia and the Ndelamaye (a Ndelie lineage) are more successful than others at growing sweet potatoes. It is said that, whenever drought or insects devastate the tribe's gardens, theirs are never damaged and that they can afford to be generous and allow the other clans to come and help themselves in their

[2] Maurice Godelier, "Le visible et l'invisible chez les Baruya de Nouvelle-Guinée," *Langues et techniques, Nature et societé*, ed. J. Thomas and L. Bernot (Paris: Klincksieck, 1972), vol. 2, pp. 263–9.

gardens. But they are feared too, for as a counterpart to their green thumbs they are also presumed to be able to cast spells on other people's gardens and prevent anything from growing in them.

Therefore, as regards the magical practices necessary to the production of tubers, men possess greater powers than women. It is also true, obviously, where hunting, salt making, and house building are concerned, for these are a male monopoly, and each man has his own appropriate magic for each of these activities. But it is not so for the gardens where reeds are grown to make pulpuls, nor for pig breeding, nor of course for the desire to have or not to have children, to give birth painlessly, and so on. These activities are the women's sphere. Women give their pigs the names of the streams or mountains that belong to their lineage and mark their ancestors' territory. They use propitiatory formulas handed down by their mothers and subsequently passed on to their daughters whenever one of their sows produces a litter, and they coat each piglet in an ochre clay with magical powers so as to help them grow better, fatter, and be more vigorous.

But all these forms of magic, both male and female, can be neutralized if man and wife make love in certain forbidden places or at forbidden times. Things get worse still if one or the other commits adultery and makes love in secret with forbidden partners.

Therefore, whenever the taro plants in a garden begin to wither even though the weather is not too hot, or as soon as a pig's flesh begins to get flabby just as it looked nice and fat, neighbors begin to harbor suspicions about the couple that planted the garden or reared the pig. Ill-wishers start to make snide comments in public. Here we see for the first time a fundamental aspect of Baruya thought and social organization, namely, that sexuality is viewed and experienced as a permanent threat to the reproduction of nature and society. Nor does this threat stem exclusively from taboo sexual relations or adultery. Even after they have made love at home, at a properly authorized time and place, a married man and woman must avoid contact with others for some time afterward, must not return to work in the fields, go hunting, or feed the pigs. The sexual act is dangerous because it pollutes, and the pollution weakens, corrupts, and endangers strength and life – starting with that rampart of life, that source of strength, man himself.

For though sexuality and sexual relations pollute, the danger does not flow in equal proportions from the two sexes. It wells forth essentially from the woman, from the substances that flow from her vagina: her menstrual blood, her fluids and secretions. Consequently a woman is not allowed to bestride her husband during coitus, as this position would risk spilling onto his belly the fluids that run from her sex. We shall leave our analysis of sexual relations between the sexes and of their underpinning representations of the body and of life. Yet these first references to sexuality, and to the woman's special responsibility for the terrible consequences that are liable to flow from sexuality, suffice to elucidate one additional inequality between the sexes, not in their access to the means of production, destruction, or exchange among men, but to the material and magical means of communication with the invisible powers that populate and govern the universe. They use, first, musical instruments, flutes and bull-roarers; and second, the sacred objects, the *kwaimatnie* owned and manipulated by the masters of the male initiations, which were given to their ancestors by the Sun, father of all the Baruya. Women are told that the bull-roarers and flutes are the voices of spirits that communicate with the men during the boys' initiations. Under no circumstances may the women see these instruments, though they can hear them echoing through the forest from afar; nor may they come near the initiation house. In either case, the punishment is death. But here we are already touching on the central feature of male dominance which is the initiate machinery. Beforehand, we need to scrutinize one essential element of man/woman relations among the Baruya, namely, their respective position in kinship relations and, through these, in the reproduction of the lineages and clans that make up their society.

The subordination of women in the production of relations of kinship

The Baruya kinship system is patrilineal, which means that a child automatically belongs, at birth, to his father's lineage and clan. Each clan possesses a stock of men's and women's names that are its alone, and one merely has to hear a person's name to know to which lineage he or she belongs. Koummaineu, for instance, is a man's name from the Nounguye clan; Watchimaiac, a woman's name from the Andavakia clan. A dead person's name cannot be reused in the following generation, but in the generation after that a grandson or great-nephew can use it.

The terminology of kinship distinguishes between parallel cousins and crossed cousins,[3] and it belongs to the "Iroquois" type. The vocabulary provides for distinctions between older brother–older sister/younger brother–younger sister, but only for Ego's own generation, where they apply to his siblings and parallel cousins. The vocabulary of kinship extends as far as the third generation of ancestors and the third generation of descendants. The

[3] For the nonspecialist, *parallel cousins* [1 and 2 in the diagram] refers to the children of Ego's father's brother or mother's sister, whereas *cross cousins* [3 and 4] refers to the children of his father's sister and his mother's brother. *Ego* is the name given by convention to the individual chosen as the point of reference in a system of kinship.

terms used to designate grandparents and grandchildren are identical and reciprocal.

Marriage with a close patrilateral parallel female cousin or with a matrilateral cross cousin is forbidden. Marriage with a matrilateral parallel female cousin is permissible. Marriage with a patrilateral crossed female cousin is permissible and even, as we shall see, prescribed when a woman has not been exchanged for the father's sister.

The clan is not an exogamous unit, since marriage with a distant patrilateral parallel female cousin is not forbidden.

Maternal kinfolk, particularly the uncle and his children, are of great importance to the Baruya. They signify protection and affection. The mother's brother is distinguished from all the mother's other classificatory brothers by adding to the term *api,* which signifies maternal uncle, the word *aounie,* which signifies breast, milk. The sons and daughters of this man are called "cousins by the breast" and are thus distinguished from all the other classificatory matrilateral cross cousins of Ego. At the opposing end of the scale, the sons and daughters of the father's sister, the patrilateral cross cousins, are called cross cousins "of the liver," *kale.*

Residence is virilocal, or more precisely patrivirilocal, inasmuch as the sons often live near their father. But it is perfectly possible for a man to go and live near his wife's brother, especially if the two brothers-in-law have exchanged sisters. People frequently take advantage of the possibility of going to live with their affines, as when several brothers coresiding near their father start to quarrel violently. Before matters get out of hand – a bloody quarrel, murder even, which could break up the lineage – one of the brothers will ask his brothers-in-law permission to come and live with them, and the latter never refuses.

The Baruya distinguish among five types of possible marriage. The first, *ginamare,* is considered the norm. It is based on the direct exchange of women by two lineages or segments of a lineage. The exchange may be organized either at the children's birth by their fathers, or by two young men, who decide to exchange sisters when the latter reach puberty.

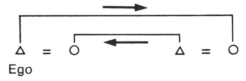

The second type of marriage derives from the first. It is called *kouremandjinaveu* (literally, *koure,* banana tree; *mandjinaveu,* to follow). This metaphor designates marriage with the daughter of the father's sister, the patrilateral cross cousin. It takes place when the father of Ego has given one of his sisters without receiving a wife in exchange. This gives him rights over his niece, and when she reaches puberty, he goes to fetch her to give her to his son. The daughter of his sister thus returns to the place where her mother once lived. She is like the offshoot of a banana tree (*koure*), which grows at its foot and replaces it after it has borne its fruit. Marriage with the patrilateral cross cousin is the complement of marriage by direct exchange. It proceeds from the exchange of women over a short cycle (one generation). But the second type of marriage, where the direct exchange of women takes place immediately and does not generate a cycle, requires two generations to accomplish the exchange of women and engender a cycle.

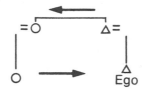

The third type of marriage, *tsika*, designates marriage after elopement. In principle, this type of marriage stands in opposition to the foregoing patterns of marriage by exchange of women. In fact, it always culminates in the application of one or another of these formulas.

Tsika means to pull. The young man who elopes with a girl "pulls" her by holding her hand and twisting one of her fingers backward. He generally tries to avoid harming her, since the elopement was planned in advance by the two youths, and the girl offers no resistance. What these youngsters are trying to do is to flout their families' decisions to give them partners whom they do not wish to marry. It is a serious affair, especially if the families were planning a marriage based on the *ginamare* principle, exchanging sisters. By her refusal, the girl endangers the marriage of one of her brothers. The young man may already have been engaged to another girl in exchange for whom his parents had already given one of his sisters. But, once decided on, the elopement takes place according to certain social rules.

The young man warns his brothers and his crossed cousins about his project, and persuades them to help him in his adventure. On the appointed day, he elopes with the girl at an agreed spot, in a garden for example, and he carries her off into the forest, where he entrusts her to his brothers and cousins for safekeeping. He then returns to the village and goes to wait in the men's house. That evening, people notice the girl's absence, start looking for her but fail to find her. Frequently rumors begin to fly the next day, sometimes suggested by the youngsters' accomplices, and the truth finally comes out. The girl's lineage gets angry. Her brothers and parallel cousins arm themselves and set off in search of the young man, who is in fact awaiting them. Insults, reproaches, shouting, and threats to kill make the encounter a violent one. It generally ends in blows. The young man is beaten. He does not defend himself, he offers his head to the blows. He is injured. As soon

21

as that happens, the young man tries to spill his blood onto the girl, brought to the scene of the fight by his brothers and cousins. He rushes to her and lets the blood from his wounds flow onto her breasts. This gesture cools people's tempers, and finally the girl is given in marriage, an obligation being placed on the couple to give one of its daughters to the wife's lineage when the time comes. At that point, the logic of the *kouremandjinaveu* match, that is, marriage with a patrilateral female cross cousin, reestablishes itself.

Things sometimes happen with a lot less fuss. If the young man has a sister not yet betrothed, he carries off the girl he wants to marry and hides her with his sister in the house of a conniving kinsman. The same scenario as above then ensues, but this time when her family comes looking for the girl, they find her hidden with the young man's sister, and he then offers his sister in compensation. Peace is made, and the marriage reverts to the logic of the *ginamare,* the logic of the direct exchange of women.

Whichever variant is the case, the *tsika* marriage places the relations between lineages under strain. It threatens the unity of the group and it compromises strategies. It cancels out years of exchanges of pig meat and reciprocal services between families who had already come to look on each other as affines. Understandably, this kind of marriage is rare.

The fourth type of marriage is equally infrequent. Sometimes a boy has no sister or female cousin to exchange. So he seeks out a couple with a daughter but no son, wanting a son-in-law to come and live with them and help them in their old age. The young man offers to help the young girl's father to build fences for his gardens; he brings him liana gathered in the forest to bind the stakes, and so on. Finally, he gains acceptance as son-in-law. This type of marriage is called *apmweraveugaimwonga,* that is, to help (*gaimwonga*) people, men (*apmweraveu*). Sometimes, a daughter born of this marriage will be given to a man from the wife's lineage. This arrangement once again brings us back to the *kouremandjinaveu* logic.

The fifth type of marriage is called *apmwetsalairaveumatna,* from *irata,* to gather; *tsala,* salt; *matna,* (in order to) take; *apmwevo,* woman. This type of marriage was never practiced among the Baruya themselves, but from time to time with distant, foreign tribes with whom they wished to establish or consolidate trading or peaceful relations. This type of marriage carried bride wealth with it, since the Baruya used to offer a certain number of salt bars and fathoms of cowries in exchange for a wife. The goods handed over as bride wealth put an end to this woman's lineage rights over the children she was about to bring into the world among the Baruya.

Finally, mention should be made of another form of marriage which used to be frequent, namely, with female prisoners of war, and which entailed no form of compensation whatever. It was not uncommon for the Baruya to capture young women or little girls from enemy tribes, killing their mothers and bringing them up in order to give them in marriage to a member of their lineage or to exchange them like their own daughters. However, when peace was restored with the woman's or little girl's tribe, her lineage would come to visit its involuntary brothers-in-law. Sometimes, it was an occasion for the two enemy lineages to conclude a closer, official alliance, in which case the Baruya would agree to give one of their women in compensation for the captive. Once that had happened, neither the brothers-in-law nor their descendants could kill each other in war. As we shall see, though, these marriages, like all marriages with enemies, often served strategic ends, helping to split the enemy, drawing over to the Baruya's side the lineages allied with it by marriage, preparing under cover of peace their treachery in time of war.

With the exception of enforced marriages between enemy female prisoners and their conquerors, all the forms of marriage practiced involve exchanges that appear to compensate for one thing or another. But, on closer examination, these forms are seen to be based not on a single principle, but on at least two.

The first three forms of marriage represent a distinct group ultimately based on the fundamental principle spelled out in the first of these forms, namely, the principle of *ginamare*, of the direct exchange of sisters. What is the social logic underlying this principle?

One woman equals one woman

The only way one can really compensate the gift of a woman is by giving another woman in exchange, whether in the same generation or in the one that follows the first marriage. Thus only a woman can equal or compensate for another woman.

For a person in our culture accustomed to the logic of commercial and monetary exchanges, the spontaneous reaction will be to interpret the countergift of a woman as a means of wiping out the debt contracted by receiving the initial gift. I believe that this would be a mistaken view of the social logic of giving. In actual fact, a debt created by a gift can never strictly speaking be canceled out. It can and must be counterbalanced by another gift, which creates an equivalent debt on the part of the people to whom one is indebted. The social logic of the gift/countergift is not really to wipe out debts but to balance them. If all that were needed to cancel a debt were an equivalent countergift, and if that were the aim of exchanging sisters, then once two men had exchanged sisters (and provided the two were equally fertile, hard working, and faithful), they could practically call it quits between them, there being no further reciprocal obligations. What in fact happens is quite the reverse. Far from breaking off or gradually dwindling to vanishing point, reciprocal exchanges of services and gifts between the two brothers-in-law in fact proliferate, thus showing that their reciprocal obligations are not

23

erased, or canceled out by the exchange of their sisters; and most brothers-in-law come to count far more on each other than on the help of their own brothers. So it would be a mistake to view these two-way exchanges of goods and services as dynamic means of paying bride wealth, or as the material equivalent of the woman received, or again as compensation for the handing over of rights over the children that she is destined to give to her husband's lineage.

On the other hand, it does look as if the Baruya apply the bride wealth or material compensation principle in the fifth form of marriage, in the case of an alliance with a tribe, with which they wish to establish or preserve relations conducive to traditional trade. In such cases, the Baruya plant one or two bamboo poles several meters tall, from which they hang fathoms of cowrie necklaces dangling to the ground. At the foot of the bamboo stakes, they heap bark cloaks and bars of salt. The life of this woman and that of the children she would ultimately produce thus find their equivalent in the various forms of material wealth produced and accumulated. In this type of exchange, the woman thus ceases to equal another woman.

One final case occupies a sort of middle term between the two essential principles: that of a young man, either an orphan or abandoned by his family and having no sister to exchange, yet seeking a wife. From the outset, he finds himself in a situation of individual dependence, since he has nothing to offer save his services to anyone willing to give him a wife. This relation of dependence is to some extent similar to the material compensation paid for a foreign wife, but it is radically different in the sense that the services rendered over the years can never cancel out the gift of a woman, and the man can only restore the balance by giving a daughter born of his marriage to a man from his wife's lineage, to the son of one of his (close) "brothers-in-law." That would reconfirm the general principle of the exchange of women. Examples of this type of marriage are rare and illustrate the limitations within which the principle of the exchange of sisters operates. It presupposes a relative demographic balance between the different wife-exchanging lineage segments, and above all a fair degree of intralineage solidarity, so that a young man without a sister can count on his paternal uncles, both close and distant, to lend him a daughter (one of his patrilateral parallel female cousins) for exchanging.

If this demographic balance is broken by sickness or war, which is capable of decimating a lineage segment and creating a large number of orphans, or if intralineage solidarity breaks down through conflicts of interest, quarrels over land, pandanus trees, pigs, or whatever, there will be an increase in the number of individuals without sisters and social backing who will find themselves from the outset in a situation of virtual dependence on anybody prepared to give them a wife. The only way they can completely overcome this situation of dependence is to have daughters themselves, whom they can give away and thus counterbalance their old debt. This then brings us to another aspect of the all-pervasive principle of the exchange of women; namely, for the Baruya, the givers of women are superior to the takers; consequently the only way to restore balance between them is for the takers to become givers to their giver.

Figure 2 summarizes the principles underlying the different forms of Baruya marriages.

This analysis brings us to a general comment whose theoretical import transcends the case of the Baruya. The Baruya conclude alliances in several different ways. Among themselves, they give pride of place to the direct exchange of women, but they are prepared to apply the principle of the exchange of women for material wealth when the marriage does not concern the everyday reproduction of their own society's internal relations, or that of relations between their society and immediately neighboring tribes, with which they are obliged to coexist positively and/or negatively. Now, the principle that equates women with certain forms of wealth is exactly the same as the one found at work in the "big men" societies in New Guinea and elsewhere. It plays only a minor, subordinate role among the Baruya, explicitly confined to relations with neutral foreign groups, neutral because living sufficiently distant from the Baruya to have no reason or opportunity for intervening directly in the workings of Baruya society. Wealth therefore becomes a principle of matrimonial exchange not at the frontiers of Baruya territory itself, but at those of the economic sphere to which they belong. Things are very different in societies where the woman is obtained in exchange for bride wealth, and where the production of certain forms of material wealth and the reproduction of relations of kinship and of local groups are internally interlinked. In such societies there are opportunities of accumulating goods in order to accumulate wives or, alternatively, of accumulating women in order to accumulate goods: an essential condition of the formation of a big man's power. As we can already perceive, the opposition between Baruya-type societies and big-man ones is not a matter of the presence or absence of the principle that equates women with wealth, but whether or not this principle is subordinate or dominant among other principles offering other possibilities of establishing matrimonial alliances.

We shall be returning to this point later on, as it is of major theoretical importance. For the time being, it is worth observing that, whatever the principles underlying the social mechanisms that ensure the reproduction of life and the production of relations of kinship among the Baruya, these principles and mechanisms imply the subordination of women. Whether brothers exchange their sisters or fathers their daughters, whether a father gives to his wife's family a daughter to replace the sister that he did not give, whether a young man refuses the marriage planned for him and arranges a kind of symbolic abduction with the complicity of the girl he plans to marry, or

	Marriages inside the Baruya tribe	

Inside the tribe	Balanced exchange:
	  Principle: woman ⟺ woman
	    (Types 1 and 2 marriages)
	Unbalanced exchange:
	  Principle: woman ⟺ work
	    (Type 4 marriage)
	    (Type 3 marriage, unbalanced
	    evolves toward a Type 2 marriage)	

Outside the tribe

(a) Friendly but not neighboring

Marriages between Baruya and women from a friendly non-neighboring tribe	Marriage involving exchange according to three possible principles
Balanced exchange: Principle: woman ⟺ wealth	

(b) Neighboring but friendly

Marriages between Baruya and members of a friendly neighboring tribe
Principle: woman ⟺ woman (Types 1 and 2 marriages) (Type 4 marriage implies that the individual leaves his kin to go and live with his affines, on whom he depends not only for his wife but also for land)

(c) Neighboring but belligerent

Marriage between Baruya and members of a hostile neighboring tribe belonging to the same culture	Marriage without exchange
Principle: by capture without compensation, but if peace is restored between the two tribes marriage by capture may give rise to compensation in the following generation. This brings us back to Type 2 marriages.	

Figure 2. Principles underlying the different forms of Baruya marriages

whether a victorious warrior decides to marry his captive – in all these different ways of marrying, men visibly exercise more power than women, and exercise this power over the women.

These observations in no way imply that women have no say in the arrangement of these marriages, that they are merely passive instruments, docilely bowing to the wishes of the men in their lineages. To be sure, a Baruya woman cannot refuse to marry and decide to remain a spinster, but she can reject the person chosen to be her husband. If so, she must make known her decision before reaching puberty or, at the latest, at her first menstruation, when for the first time she goes down to the bottom of her village to await her initiation ceremonies in a menstrual hut. She must then send back the gifts of bark cloaks sent her by her fiancé's family, thereby signaling her rejection of the marriage. It is a serious decision, and a difficult one to make if the marriage of one of her younger brothers depends on her own marriage, and almost impossible to make if one of her older brothers has already obtained a wife against the promise that she will be given to his affines in exchange.

Another example of the woman's role concerns decisions on a daughter's marriage, hence the establishment of new advantageous alliances for her husband's lineage. It frequently happens that when a daughter is born into a family her parents are connected by another family already planning to marry her to one of its sons. But no commitment can be entered into without the approval of the child's mother, who can dismiss the projected marriage without her husband really being in any position to oppose her wishes. This approval role means two things at least: first, that mothers make common cause with their daughters and intervene in their matrimonial fate; second, since the mother consults members of her own lineage, that the maternal lineage plays a part in a patrilineal society in the conclusion of marriages between patrilineal lineages.

However – and this is further evidence of women's general subordination to men – once married, a woman cannot leave her husband. There is no divorce among the Baruya, although the man is perfectly entitled to repudiate a wife and give her to one of his brothers, real or classificatory, or even to a man from another lineage if he has some specific obligations toward the latter. At the husband's death, his wives are shared among his brothers and his patrilateral parallel cousins. However, it does happen that an already aged woman, with grandchildren, may refuse to be "inherited" and goes to live near one of her daughters, helping her to tend her gardens and above all to raise her pigs. So there is no divorce, and adultery is severely punished. In all the lessons in morality that the Baruya give to their young boys and girls in the course of initiation ceremonies are the most dreadful threats of death for anyone who strays into adultery.

A last look at the principle of female equivalence

To conclude this analysis of the place of men and women in the process of production of life, in other words the process of production of new members of society, with their relations of kinship, we need to take another look at the central fact that the marriages that create these relations are founded on the principle that only another woman is worth a woman, that all women are equivalent. What does this equivalence signify? How does it appear in practice and what characteristics does it entail?

It postulates that any girl, provided she is in good health and suffers no serious physical or mental impairment, can be exchanged for any other. It implies taking little notice of each individual woman's particular characteristics, and treating her as an abstract means of exchange. This attitude finds practical, instantaneous expression in certain situations where groups exchange what can only be called credits in women among themselves. Among the Baruya, it often happens that lineage A owes a wife to lineage B, while at the same time lineage B owes a wife to lineage C. The three groups will then reach an agreement among themselves under which group A will transfer one of its women directly to lineage C, thus compensating B's debt toward C and A's debt toward B. In this instance, the abstract postulate of female equivalence is made manifest immediately, since the woman circulating among the group becomes the equivalent not merely of a woman who has married or will marry one of its brothers, but of any one of the women remaining to be exchanged within the sequence of alliances into which her marriage fits. She thus immediately becomes the abstract equivalent of any woman remaining due within this chain, much in the way a special category of goods might become transformed into money, some general equivalent, when it ceases to be bartered for some other unvarying category of goods.

The practice of transferring wife debts is of great interest for the theoretical analysis of relations of kinship. For a group, transferring a debt and a woman to a group with which it has not directly exchanged women engenders effects within a system of restricted exchange analogous to those of a system of generalized exchange. In restricted exchange, two groups, A and B, find themselves simultaneously both giving and taking women. If group A can transfer the wife it normally owes to B directly to C, then each group ceases to be both giver and taker vis-à-vis the others. A has received a wife from B and has given one to C. The givers are no longer the takers. A system of restricted exchange can produce effects analogous to those of a system of generalized exchange.

To simplify these relations:

In a general situation based on gifts, where

$$B \rightarrow A$$
$$C \rightarrow B,$$

which, according to the formula of a restricted exchange, entails the counter-gift

$$A \rightarrow B$$
$$B \rightarrow C,$$

the debt-transfer formula permits the counter-gift

$$A \rightarrow C.$$

It is as if the Baruya were practicing a $B \rightarrow A \rightarrow C \rightarrow B$–type formula. Under the terms of this formula, takers are no longer givers, and exchanges are balanced when the exchange cycle is completed. But in a genuine generalized exchange formula, the next cycle starts all over again in the same direction, whereas the debt-transfer formula can only function as the occasion arises, without any need to repeat it among the same groups or in the same direction. The debt-transfer formula is therefore confined within the limits of the principle of restricted exchange. It stretches them and bends them, but does not abolish them.

Whatever the outcome of this theoretical discussion, the postulate of female equivalence also implies that women are mutually equivalent not only in abstract logic, in the political balance of matrimonial exchanges, but in the practical logic of work performed and services rendered; it implies that they have all been trained to work hard, do what is expected of a woman in society, and thus to recognize the authority of men and primarily that of their fathers, brothers, and husbands. It also implies that they are expected to be fertile and to become good mothers. The education that they receive before marriage is intended to prepare them to comply. But family education alone is not enough for Baruya boys or girls, as men and women are not allowed to marry until they have been initiated.

To sum up, male dominance over women among the Baruya appears to rest upon the following foundations:

Women are excluded from ownership of the land, but not from its use.

Women are excluded from the ownership and the use of the most efficient tools for clearing the forest.

Women are excluded from ownership and the use of weapons, the means of destruction, and hence of hunting, warfare, and recourse to armed violence.

Women are excluded from the manufacture of salt and the pursuit of trade relations with foreign tribes. They depend on men to obtain salt bars, which they are subsequently free to use, however, in order to buy clothing, adornments, and so on.

Women are excluded from ownership and the use of sacred objects, that is, the material supernatural means of controlling the reproduction of strength and social life.

Last, in the process of production of relations of kinship (which are simultaneously the conditions of reproduction of the social groups that make up Baruya society) women occupy a subordinate position relative to men, who exchange them among themselves and between the groups that they represent.

Baruya women are thus materially, politically, and symbolically subordinate to men – to use categories specific to our own culture. This subordination in no way implies that women are bereft of rights, and that they have only duties. They do have rights, which men are obliged to know and acknowledge. Indeed, a fair proportion of the male ceremonies is devoted precisely to instructing the young initiates in the rights of women and in their duties toward them.

The very fact that one sex is subordinated to the other presupposes that the dominant sex also exercises various forms of violence on the other sex: physical violence (blows, injuries), psychological violence (insults, contempt, ideologies that denigrate and belittle). But permanent subordination also implies the existence of some measure of consent on the part of the dominated, together with social and ideological devices designed to obtain this consent. However, the existence of consent in no way implies an absence of resistance and opposition on the part of women to the order by which they are dominated.

We shall be returning to all these points – violence, resistance, and the repression whereby the men meet this resistance. Beforehand, we need to investigate the social mechanism whereby the unequal rights and duties of the two sexes are legitimized, instituting and amplifying male domination and the subordination of women, of all women to men, to any man whatever; in a word, we must now take a look at the machinery that produces domination on the one hand and consent on the other, that is, the male and female initiations.

3

The institution and legitimization of male superiority

Initiations and the separation of the sexes

During the course of their lifetime, the Baruya pass through various phases of a cycle specific to their respective sex, each phase of which has a distinct name and confers a specific status. These phases are represented by Figure 3.

The male life cycle

At birth, a man is a *bwaranie,* a baby; his mother carries him in a string bag and breast-feeds him. He has no name before the age of twelve to fifteen months, when he learns to walk and cuts his first teeth. Until then, his mother is supposed to hide her baby's face from her husband. Whenever the latter is at hand, she covers the baby with a kind of little string bag which conceals his features while allowing him to breathe. When the *bwaranie* looks as if he has a good chance of surviving, the father's lineage gives presents to the mother's lineage, and he receives his first name, which he will bear until initiation. He becomes a *keimale* (boy), and then, at the age of six or seven, a *keimalenange* (literally, big boy).

Till then, he lives in the world of women, dressed in a long *pulpul* similar to the skirts worn by little girls. Indeed, he plays with his sisters, female cousins, and female neighbors. From the age of six or seven, little boys tend to go off and play among themselves, shooting miniature bows and arrows in the forest, whereas little girls generally stay with their mothers, and start to help them in the garden and look after their younger brothers or sisters. The separation of the sexes begins to take shape.

Then, one evening, a man comes to fetch the boy, at around the age of nine, and locks him up in his house along with all the other boys of his age. Now comes the moment of separation from the female world. This man is the master of the first initiation ceremonies (he will turn them into *mouka*).

31

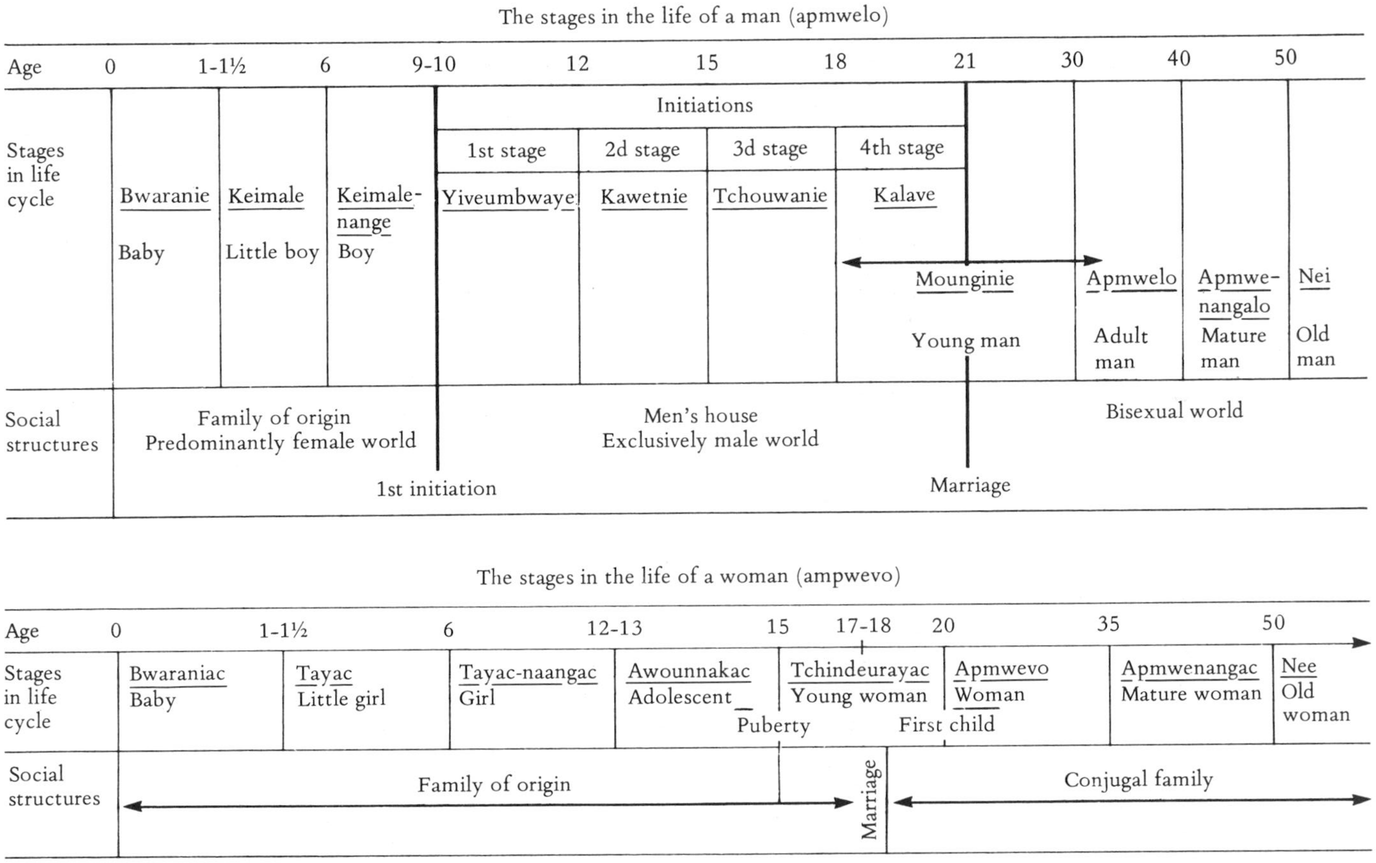

The stages in the life of a man (apmwelo)

Age	0	1–1½	6	9–10		12	15	18	21	30	40	50
					Initiations							
					1st stage	2d stage	3d stage	4th stage				
Stages in life cycle	Bwaranie	Keimale	Keimale-nange		Yiveumbwaye	Kawetnie	Tchouwanie	Kalave	Mounginie	Apmwelo	Apmwe-nangalo	Nei
	Baby	Little boy	Boy						Young man	Adult man	Mature man	Old man
				1st initiation					Marriage		Bisexual world	
Social structures	Family of origin Predominantly female world				Men's house Exclusively male world							

The stages in the life of a woman (ampwevo)

Age	0	1–1½	6	12–13	15	17–18	20	35	50
Stages in life cycle	Bwaraniac	Tayac	Tayac-naangac	Awounnakac	Tchindeurayac		Apmwevo	Apmwenangac	Nee
	Baby	Little girl	Girl	Adolescent	Young woman		Woman	Mature woman	Old woman
				Puberty		First child			
						Marriage			
Social structures	Family of origin						Conjugal family		

Figure 3. The stages in the life of a man and a woman

His wife, his daughters if they have reached puberty, will look after the little boys for a few days. At the top of the village, near the men's house, the men have built *moukaanga,* the house of the *mouka,* where the boys will enter a few days after their brutal separation from their mother. At the conclusion of a month of ceremonies, during which the person in charge of this first stage of the boy's initiation will pierce his nose, the *mouka* becomes a *yiveumbwaye* for the next three or four years; from now on, he will live in the men's house, the *kwalanga.* He is now dressed half as a man, half as a woman. His *pulpul* is still cut like a skirt, and beneath his wide bark cloak, he does not wear the little loincloth that normally hides men's buttocks. This is so as to force him to flee women's presence out of a sense of shame. For the next several months, he is forbidden to speak in the presence of his elders, who poke fun at him, insult him, humiliate him, remind him that not so long ago he lived among the women; from time to time, they will grab hold of him and beat him with sticks or nettles. Sometimes he will defecate from fright. Since becoming a *mouka,* the initiate may no longer utter his own name or that of his coinitiates. Except in the event of the boy having behaved badly – such as a major theft in some garden, or a fight with serious consequences for some other child – an initiate's father will no longer strike him. His punishments will be inflicted on him by third- or fourth-stage initiates, who live in the men's house and to some extent act as the representatives of the entire male body in dealings with the younger boys.

At around twelve years old, while the *tchouwanie* and *kalave* (third and fourth stage) initiation ceremonies are in progress, the *yiveumbwaye* become *kawetnie.* After a variety of rituals that take place in the forest or close to the men's house, by day and by night, the *yiveumbwaye* discard their half-feminine *pulpul*s and their old cloaks in some hidden spot in the forest. The men in charge of the second stage of initiation hang them up high on the trunk of some giant tree, leaving them there to rot. The master of this ritual, before hanging up their clothes, calls down the protection of the tree's spirit, gathers a little of its sap and bark, and smears it on the tuft of hair remaining on each child's shaven crown, where, according to the Baruya, the spirit lives. Next, for the first time in their lives, the boys are dressed properly as men and receive the feather adornments and other signs of their rank.

At around fifteen the *kawetnie* become *tchouwanie.* The ceremonies marking this transition last almost five weeks, and these, along with those marking the *mouka*'s break with the world of women, are the most important in the entire Baruya initiate cycle. For this occasion, the mature men or *apmwenangalo,* the great men who have already fathered several children the oldest of whom are already initiates, erect a gigantic ceremonial house that can accommodate the several hundred men who will be attending over the coming weeks and the new *tchouwanie* and *kalave* for sleeping at night.

For the Baruya, the *tsimia,* or great ceremonial house, is like the symbolic

33

body of the tribe. The thatched roof seems to them like the skin of this body, and the bones and skeleton are symbolized by the poles holding up the roof. The central pole upon which the edifice rests is called the "grandfather." Once it has been erected, a live opossum is cast from the top and is killed as it crashes to the ground. The dead animal is given to the oldest man in the valley, both to notify him and console him for the fact that he is destined to die before the following initiation, three years hence. Each pole holding up the *tsimia* represents a new initiate, and the great man who plants it murmurs his name as he drives it into the ground. The poles are all planted simultaneously, by dozens of men packed shoulder to shoulder in a vast circle which then becomes the perimeter of the *tsimia*. The men are grouped by village, but with no distinction of lineage or clan. The *tsimia* is thus the house of all the men of all the villages, of all the lineages together, transcending distinctions of kinship and residence. In this respect it is indeed, as the Baruya say, the (symbolic) "body" of their tribe, the embodiment of their unity against enemies, and of their solidarity against women.

On the day of the *tsimia*'s completion, men secretly lead the future *tchou-wanie* and *kalave* into the edifice, each bearing a stick or a noisy rattle, just before hundreds of women, grouped by village, bring bundles of grass to cover the roof.

The women, guided and supervised by the male shamans, start running toward the building, shouting as they cast their bales up to the married men perched on the roof, ready to set to work. Suddenly, at a discreet signal from the men, the initiates hiding within the walls set up a fearful din. The young women and children, taken by surprise, shriek with terror. The married women know what is going on, but they tell the young that they are hearing spirits that have entered into the edifice and are communicating with the initiates.

That same evening, in the now completed *tsimia,* representatives of two clans, the Nunguye and the Andavakia, set light to the new fire which is to burn throughout the ceremonies. They do so by striking flints together (or at least they did so, for the ritual stones have since vanished in the fire that consumed the village where they were kept; this fire was ordered by a young Australian officer who wanted to punish the Baruya from this village for having taken up arms to avenge the suicide of one of their married sisters in another village). By lighting fire with flints, these men reaccomplish the act of their supernatural father, the Sun, source of warmth and light.

A Baruya myth explains that, a very long time ago, the sexual organs of men and women were not pierced; they were "walled up" in a manner of speaking. The Sun put an end to this situation by casting a flint into a fire. The stone grew hot, burst, and its splinters pierced the man's penis, the woman's vagina, and their anuses. Since that time, men and women have been able to copulate and reproduce.

34

The most solemn ceremony, performed by the master of the rituals, a Baruya from the Baruya clan which gave its name to the tribe, is the placement on the initiates' heads of the very symbols of male domination, an overhanging hornbill beak, topping a ring of rattan completed by two sharpened pig's tusks whose tips are pressed into each initiate's brow.

At the moment when, standing motionless and silent, they receive these insignia and their "sponsors" and kinsmen dress them, the master of this ceremony delivers a long speech to remind them that henceforward they are men, that soon their elders will be finding wives for them, but the task will be a difficult one if the fathers of marriageable daughters learn that so and so is lazy or a thief. He reminds them that, once married, they will have to clear the forest and lay out gardens to feed their family, that they will be expected to fulfill all their responsibilities toward their wives, children, to all their consanguine relatives or affines. Above all, they must henceforward be prepared to fight to the death to defend the Baruya and their territory. Unlike the *kawetnie,* the *tchouwanie* are permitted to fight among the men, whereas when younger they had been expected to remain far from the battlefront.

The master of ceremonies who gives this speech is the most prestigious of all. He belongs to the Baruya clan, which is to the tribe as a whole what the central pole is to the ceremonial house. It goes without saying that this ceremony and this speech take place far from the women's ears and eyes, at the top of the mountain. It is only afterward that the new initiates, wearing their new insignias and their symbolic headdress, slowly descend toward the *tsimia,* displaying themselves before the admiring women and children lining their route. Magnificently painted and adorned, they parade before all the women of the tribe thronging the path, and then return to the ceremonial house where they will spend an entire night putting up with the pain of these tips pressing into their brows, walking around the central pole of the *tsimia,* becoming faint from fatigue and hunger, until daybreak. They are then told that the hornbill beak is their penis, and that the toothed circle is the woman's vagina. They are also told that their new name, *tchouwanie,* is one of the secret names, unknown to the women, of the woman's vagina.

Around this time, or in the months that follow, a *tchouwanie*'s parents must, if they have not already done so, find him a wife. One day, he is told that he is to marry such and such a young woman, who is the younger sister of one of his coinitiates, and in exchange he must hand over one of his younger sisters or female cousins. From that time on, he will start to help his future father-in-law clear his gardens, and his future brother-in-law will come to help his father. His sister will go and help her future mother-in-law and his future wife will visit his mother. He, in the meantime, will not be permitted to meet his betrothed before their marriage, which will take place several years hence.

Until the young man's parents have found him a wife, he must remain a *tchouwanie,* and he may not become a *kalave* like his other coinitiates at the next initiation. For the first time in almost ten years, he will cease to progress in step with all those who suffered the *mouka* ceremony alongside him, all those who cried, suffered, went hungry with him. This halt may happen if a boy develops more slowly than his fellows, of if he is too small or too skinny. Often though, it happens because he is fatherless, and because his mother's second husband cannot be bothered with him. He may then sense his loneliness and how little the other members of his lineage are concerned to find him a wife, and he may then decide to commit suicide, wandering off one night to hang himself in the forest.

Usually though, things pass off smoothly and the *tchouwanie* becomes a *kalave. Kalave* is the name of a species of white parrot, one of whose feathers the men wear in the center of their headdress. The *kalave* carries the village banners at ceremonies, beats the initiates in the first two stages and rubs them with nettles, and keeps a constant watch over their training. One day, somebody comes to tell the *kalave* that his fiancée has had her first period, and that she has gone down to the bottom of the village, to the area reserved for the women, to isolate herself beneath a shelter of leaves and branches and await the preparations for her initiation ceremonies, neither drinking nor eating.

For the Baruya, menstrual blood first begins to flow from a woman's belly when Moon, the brother of Sun (in certain versions of their myths, Moon is Sun's wife), pierces her vagina afresh. The two young people must then undergo the *tchangitnia* ceremonies (from *tsala,* salt; *gitnia,* to chew), the ceremonies of puberty. They will undergo these ceremonies separately, without meeting, the one in company with other initiates who are living in the men's house of his village and whose fiancées have already reached puberty, the other in company with all (or almost all) the women from all the villages. We shall discuss the young woman's ceremony in detail later on. For the time being, suffice it to say that it is a collective ceremony of initiation by all the women of the tribe, but has no master of rituals or manipulation of sacred objects.

As for the young man, he awaits the night on which his fiancée's initiation ceremony is to take place. For some days, he is forbidden to eat sugarcane, to drink, to chew areca nuts. It is his father who imposes these taboos on him. Then, at the first glimmer of dawn following the night during which he heard the chanting and dancing of the female ceremonies from afar, and a little before the girl is brought to the river to proceed with her intimate ablutions, the young man, dressed in new clothes, rushes into the forest, and climbs the mountain with a handful of coinitiates and the men in charge of this ceremony, who belong to the Boulimmambakia lineage. They climb far and high, up to the foot of an immense, straight tree whose thick sap looks like sperm. The Boulimmambakia paint the initiate's belly with this sap and secretly utter a magic formula designed to strengthen the man's sperm and at the same time to close up the woman's vagina, so that the sperm that will flow into her will not trickle out and be lost, and she can become pregnant as quickly as possible. After that, they perform another magical rite around a many-rooted plant, almost impossible to uproot, to prevent the girl from turning away from her fiancé and tearing herself away from her commitments.

Later, at the foot of another tree, the men pray to the Sun, their arms outstretched toward the treetop, snapping their fingers in salute to it and emitting a musical whistling that sends their breath up into the sky to mingle with the wind. Then the fiancé cries out his future wife's newly acquired initiate name and proclaims: "You, X, I am now your elder brother. You no longer belong to your father, but to me."

This is an extremely secret ritual. The young man only learns it when his fiancée reaches puberty. The women know nothing of it. Having uttered the woman's new name in the depths of the forest, the young man will henceforward be forbidden to pronounce it either in public or in private. For, once married, he may never call his wife anything but "Wife." She may never call her husband anything but "Husband," either in public or in private.

This ceremony culminates not in the heart of the forest but on the ceremonial site of the men of the young man's village, a clearing at the forest edge, in the middle of which stands a pandanus, the male tree par excellence. The young man is dressed and adorned, he is given taros to eat, in which are concealed magic leaves to give him strength. As mentioned, his belly is painted, this time with clay and sap, to make him fertile, so that the sap-bearing trees will give him sperm and children; he is reminded, among other things, that he should never leave his wife for another woman, on pain of death.

The next day, life resumes and goes on as usual for some months or possibly even years. One day, the father of the young *kalave* comes to tell him to gather up all the material needed to build a house. This instruction is the signal that he is about to get married. Some days later, after the men have collected the building material – except the grass for the thatch, which is women's work – all the young men come to build the house in an atmosphere of jollity. A shaman paints the poles of the house with magic clay to protect it against evil spirits. Then comes the marriage ceremony, during which the two young people, placed far apart, listen to public exhortations to remain faithful to each other, to be hard working, to think no more of having fun or stealing from other people's gardens as little children do, and so on. Men from the bridegroom's lineage build the hearth in the new house. Then the young man spends a few nights there, sleeping with the little boys from his village. The young woman does the same with the little girls. At last, they can sleep alone beneath the same roof, but they are not allowed to make love until the soot has blackened the freshly gathered green thatch. They caress each other, discover each other, and, above all, the young man allows his young wife to drink his sperm so as to make her strong and healthy before making love for the first time. Henceforward, the young man will only return to the men's house to live and sleep when his wife is menstruating or giving birth. In the past, however, in time of war or serious epidemic, the men came to live with the initiates in the *kwalanga,* the men's house, in order to ready themselves for combat or to help the shamans fight against the evil spirits, carriers of sickness and death, and drive them out.

Since becoming a *tchouwanie,* the adolescent has been a *munginie,* a young man, which he will remain until he has fathered three or four children.

A man grows in status at the birth of each of his children, and a special ceremony is performed for him and on him at the ceremonial site in his village. This occasion is attended by all the men in the village together with kinsmen and friends living in other villages, who travel to join in. This ceremony is particularly important at the birth of the first child, continuing and completing the young man's initiation.

In the morning the man goes to the river to wash his body in order to purify himself of impurities from the female sexual organ. Stripped of all clothing and adornment save the *pulpul,* he goes with his coinitiates to the ceremonial site, where he is pushed into a kind of tunnel made of leaves and branches, rather similar, though shorter, to the one through which as a young initiate he had so frequently been forced to pass, pushed and supported by his sponsor, and at the far end of which the older initiates and the (young) married men used to wait to beat him with nettles. This time, after he emerges from the tunnel, the mature men await him and rub his stomach and belly with nettles. He is then placed between two rows of large branches arranged on the ground in a kind of path. This path is the image of his own wife. He must remain inside it; he may not overstep it, for that would symbolically signify that he was walking on other people's paths, stealing their wives.

He is then presented with a packet of yellow mud. A man from either the Andavakia or Nunguye clans then launches into a violent harangue:

What is this? Mud to paint yourself with, to make yourself handsome? No, it's shit from the baby that has just been born. As long as this shit has not hardened, you shall refrain from making love. You have been with women; now we take you back; we put you back in the men's house. Think of this child; think to prepare gardens for him and his mother. When your son learns to walk and play with a child's bow, when your daughter can carry a small string bag on her head, then you can stick your cock out again.

The master of the ceremony then distributes magic nuts which the men suck in order to purify their mouths. These nuts give the men strength and sperm. The magic power filters down from the roots of their teeth to their penises. Then, while painting the man's body with red clay, the master of the ritual secretly utters a magic formula which calls upon a wild banana tree whose trunk is filled with juice, with sap. He calls upon it so that man and wife will have juice in abundance, the man sperm, his wife milk. All then pray to the Sun, their hands raised, snapping their fingers and whistling again. Secretly, the master of the ritual calls upon the eagle, the Sun bird, to bear the spirits of the men to the mountaintops, and to make them greater and stronger. The ceremony ends with a victory cry, the cry that the men utter on the battlefield when the enemy is killed or put to flight.

A simplified version of this ceremony takes place for each birth. When the *apmwe* has had at least four children and reached the age of thirty-five or forty, he becomes a mature man: an *apmwenangalo*. Meanwhile, he will have removed the taboos, one by one, that had prevented him from eating in the presence of his sponsor and his mother and from speaking to them.

His sponsor is the man who, years before, had helped him make his entry into the world of men. He is the ex–young man who for days and nights "like a mother" had cared for him in the men's house, holding him on his lap throughout the long sessions of harangues, the "lessons" given to the initiates by the married men. It was he who saw to it that he slept, dressed, and ate well and properly. It was he too who, hiding him beneath his cloak, had accompanied him when he urinated or defecated in the pit dug close to the *moukaanga*.

To his mother, now an old woman, he offers game he has caught in order to remove the taboos that have for so many years forbidden him to speak or eat in her presence. His mother is the first woman a Baruya leaves in his life, and the last with whom he is reunited.

At last, at around thirty-five or forty, when his first sons are already *ka-wetnie* or *tchouwanie,* second- or third-stage initiates, the man becomes an *apmwenangalo*. From now on, it will be he who will plant one of the poles of the *tsimia* at each initiation.

From around fifty on, as the mature man enters old age, he will play a less and less prominent role in society, unless he has been a great warrior or a great shaman, whose glory and experience can never die. As an old man, he is referred to as *nei* or *ate:* grandfather. He becomes increasingly dependent on his sons for his subsistence. He comes "to sit in their hand." Finally, if he lives to be the oldest man in the tribe, it is to him that the others will offer the opossum killed on being cast from the top of the *tsimia*. All that now remains for him to do is to die before the next initiations.

The Baruya used either to bury their dead or to expose them on a platform, according to clan, sex, age, and function. The great warriors were laid out with their bow and arrows; taros and sugarcane were planted beneath the platform; the dead man's juices would drip down onto them, and they were subsequently replanted in other gardens. The shamans were buried. The dualities of hot and cold, light and dark, day and night account for these two forms of funeral. Once an exposed body had decomposed, a second funeral was arranged. Widowers would cut off a dead wife's fingers, dry them over a fire, and wear them as a necklace. A dead person's lower jaw was cleaned and worn beneath the armpit by the surviving spouse. The remaining bones were placed in the hollow of a tree on the hunting grounds that used to belong to the dead man and his ancestors. There, his spirit would watch over the game, the natural resources of the land, attacking men from other lineages who slipped into his territory in order to steal his game, protecting his descendants provided they showed him respect (or provided he was well disposed toward them). Women's spirits also went to join the spirits of their ancestors and their dead brothers, watching with them to ensure that proper use was made of their territory's resources.

On their arrival, the Europeans forbade the exposure of the dead and second funerals. Today, after independence, the Baruya no longer expose their dead, and they now plant flowers on tombs as in European cemeteries, something the Baruya had never done before. They used to plant flowers in the gardens or at the foot of trees in the forests, whose benevolent spirit was supposed to make man and soil fertile.

The woman's life cycle

At birth, a little girl is a *bwaraniac,* a baby, and her father is not allowed to see her face until he has given presents to her mother's lineage. At twelve-to-fifteen months she becomes a *tayac,* a little girl, and then as she grows, at eight or ten, she is called a *tayac-naangac,* a big girl. At around twelve or thirteen, when her breasts begin to bud, she is known as an *awounnakac,* from *aounie,* breast.

Throughout this period, she lives primarily with her mother, although until the age of five or six, she plays with the boys of her own age. Then, gradually, she stops doing so, instead accompanying her mother in the gardens, and helping her with the many domestic chores. As her breasts swell and puberty sets in, a man comes one day to fetch her together with the other girls of her age, takes them near the village, and, without ceremony, pierces their noses. Needless to say, it is with the approval of the girls' mothers that this man comes to pierce their noses. To do so he has no need to possess a sacred object, a *kwaimatnie,* or to have any responsibility in the initiation of the boys. He may be a maternal uncle or a kinsman on a girl's mother's side.

At around fifteen or sixteen, the girl has her first period. As soon as the blood begins to flow, she tells her mother and goes down to the bottom of the village to the area reserved for the women. Her mother, her older sisters, and female cousins come to build her a hut of branches and grass. She stays there for a week, without eating and almost without drinking, awaiting the beginning of the *tchangitnia* ceremony; the male part, which concerns her fiancé, was described earlier. During this week of seclusion and fasting, she receives frequent visits from the little girls of her village, but she smiles without talking to them, or murmurs a few words in a low voice. The women from the lineages of her father, mother, and future husband make her a large quantity of *pulpul*s which she will proudly wear after her return to her village. One morning, her future father-in-law sends her a gift, a dozen bark cloaks. The young girl's acceptance of these will have decisive consequences for the rest of her life, since in so doing she accepts as her husband the man to whom she has been promised. A refusal at this point therefore represents her last chance of changing her destiny and satisfying her own desire, if she so wishes. However, as we have already seen, this refusal entails so many social conflicts that it is a rare occurrence; it did sometimes happen, though, even before the white man's arrival. Once a young girl has accepted the cloaks, she places them on her head, one on top of the other so that when she leaves the menstrual hut to go and rest outside, she looks like a stiff mannequin.

At length comes the day of the great ceremony. In the afternoon hundreds of women from all the villages in the valley converge toward the ceremonial site, trailing their small sons and daughters with them and carrying string bags filled with food and blankets for the night. The site is a vast area of trampled grass, forming a kind of clearing concealed in the undergrowth at the top of a cliff overhanging the river. In the middle stands a pile of dry tree trunks which the great men have discreetly cut down not far from here and brought to the site. Once kindled, these trunks make a huge bonfire which burns all night, its tall red, leaping flames lighting up the scene, the brown bodies, the groups of women and their dancing. The ceremony begins around eleven in the evening, and goes on till dawn, and then continues on the river bank where all the women reassemble with the initiates. It is not until the middle of the afternoon that the women bring the young girl back to her village, before returning, amid giggling and laughter, to their respective villages.

The ceremony is strictly out of bounds to men, who often tease the women by claiming to have hidden all night and watched them and boasting that they have seen "everything." Despite this prohibition, the women have allowed me to attend their ceremonies on many occasions. I had expressed the wish to do so to two of my female informants who had been working with me. One of them is Djirinac, among those to whom I have dedicated this book. For over a year, I heard nothing more about my wish, even though my friends had promised to convey it to the other women and to talk it over with them.

One evening – an evening on which I knew the women would be celebrating the initiation of a friend's daughter, Ymbaingac, who was a leader among the teenage girls and a lively, bold, insolent, quick-witted girl whom I liked a lot – my two friends, accompanied by some old women, came to seek me

41

out and took me down to the bottom of the village where they left me in company with Ymbaingac, her female sponsor, and a handful of coinitiates in the menstrual house. Despite the fasting and her apprehensions about the coming events, Ymbaingac spent the evening joking and sleeping. Then, around midnight, other women came to fetch us and we went down in silence to the hidden clearing at the cliff's edge.

I must point out straightaway that, as a result of my attendance at the women's rites, I was excluded for some hours from the world of men. When I returned to the village, having spent the night and day among the women, there was not a man to be found in the village, and their disappearance was to be expected; they had abandoned it to the women and were gathered in the men's house. I was quite taken aback, though, when after some time two young men arrived and called me by my name, but refused to come near and warned me not to approach them. They then explained that they had been sent by the men to tell me that I could not live with them again unless I agreed to undergo a purification rite. I acquiesced, and the two messengers went off into the forest, saying that they would be back in an hour or two. Some hours later they did indeed return, carrying two freshly killed birds. They came up to me and asked me to undress, and I did so. They then set fire to the birds' feathers and waved them like torches beneath my armpits, and around my crotch, close to my genitals. The smoke and stench of burned feathers and flesh chased away the smells and pollution of the women, which had clung to my body, and I was thus able to resume my place in the men's world.

In fact, as I understood later, they had performed on me a rite that the women perform on themselves each time they resume married life after having been separated from their husbands for a while in order to give birth or await the end of the menstrual period. On each occasion, the husband goes hunting the day before his wife's return, kills a bird, and leaves it near the entrance of their house. On arrival, his wife finds the bird, sets fire to the feathers, and purifies herself by waving the burning bird along her body, her belly, her hands, around the hearth where she cooks the family's food and, finally, along the walls of the hut.

These were the conditions of my attending the ceremonies, and here, in summary, is what I saw and heard. The young girl is brought close to the gigantic bonfire which her sponsor and other young women have just lit. She is made to sit down right at the edge of the flames, on her sponsor's lap, the latter being seated on the ground. On either side of the couple sit all the pubescent girls in the valley not yet married or who, if they are married, have not yet had children. The heat is fierce, and although the girls are sheltered beneath several bark cloaks, they sweat profusely. This fire and heat are meant to purify them, to eliminate the water from their body, to make them tough and firm, and to give them a glossy new skin.

Then begins a long series of harangues aggressively delivered to the young girl by old women armed with long digging sticks, which they brandish about the head, while hopping backward and forward, as warriors do when they defy their enemies and dodge their arrows. The girl and her companion listen silently to these harangues as each lesson is driven home with light, symbolic taps on the head with the stick by one of the old women, who suddenly stops jumping and rushes threateningly upon the initiate. What these old women are shouting at them are the tablets of the Baruya law, the commandments of male domination over the women and of the submission of the younger to the elder:

Do not resist your husband when he wants to make love; do not cry out, or you will be heard and from shame he will hang himself.

Be careful of your husband's coinitiates. If they come when your husband is not there, they may try to make love to you, your husband will find out, will kill you and them as well.

Do not laugh if your husband's *pulpul* is not put on straight and lets you glimpse his genitals. He would be ashamed.

Do not cut down the sugarcanes he has planted without his permission, unless guests pay a visit. Then you should rush to cut them down and give them to drink. Cook sweet potatoes for them. Your husband will be pleased.

Do not kill your child when you give birth to it. Men are more inclined to become attached when they have children; they think more about clearing gardens for them and for you.

[. . .]

In the middle of all these speeches, a girl disguised as a man, as a warrior, makes her entrance. She is the sister or a classificatory sister of the fiancé of the girl who has just had her first period; she represents her brother, the husband-to-be. Then the old women cry out, pointing to the man-woman: "Look, look who's coming, look . . .[then follows the name of the young man she is destined to marry]." The fiancé's sister chews some salt and the leaves of magic plants, and spits this "sauce" onto the leaves of a variety of banana tree whose fruit is said to make women more fertile. They then give this sauce to the young initiate to eat, and then to the other women. Needless to say, there are several meanings to this rite, some of which I know because the women revealed them to me, but not all of them. It has something to do with the reeds that the women plant in order to make *pulpuls*, the *pulpuls* that hide men's and women's sexual organs. It also signifies that the woman must not withhold her vagina.

Lastly, and above all, it refers to sperm, as does the following ritual.

Young women prepare pieces of sugarcane, stripping off the bark. They put these into the girl's mouth and give them to other young women as well to suck. Here too, the meaning is clear once one knows that the sugarcane is planted exclusively by the men in special gardens and that it represents the penis. The juice that her mouth expresses from the pieces of sugarcane is like the sperm that the man ejaculates not only in the woman's belly in order to make children, but also in her mouth when he gives her his sperm to drink, whenever she needs to recover her strength, after childbirth or menstruation. This is the secret revealed to the young girl on that night, not only by means of gestures, but also through songs that tell her never to refuse, later on in life, to drink the sugarcane juice. We shall be coming back to this matter for it lies at the heart of the Baruya thinking that legitimizes male power.

Then, in the dark surrounding the clearing lit by the bonfire, the young women go off to prepare themselves. Several times during the night, they spring out of the shadows to dance and mime around the fire before the eyes of the young initiate, a series of scenes illustrating a principle or behavioral norm expected of a woman. They dress up as warriors for each of these dances, holding in their hands the long reed stalks that the little boys use as spears in their games. They come before the young initiate and her friends, and at a given signal, they fling the spears in the girl's face. The girl remains motionless, but her sponsor and the other young women, while remaining seated, gather up the projectiles and reply in kind. This scene mimes the fate awaiting the girl should she ever deceive her husband. He would come to seek her to kill her with a bamboo arrow, *biaka,* the arrow used to kill pigs, wild and domestic, and enemies. Formerly, the Baruya used to paint the image of a woman's vagina onto the tips of these arrows as a reminder of the punishment awaiting the adulterous woman and her lover.

Other dances and songs follow all through the night. In one of them, the woman is told never to stand when her husband is seated and eating sugarcane. Otherwise, her sex would poison the juice of the sugar. She must squat or sit, and wait until he has finished; if not he is liable to suspect her of wanting to poison him and may seek revenge by casting an evil spell on her. Another song advises the young woman to resist her husband if he tries to make love with her in some forbidden place or time, on the way to the hunting grounds, for example, or the day set for cooking a pig in the oven dug in the earth.

While they mime these scenes and sing group songs, the old women continue to threaten the girl, and other women make her ashamed of herself by reminding her of incidents from her childhood, her misdeeds and shortcomings. Here are some translations:

A woman: You must help your father, and bring him a basket of sweet potatoes.

Another: When the women go to cook their food together, help them, peel the sweet potatoes, bring banana leaves to line the bottom of the oven.

Another: You should help your father-in-law and mother-in-law. They are growing old now.

Another: When people build a new house, help them; bring them bales of straw.

Another: Get home before your husband; that way he won't suspect you of screwing around outside.

Another: Now you can no longer go around exciting men. Now that your vagina is open, they are liable to take that as an invitation to screw you.

44

Another: Now, when you walk along the road, don't look at your arms or your skirt; walk straight ahead and do not shout like a man.

Another: Don't run the way you used to when you were little, to catch field mice in the gardens.

Another: I heard you tell old Bousaraiac: "If you scold me, I'll hit you." Now you must no longer talk like that to old women.

Another: Do you imagine that all men belong to you, and that you can choose one the way you would pick out the best sweet potatoes, leaving the half-rotten ones? You must obey the rules. These young men are the sons of many different women and we have chosen a husband for you. Now you must respect the law.

Another: If you don't want to marry Djonongaliac's son, there are many people in his clan and they will kill you.

Another: If you don't want to marry him, then just have a go at trying to scatter the fire your sister has lit for you; just try to wreck it.

Another: Why are you afraid of the fire? Come on, there's no point covering your face. You used not to be afraid of us in the village. You used to show us your behind. So you shouldn't be afraid of the fire now.

Another: We've been watching you a long time. We don't think you're capable of having more than two children.

Another: I overheard you say: "I don't want to cook for my father." All you carry on your back is a small string bag. Is that a way to carry on? You're behaving like a man. Now you've got to learn to carry a heavy bagful of sweet potatoes.

Another: Hey, little girl, you see this little [metonymy!] fire over there; that's an image of your home. You've no right to sit around doing nothing at home and let the fire die out. You must build a good fire every day. If your man returns home and there's no fire, his friends and coinitiates will poke fun at him. He will be ashamed.

Another: You see, a long time ago we told Nungwakac what we're telling you today; now she's got ten children and lots of pigs, and each time she makes a *mumu* [big oven] to cook for her family. She listened to us.

At length, with the first glimmer of dawn, the young initiate, her sponsor, the other girls who have had their first periods in recent months, quietly slip away from the spot while, around the dying embers, hundreds of women are stretched out asleep, covered by their bark cloaks, children pressed to their bellies, in the grass damp with chilly dew. They silently go down to the river. There, at the water's edge, the sponsor rolls about in the mud with the young initiate, apparently miming the act of copulation. Then everyone washes and stays squatting in the water. They are covered with branches and leaves, which are sprinkled with water from time to time while they await the arrival of the main body of women. During this time, apparently, the young women who have just given birth and whose breasts are still swollen with milk hide beneath the leafy branches and give their breasts to the young initiates to suck.

Then, for hours on end, throughout the morning, all the women dance and beat themselves with nettles or whip themselves with branches, pretending to feel nothing. The little ones are beaten too, as they are tied to their mothers' backs so as not to slide off to the ground during the dancing. At a given signal, the young initiates spring out from beneath the heaps of branches to dance, and the women while singing start to beat them. The young girl is given a lump of wood to bite on as hard as possible, while women rub her face, breasts, and belly with nettles, which burn her horribly. The lump of wood is meant to stifle her cries in the presence of her sponsor. It is after this trial that the young girl's mother calls her daughter by her "grown-up name," her initiate name. She is then dressed in her new skirts; the women from her paternal and maternal families lend necklaces of shells to be passed around her neck, and the dozen bark cloaks presented to her by her fiancé's family are then passed over her head.

Then comes the girl's first meal. Dozens of taros and sweet potatoes are heaped at her feet with prodigality. She herself will eat but one or two of them, into which leaves with magical powers have been inserted to give her strength. At last it is time to return to the village, in a slow-moving procession. But suddenly a group of young men in the fourth stage of the initiation, with bloodshot eyes, spring from the undergrowth and charge the women, waving branches bristling with spikes or clubs. In the ensuing melee, amid the cries and shouts, the married women defend themselves roughly with their digging sticks. We shall be coming back to this ritual. Finally, the young initiate and her companions reach the village. Exhausted, they collapse onto the ground to sleep, having first spread out in a vast green circle the dozens of skirts that have been given to them and that until now they have been wearing one on top of another. Women living farther away set out for home fairly early so as to be able to get a little sleep before preparing, as always, their husband's meals and food for the pigs.

The following day, the women from the girl's lineage and from that of her husband-to-be gather to eat, with her and their children, the game brought by their brothers, fathers, and husbands, who have been out hunting in the forest for the past few days. The meal takes place close to the future father-in-law's home; it is he who prepares and cooks the game before offering it to the women. In the days that follow, several final rituals take place to remove the prohibitions on the eating of areca nuts, drinking water, and so forth imposed before the ceremony. One evening, the girl and her coinitiates are shut up in her sponsor's house. The sponsor burns the remains of the sugar-cane on the fire, and everyone suffocates for hours in the shifting thick smoke. This is supposed to remind them not to start fires just anywhere when preparing their garden; but there are other, more secret, meanings, since the sugarcane is the man's penis.

Are the women's initiations genuine initiations?

Having thus all too briefly described some of the rituals to which the Baruya, both men and women, submit, it is now important to examine their explicit and implicit meanings. First of all, it is important to note the differences between the two series of initiations, between the procedures adopted to imprint upon individuals the social characteristics expected of their sex.

What strikes one first is the difference in the amount of energy that society expends to make a man and a woman suitable for marriage. It takes ten years of sexual segregation, four major ceremonies at intervals of several years, the first and third of which last more than five weeks, to separate a boy from his mother, to sever him from the world of women, and to prepare him to cope with women again when he marries. On the other hand, it takes a little less than a fortnight to turn an adolescent into a girl ready for marriage and childbearing.

What is more, whereas the boys, once separated from their mothers, are plunged for at least ten years into an utterly different, exclusively masculine world, from which they will emerge reborn, young girls spend only a few days in an exclusively feminine world, thereafter returning to live the same life as before, at the side of their mothers, the only difference being that they will now start to visit another family, that of their future parents-in-law more frequently, and will start performing services for them. So it is the fate of a woman to leave one family, her father's, for that of her husband in order to found another.

The few days that the girl has spent with the women, and this interlude recurs each time another girl has her first period, interrupt an everyday life made up of work in the fields, wood gathering, looking after the little children, cooking each day for the family, and raising pigs, but they do not change her life. Whereas the boys' initiation represents a complete break, accomplished by the men, against the women, with the Sun's help. It is followed by a new birth, this time accomplished by the men unaided. The girl's initiation is the consecration of a break initiated by Moon, younger brother of Sun. Master of all that is humid, the Moon pierces the sex of women and makes their menstrual blood to flow. Men too contribute to this break, since some months before the girl has her period, when her breasts are already firmly outlined, a man, a "maternal" uncle, comes to pierce her nose and open it. But the break is not followed by a prolonged spell in a world cut off from men; nor, apparently, does it involve a genuine rebirth or renaissance of women into the world.

Indeed, one may legitimately wonder whether the girls' puberty ceremony is a real initiation ceremony at all.

On closer inspection, the answer is bound to be yes, for the following reasons. First of all, in both symbolic practices we find a number of common ritual elements that play an essential role in what undeniably appears to be a boys' initiation. The first fundamental fact is the name change. There is a childhood name, and there is the one that one bears after these ceremonies, and it is by this second name that one is thereafter known in society. Everyone is expected to forget the old name as quickly as possible, and no one is allowed to utter it. It is a deep insult to call a man or woman by his or her initial name. It is as if one were accusing him or her of being a child, never having grown up, of having stayed irresponsible.

As with the boys, this change of name and status is accompanied by violence; boys and girls alike are assisted by an older boy or girl who represents the maternal world and helps them come through the test, agreeing to submit once more, with them and for their sake, to an ordeal through which he (or she) has already passed. Boys and girls subsequently have certain obligations and prohibitions toward their sponsor, similar to those laid upon a man regarding his mother.

In either case, the change of social status implies the imposition of certain constraints in posture and uses of the body, on speech, diet, clothing, and so on. At one stage, the individual is forbidden to eat a certain plant. This prohibition is then removed and replaced by others. Women, however, are subjected to far fewer dietary prohibitions than the men, and old women are subject to practically none at all. But other elements in the girls' puberty ceremony are clear evidence that it does indeed produce a break with the past and aspires to bring a new being into the world: first of all, the exposure of newly pubescent girls to the fierce heat of the fire, which is supposed to purify them and "change their skin," that is, to renew the body; the permanent presence of a sponsor to provide them with physical and psychological support in withstanding the test and in crossing the line between the two states; then, most important, the revelation that they will be drinking sperm, which will henceforth give them their strength; last, the sending of the girls' spirits into the treetops by an older girl, who raises their bark cloaks and flaps them toward the skies, as do the initiation masters in the different stages of the male initiations. Now, up to that point, the girls had never attended the last ritual, which the Baruya hold essential to the preservation of the strength and life of the group, namely, calling down on themselves the protection of their father, the Sun.

These revelations of hitherto unknown details, which are now presented as essential to the life and growth of individuals, to the survival of the group, do indeed make the girls' puberty ceremony an initiation, but not into an entirely new world since, as before, these girls will be returning to a world dominated by men. Consequently, the women attach importance to these ceremonies and are eager to take part in them. For it is the only "legal" occasion (in men's eyes) that they have to meet among themselves, in the absence of all men, with no barriers as to lineage and village of origin. This is not to say that they gather together to overthrow the social order, the male order, and the women's harangues to the young initiate are clear evidence that women do not take advantage of these collective ceremonies to set up a countermodel to the model of male domination. On the contrary, although the men are nowhere at hand and play no direct part in the proceedings, the women cooperate with them to impose on the sometimes rebellious young girls a set of rules that binds them over to men whom they may not want, and subjects them to a social order that is the order of male domination.

The occasions of freedom for the women – that the women sometimes get together among themselves, even for a short while; that they act, think, and speak beyond the men's direct control – arouse contradictory reactions, revealing the men's deep-seated fear that this freedom may go too far and pose a threat to them.

In public, the men never tire of belittling the importance of female ceremonies. "They're nothing at all; they're insignificant compared to our great ceremonies; they're grotesque, we've heard them singing in the distance, but their songs are just gibberish." They further claim: "We know all about it; we've seen everything; it's just a lot of clowning around." Now what no man, to the best of my knowledge, has ever seen or would dare to go and see, is the ablutions of the young girls in the river, at dawn, or the rituals that they perform at daybreak on the following days, in a little stream, *Yuwaric,* reserved for the women. But their feelings are mixed, with anger and agression uppermost. Yet, so far as I know, no woman has ever dared to mock the male initiations in public. In fact, the men are pretty certain that the women take advantage of their absence to make fun of them, humiliate them, to "heap all their filth" onto them. So powerful was this feeling that, before the white man's arrival, the men used to allow a group of *tchouwanie* and *kalave* to lie in ambush as the women made their way back to the initiate's village after each initiation; the youths, their eyes bloodshot, would rush down upon the women and children to flail them with thorns and sticks, spewing out insults. The women used to give as good as they got, laying about with their hard, pointed digging sticks. The married men used to be on hand, however, to stop the tussle from degenerating into murder. Having done that, intoxicated with their set-to with the women, the young men would climb back to the men's house, singing as they went, to beat the little initiates only recently taken from the women's world; or, in time of war, they would rush toward their enemies' territory to provoke or kill a few of them. War against external enemies, war against women, their internal enemies; nothing could better illustrate these two aspects of male domination than this outbreak of violence that followed whenever the women had gathered among themselves, celebrating the fact that one of them, in her turn, would soon be giving life, so asserting their fundamental link with the production of children and the continuity of society.

What is highly symbolic of men's intention to reassert their superiority on this occasion is the fact that if a woman ever dealt a head injury to one of the men, then the men solemnly removed the bouquet that usually decorates the highest point of the men's house, to indicate that it was now nothing but a "women's house." The bouquet was replaced after the injured man recovered.

Of course, when I attended the women's ceremonies, I did hear them making fun of their husbands and discussing them with very little of the respect that they show toward the men in public. But it took place somewhat on the fringe of things, in the chatting and joking that went on among the married women, in between the dances and sketches making up the ceremony, which they knew by heart. The message contained in these dances and sketches or mimed scenes did not deride the male order, as the men claim, nor did they incite to rebellion or propose a female countermodel of the social order; instead they explicitly encourage women to consent to male domination; they represent a remarkable plea to the young women to accept this order, a reminder that what is is what ought to be, that their customs comply with the order of things, and that this order is legitimate.

The girls' ceremony is thus not devoid of any relation to the male initiations. Nor is it a poor copy of what the men do, still less an ineffectual means of standing up to them. In fact, the female initiation emerges as the complement or projection of the men's initiation into the world of women; it is the women's share in the task of promoting a single order and law, that of male domination. In this female initiation, the women produce their own consent to the order by which they are dominated. In one sense, this ceremony is merely another aspect of the men's strength, and an essential aspect of it, in that it is the work of the women themselves. The women thereby add to the power that men derive from their permanent repression of women (and initiates).

It could be that the women themselves tend to legitimize men's open contempt for their ceremonies and their condescending claim that these are not true initiations. For the old women, brandishing their sticks at the girls and their now married former playmates disguised as warriors, hurling symbolic arrows at them, are imprinting into the girls' minds the same social order as the one they have known since birth, namely, the order of submission to the men. What is new to them, making all these efforts necessary, is that they are now being asked to do for other men, of whom they know very little and whom they certainly have not yet come to love, what they have already been doing for their brothers and father. They are being asked to do again, and to do it well, what their mothers, and all married women, have always done in the past. And they are constantly reminded that, by obeying, they will not only be serving directly the interests of their mothers and their family, but indirectly those of all the Baruya as well. In so doing, they will deserve the men whom they serve and who serve them in return, by protecting them, helping them to raise children, and so on.

What the girls discover then, once Moon has pierced them and separated them from their childhood, is not, as with the boys, a totally new world; it is rather, over and above the obligations of their youth, which still stand, a whole series of new duties, primarily sexual and material, but of such social importance that this time society as a whole has an interest in ensuring respect for them. This is the price that they must pay one day to become real women, mothers of many children, hard working, proud of their sons, their gardens, and their pigs, proud of all that they do for their husband, sons, brothers, and father, in a word, respected women, "great women."

All these relations are expressed, interpreted, and legitimized in the Baruya world of the conceptual[1] and, above all, in their theory of life, sperm, and the various bodily substances. It is around these ideas or presentations that their symbolic practice is organized and their everyday practice, their social order, justified. In order to penetrate more deeply the significance of these male and female initiations, we must first take a close look at the way they view the process of reproduction of life and of the role of each sex in that process.

The Baruya vision of the process of the reproduction of life; the significance of bodily substances

For the Baruya, a child is first and foremost produced by the man, by his sperm, his "water." But the man's sperm, once locked inside the woman, mingles with her liquids, her "water." If the man's sperm prevails over the woman's water, the child will be a boy and vice versa. But the man, not content to make the child with his sperm, continues to "nourish" it by means of repeated coitus, and makes it grow in the woman's belly.

But men are not alone in making children in women's bellies. Each child has two fathers, his own human father and the supernatural father of all humans, the Sun. All that the man does in fact is to make the child's body. It is the Sun that makes his eyes, nose, mouth, fingers, and toes. Just as the Sun paved the way for life by piercing the man's penis and the woman's vagina, so it completes the process by rounding off the work begun by the man.

I am divulging here practices and theories that the Baruya have striven fiercely to keep secret, prudently, obstinately concealing them from the whites, whose contempt and aggressiveness they fear more than anything else. Immediately after the European conquest the Baruya came into contact with missionaries who exhorted them to cast aside their ancestral customs, saying they were based on ignorance of the true God, of truth, and inspired

---

[1] The conceptual: *idéel* (the translator feels that the near-equivalent most readily comprehensible to the English-speaking reader is conceptual, although it is a neologism in the French). It is the system of ideas, values, beliefs, and representations that go to make up a society. It should not be confused with its system of ideals. See Maurice Godelier, "La part idéelle du réel. Essai sur l'idéologie," *L'Homme* 18 (3–4) (1978): 155–88.

by Satan, who was black as they and condemned them irremediably to Hell. The Baruya reacted by shrouding in still deeper mystery their practices, already surrounded by the secrecy of things revealed to initiates (boys or girls) alone, secrets that, by definition, could never be shared by all the members of society, still less so with outsiders.

The first of these secrets – as we have already had occasion to see – is that sperm is life, strength, the nourishment that gives life strength. Therefore men give their sperm to drink to their wives weakened by menstruation or childbirth. But sperm also makes women's milk, develops their breasts, and makes them nursing mothers. Consequently, before making love to his wife for the first time, the young bridegroom must give her his sperm to drink, and he must go on doing so until she is sufficiently strong, until the soot has blackened the walls of their new home.

The second secret is more sacred still, and no woman must ever know it. Sperm gives men the power to make boys be born again outside the mother's belly, apart from the world of women, in the world of men and by their efforts alone. This holiest of secrets is that, as soon as the young initiates enter the men's house, they are nourished on the sperm of their elders, and that this sperm is drunk repeatedly over many years in order to make them grow bigger and stronger than the women, superior to them, capable of dominating and managing them.

This custom is no longer in use today, having disappeared practically immediately after the arrival of the Europeans in 1960. It does still survive in certain tribes belonging to the Anga group, living farther to the south, in the mountains and forests even less accessible than those of the Baruya to the influence of the Europeans and to state administration. Gilbert Herdt, an American anthropologist who has lived and worked with one of these tribes, the Tsambia, has observed it in detail and has recently described it in his book *Guardians of the Flutes* (1981), which on many points coincides with my own findings concerning the Baruya. But Herdt was also conscious of the sacred character of the practices he was observing, of the secrets being confided in him, conscious too of the contemptuous, hostile, and sometimes even positively aggressive attitude of certain missionaries (belonging to the German Lutheran Church, who on many occasions had tried to persuade the Australian administration to prohibit these initiations, and had even, after independence, proclaimed its intention "publicly to shame" all these tribes for their barbarous customs, by revealing to the women what the men did, among others). Herdt has therefore decided to publish his findings though changing the name of the tribe in question so as to prevent identification. Such are the contradictions of the white man's world! Let the reader who is part of that world be mindful of this situation and draw the appropriate conclusions.

Our examination reveals an overarching unity of the different aspects of

Baruya thought and social practice in their efforts to control and organize the process of the reproduction of life in order both to ensure its successful outcome – the birth and growth of children – and to establish male domination, and in so doing infuse sexuality in all its aspects, heterosexual and homosexual, with meaning, instilling it with both social and cosmic significance.

To make a child of either sex, the Baruya believe that the men must first exchange their sisters and that they must then pour their sperm into their wives' mouths and bellies in order to make children, nourish them and nourish the mothers, and to fortify both children and mothers. But without the Sun's intervention in the woman's belly in order to complete man's work, the fetus would emerge noseless, eyeless, and fingerless.

At birth, babies are not properly completed. In the case of a girl, Moon must pierce her again in order to open her to men and make her capable of being fertilized. If it is a boy, the men and the Sun must separate him from women, and make him be born a second time among them. The men then nourish him with their sperm, and the Sun periodically comes down at each initiation to complete their work and to help him to grow to manhood through the four stages of initiation.

Now, the next question is, who among the men is fit to take the place of the boy's father (and mother) to continue this "nursing"? Married men are ineligible. For the Baruya, it would be the worst possible humiliation, the worst form of aggression to give seed from a penis that has penetrated a woman to the young boy to drink so shortly after his forcible removal from the world of women. It would be tantamount to treating the boy's mouth like a vagina, and communicating to his mouth all the pollution that comes from women's genitalia. Consequently, only the unmarried young men, the *tchouwanie* and the *kalave,* the eldest among all these virgin boys, could and should give their sperm to the new initiates. The initiates had no option but to accept the penis thus proffered. Those that refused to do so, terrified by the secret import of the gesture, by its importance to them as to all the Baruya and by the punishment awaiting them should they ever divulge it to the women and to the not-yet-initiated little boys, were coerced. Tradition relates that some who refused broke their necks in their efforts to resist. They were buried and their mothers never learned the true cause of their death, being told that they had fallen out of some tree in the course of a hunting party.

Needless to say, this initial violence was followed by more relaxed, more easygoing relations. Couples would form in the men's house and the older partner would look after the younger one. After having used his mouth, he was supposed to go hunting and offer him some game, just as the married men offer game to the initiates at the conclusion of each great ceremony marking the transition from one stage to the next, or to their wives after childbirth. One point needs to be made clear, namely that like all Anga

53

tribes, the Baruya never performed sodomy. Their homosexuality was confined to caresses and fellatio. The very idea of ejaculating into someone else's anus struck them as both grotesque and repellant.

Although all married men were excluded from these homosexual relations, not all unmarried men were permitted to give their sperm to a young initiate. The initiate's direct maternal and paternal kin could under no circumstances become his partners. The exchange of sperm, of the vital substance, between men was thus permissible only beyond the perimeter of relations established by the exchange of women. Male society, the order of male domination, stands above social relations of intimacy and mutual help engendered by the exchange of women; it is above relations of kinship and their obligations which, though undoubtedly fundamental, are confined to the handful of lineages that make up a person's kinfolk, by the very limitations of these relations.

Now, what happens in this exchange of vital substance between men? The older boys give their seed to the younger ones, just as they themselves had received the same gift from those now married. The circulation of life and strength works according to the principle that the givers of sperm are not takers, a kind of principle of "generalized exchange" of life between all men down succeeding generations, but on condition that these men have never had sexual relations with women. Thus they give life to other men before marrying and going on to make it in the bellies of their lawful wives. There thus emerges here a complete cycle of exchanges between the men who create, build, and practice solidarity among themselves, regardless of generation and lineage, transcending the frontiers between them, outside the world of women and against them. So all unmarried young men thus help the sons of married men not belonging to their own lineage or that of their mother to become men. They thus give back what they themselves have received from older men, who have now left the men's house to marry. Whereas relations of kinship work on the principle of direct exchange of women, the takers being givers as well, the political and ideological relations between men work on the basis of general exchange of vital substance. The takers can never be the givers since the relationship between the two is asymmetrical, the givers (the older) being superior to the takers (the younger). These relations between men are also relations between lineages having no direct bond of consanguinity or marriage.

For those who somewhat facilely and, to be frank, mechanically contrast societies characterized by the restricted exchange of women with generalized exchange societies, as if the former were ignorant of the principle on which the latter rest, the example of the Baruya clearly offers a means of rectifying their view. Although the Baruya prefer the principle of restricted exchange of women in order to establish relations of kinship between lineages and individuals, they apply a kind of principle of generalized exchange of sperm between all the men not belonging to the sphere of the exchange of women in order to establish manhood and male domination. Both principles of exchange thus exist in their thought, but are applied in distinct areas of their social life. I should point out, however, that I am using these words "generalized exchange" only metaphorically, to refer to the gift of sperm between men belonging to consecutive generations. When Lévi-Strauss speaks of "generalized exchange" of women, he is referring to a principle that goes beyond the distinction, the asymmetry between givers and takers of women, beyond the force that pushes exchanges in a given irreversible direction. He is referring to the fact that these exchanges take place within a closed circuit or loop. A gives a wife to B, B to C, C to A, and so on; consequently the loop may take some time, several generations even, to reach completion.

Here, clearly, there is no looping in the circulation of sperm between consecutive generations of men who have as yet had no sexual relations with women; for the loop to occur the youngest men would have to return their sperm to the givers of their givers. What in fact happens is that the vital substance circulates continuously downward from generation to generation; the generation that gives is superior to the one that receives, and inferior to the one that gave to it. This asymmetry of gift/countergift relations limits the comparison between the general exchange of sperm and generalized exchange of women among men [Figure 4].

Incidentally, it would be absurd to believe that social evolution leads from the simple to the complex, for, as we see here, simple and complex principles of exchange coexist in social organization and practice, but not in the same spot or for the same purposes.

Baruya reality is still more complex because the generalized exchange of vital substances does not occur solely among the men. The women too do the same thing with their milk. This practice casts a different light on the relations between men and women in this society. It shows that the women too try to nourish themselves, to fortify themselves and grow without the help of men. This attempt clearly throws into relief the tension, if not to say opposition, that exists between the sexes, endlessly giving proof that not only is the subordination of women to men neither total nor definitive, but that, on the contrary, it helps maintain a state of competition and struggle between the sexes.

Before going any further, let us take another look at milk. It was several years before the women explained to me the significance of certain practices. For example, the woman, when traveling at night, instead of carrying her baby on her back, covered by her bark cloak, carries it on her stomach, swinging in its string bag as she stumbles over the ruts along the path. Also, the woman never gives her breast to a baby without first squirting a little milk onto the ground. Last the woman, while working in the fields, never leaves her baby alone, hanging in the shade of a tree, but always in the company of

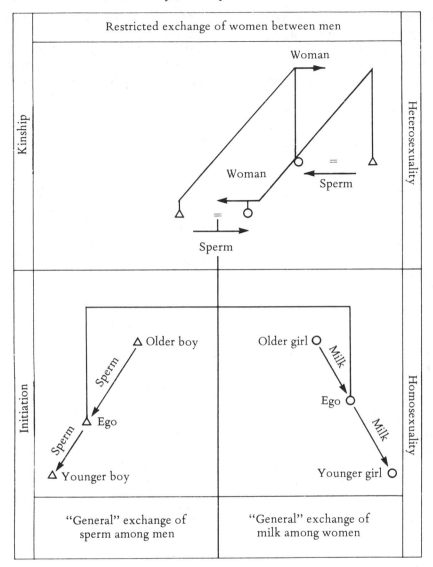

Figure 4. Kinship and initiation among the Baruya

a little girl, a younger sister or older daughter, who watches over the baby and stays in the garden less to help with the work than to stay close to the child. It is not easy for a man to observe these little facts but all flow from the regard of the women, whether dead or alive, for the milk of other women.

Dead women are avid for the milk that a mother squirts before putting her breast in her baby's mouth to clean away the dangerous, mortal traces that dead women or dead babies may have left behind when sucking milk without her even realizing it. At night, a mother carries her child in front of her, fearing that dead women, their breasts filled with milk, may rush upon the baby to give it their mortal milk to suckle. For the same reason a little girl is always posted beside the baby: Her presence frightens off dead women avid to give their milk to the child.

Living women too may wish to give their milk to the child, although on this point I know very little. Most of what I know comes from the men, and what they had to say was not all that specific. Young women did tell me, however, that the women used to give each other milk to drink. I myself observed how, when alone, they used to fondle and weigh each other's breasts. I could not help but compare these caresses with the way the men often caress each other, slipping a hand beneath a friend's *pulpul* to caress his testicles, or squeeze his penis between forefinger and thumb. The women's secret, then, is that young women who have just had a child and whose breasts are still swollen with milk give their breasts to squeeze and drink to younger, nonpubescent girls. Just as the men give their penises to other men to drink and thus withhold a portion from the world of women, so women apparently give their milk to other women and so withhold a portion from the child whom the men have made in their bellies. This aspect of the women's behavior suggests the existence of another world in which women, notwithstanding their general subordination to men, conceive or lay claim to some form of autonomy, to a power of autonomous growth rather similar to the one that the men claim for themselves and imagine that they possess. So it would appear to be milk that the young pubescent girl, hiding beneath a huge pile of leaves and branches, drinks from the breasts of one of her elders, in the dawn that follows her great nocturnal initiation ceremony, squatting with the other women in the river water, where they have come to wash and purify themselves. But I do not know this point for certain, and I cannot be altogether categorical.

The Baruya theory and male symbolic practices contest or minimize the claim to autonomy, which apparently underpins certain aspects of the women's behavior. According to the men, a woman can only have milk and fine breasts after her young husband has nourished her abundantly with his sperm. For a Baruya, his wife's milk is none other than his sperm transformed into a substance to nurture his child; by giving her milk to young girls about to marry, a wife merely anticipates what the young bridegrooms are about to do, when they too fortify their brides with their sperm. To the extent, therefore, that women share more or less fully the ideology according to which everything comes either directly or indirectly from the men, they will view the generalized exchange of milk between generations of women as evidence that they really are as inferior to men as the latter would have them and claim them to be or, on the contrary, proof that they are much less so, even if they cannot say so in public. The fact that each sex enjoys the possibility of interpreting the same ideas in its own distinct way provides an outlet for the tensions and conflicts that inevitably arise when one part of society (in this case, one sex) is dominant over the other. So what we have here is not really a female countermodel, or a set of ideas distinct from the official view arguing in favor of a different society in which this oppression would be banished; it is a different, partially opposed (but only partly) manner of shedding light on the same ideas and experiencing the same practice.

For in thought at least, things can go no further; they can take on no stronger, more radical meaning. Do things not in effect correspond to official Baruya thinking? Is it not true that boys have no need of women to produce sperm, and that they have no need, as the women do, to wait for Moon to pierce them, to be married, nurtured, and fertilized by a man's sperm in order to produce their substance and give their strength? These things happen without women whereas for women, quite plainly, they cannot happen without men. However differently the women may interpret the same facts, they cannot deny that sperm, of all these bodily substances, is by far the most powerful and nourishing, and that it accounts for and legitimizes male domination. The man's body and his penis are ever present to attest the superiority of man over woman, of all men over all women, and to bear witness in his favor. But this superiority is under constant threat from another substance, which this time flows exclusively and regularly from the woman's body, once Moon has pierced her and she has had her first period, namely, menstrual blood.

The attitude of the men toward menstrual blood, whenever they talk or think about it, verges on hysteria, mingling disgust, repulsion, and above all fear. For them, menstrual blood is dirty, and they rank it with those other polluting, repugnant substances, urine and feces. Above all, though, it is a substance that weakens women whenever it flows from them, and it would destroy men's strength if ever it came into contact with their bodies. Hence the total segregation of the sexes whenever a woman has her period; this attitude also explains why she is forbidden at such times to prepare food for her husband's family and even for herself with her hands, which cannot avoid touching her sex and handling the wads of leaves that she uses to absorb the blood. Therefore women are confined in a temporary shelter at the bottom of the village, among the bushes and undergrowth in the area reserved for their use, and, finally, are obliged to purify themselves before returning to conjugal life. It is because blood, for the Baruya, represents strength and life that any loss of it, any flow of blood, makes them frightened and shrink from it.

First, there is the blood that flows from wounds, those received and those given. When the Baruya used to kill an enemy in battle, they would plunge their weapons into the blood that flowed from the wounds and utter their victory cry. Or, they might sacrifice an enemy warrior captured live, piercing his body with a sacred bamboo knife, daubing their bodies with the blood that flowed. Then they would finish him off by tearing out his liver, which they then cooked and ate. Afterward they could not return to their village and resume normal life without washing themselves and ritually purifying their body of all trace of blood, of this blood of another man, which for them signified victory.

But in addition to the blood that flows from wounds, there is another more dangerous kind, which oozes suddenly and flows from the bodily orifices, the nose, the ears, the mouth, the anus, blood vomited, urinated, or defecated. This blood, more surely so than the other, is a sign of death, of looming yet secret, invisible death. It is the death that the shamans inflict, whose spirit devours your liver, or the death deliberately contrived by an enemy, internal or external, who casts a spell on you or kills you by sorcery.

Menstrual blood is more dangerous still. It too flows suddenly from an orifice, but instead of bringing about the body's death, it merely weakens it temporarily. Its lethal part is aimed at men and represents a permanent threat to their strength and vital force, against all that underpins and justifies their social domination.

Women, moreover, are intermittently dangerous not only on account of their menstrual blood, for in that case all the precautions taken during menstruation ought to be sufficient to protect men from the risks that their bleeding entails for them. In fact, the Baruya view women as a permanent danger by virtue of the very shape of their sexual organ, by the inevitable fact that it is a slit that can never altogether keep back the liquids that it inwardly secretes, or the sperm that man places in it. Despite herself, despite all the precautions that she takes, a woman can never totally prevent drops of sperm and/or drops of her vaginal liquids from flowing from her sex when she sits down or from falling to the ground when she stands. (Baruya women, needless to say, wear no undergarments.)

Now, for the Baruya, the ground teems with worms and snakes that slither through the grass and catch these falling secretions and carry them away through cracks in the ground down to the abyss, where evil, chthonic powers dwell. These then make use of these substances, stolen from humans though made available by women, to send sickness and death not only to men or women who have just made love, but also to the plants that they cultivate and the pigs that they breed. They thus do what people wishing to kill somebody by means of sorcery do, furtively making off with a piece of sweet potato that their intended victim has just spat out, or one of his hairs, or again a piece of fingernail, and using it to cast an evil spell on him. Therefore the Baruya never leave their hair, nail clippings, or leftovers from their meals lying around.

So, through her sexual organs, women act as a constant magnet to the evil powers that populate the invisible part of the world. They attract them and help them, without even being aware of it, to endanger nature and society. Sometimes, though, they conspire with them actively and deliberately, such as when a woman wanting to kill her husband collects his sperm as it flows from her sex and throws it into the fire. Women, through their genitalia, act as much upon the cosmic order as upon the order of society, and all the more powerfully upon the social order because they also act directly on the balance of (super)natural powers. For if nothing grows in the fields, and if the pigs' flesh turns watery when cooked, then people can no longer meet their social and moral obligations, which is to share their pig, to give or to give back what has been given them, to help, and to be helped. For an individual this situation is a disgrace, but for society it spells the breakdown and possible collapse of all the necessary solidarity, the denial of all obligations rooted in relations of kinship and neighborliness.

Therefore women imperil the social order in two ways: directly, by means of their menstrual blood, which threatens to impair men's virility, and consequently their domination of society; and indirectly by the shape of their sex, which makes it an accomplice of conspiracies to ruin the efforts of human beings to produce their material conditions of existence, that is, fine gardens, nice, fat pigs to help them not only to live comfortably, but also and above all to maintain their position in society, to reproduce in it, and, consequently, to reproduce it (society).

It is easier, in the light of this analysis, to understand the vast array of taboos, complex precautions, and propitiatory or purificatory rituals with which the Baruya surround the uses of their body and their sex organs. A woman must avoid stepping over an object lying on the ground. Under no pretext, and on pain of death, may she step across the hearth, even extinguished, of her home. Her sex might open and pollute the place where she cooks the food destined for her husband's mouth. Hence too, but this the women do not know, the men perform the secret rituals to stop up the women, to keep the man's sperm inside her vagina, not only to fertilize her more surely, or if she is pregnant to nourish the fetus inside her belly, but to avoid providing the chthonic powers with the material they need for their evil doings.

Sexual relations between the sexes

A profusion of taboos surround sexual relations between husband and wife. They are not allowed to make love when it is time to clear the forest and plant their gardens, or to cut the salt cane, or to kill and eat their pig, or before the husband is to go off hunting; when it is time to build a home for a newlywed couple, to rebuild that of a neighbor or one's own house, or during male or female initiations, and so on. Space too is marked out by various taboos. One must never make love in a garden, in swampy areas infested with worms and snakes, near the places where the spirits live, near cemeteries, and so on. Last, couples must absolutely refrain from making love after the birth of a child until it has cut its first teeth and, in the case of a boy, can play with a miniature bow or, if it is a girl, is capable of carrying a little string bag on her back.

It is considered good form, especially for the young, to refrain from mentioning sexual matters in public, and if one does so, to talk in metaphors and even to resort to a secret language, while spitting abundantly to purify the mouth. But as in all sexually repressive societies, alongside this verbal puritanism both men and women indulge in obscene language, especially when exchanging insults in a quarrel. They also have a whole range of dirty jokes, sexual allusions and provocations, particularly common among cross cousins, both female and male. These jokes are socially permitted and leave those present unmoved, or make them smile if someone happens to crack a "good" one.

How do the Baruya make love? During copulation, the woman is, as we have already seen, forbidden to bestride her partner, as the fluids in her vagina may spill onto the man's belly. And, of course, although the woman sucks her husband's penis, his mouth never comes near the woman's vagina. Like the idea of sodomy, the very thought is "unthinkable."

Adult Baruya generally take great care to hide their private parts. Neither man nor woman can comment, still less make a joke, if some man or woman should happen unintentionally to give people a glimpse of them. The person may go and hang himself or herself out of shame, and such hanging happens fairly frequently, especially when, in the middle of a husband-and-wife set-to, the man pushes the woman and makes her fall over backward, legs apart, in the sight of a crowd of neighbors contemplating the scene without intervening.

The Baruya never kiss. Husband and wife are not allowed to touch each other in public, but mothers, aunts, and sisters love kissing babies' bodies noisily. Large breasts are appreciated, and a woman who allows a man to brush against or touch her breasts is regarded as making a pass at him. The Baruya man regards his baby as an unclean thing. It is kept out of his sight, and should he happen to see it by chance, he spits on the ground. Indeed, children are not given a name until they are sure to survive, and a baby that dies in the first few months of life is buried by its mother without ceremony. Until the last few years, no man would ever have dreamed of holding a baby in his arms. No father would ever have wiped his child's behind. That is the mother's job, as is cleaning up the little one's urine. The men wipe their children's noses with their thumb. It is interesting to contrast this attitude

61

with the care and attention with which they surround their hunting dogs, carrying puppies in their cloaks, feeding them with pieces of sweet potato which they chew for them, the way women do for their piglets.

To come back to the question of bodily substances, what arouses most disgust, after menstrual blood, is feces, both that of human beings and that of the dogs and pigs that roam about the village. Anyone coming upon them raises a terrific song and dance, shouting, exclaiming indignantly, pulling faces, stepping ostentatiously around the offending matter and calling out the woman of the nearest house to clean up her child's mess or get rid of her dog's or pig's droppings as quickly as possible. The woman usually protests that her children or pigs had nothing to do with this filth. Yet another argument ensues, but in vain; somebody, a woman, will finish by cleaning up.

Clearly then, for the Baruya, making love poses a threat to the reproduction of nature and society, and this danger is consubstantially linked to the sex act itself, since it flows from all sexual relations, however legitimate. The taboos that surround sexual relations can merely circumscribe or ward off this danger, but they cannot abolish it. It is as if there were a profound contradiction between the sexual activities necessary to the reproduction of life and all those other activities necessary to the reproduction of society. Accordingly, once a couple has decided to make love, it must suspend all its activities for a while, both beforehand and afterward. It must choose its moment, stay at home when the rest of the village has gone off to work in the fields; in a word, it must cut itself off from society. Yet at the same time it makes use of society, discreetly arranging with the wife's mother or sister to feed the pigs in the evening.

Needless to say, making love with someone else's wife or husband entails far graver consequences which are not confined to the ensuing social disorders. For illicit lovemaking frequently takes place standing up, in hiding, anywhere and at any time; therefore it necessarily breaks the taboos that normally diminish the dangers inherent in heterosexual relations.

However, the dangers implied by these relations do not flow equally from the man and the woman. The main burden of responsibility lies with the woman, by virtue of the role that she plays in the reproduction of life. One can readily sense the thrust behind the attitude toward the body, behind the language of the body and bodily substances. It shackles the victim of male domination to her fate by turning what makes her different from men against her, ultimately making the victim the sole guilty party.

To sum up, male and female initiations are two complementary aspects of a social practice that establishes and legitimizes the domination of men over women. The men have something – sperm – that the women do not have; it is the source of strength and life, and makes men the representatives, the pillars and legitimate rulers, of society. The women have something – menstrual blood – that the men do not have; it threatens to sap men's strength and destroy their superiority. Women also have a sex that opens, and opens the door to the cosmic powers hostile to mankind. It is therefore necessary to separate the boys from girls in order to preserve, protect, and nurture the source of their strength and superiority as well as the strength of society at large.

So far then, relations between men and women among the Baruya appear to take the form of a rigid and fairly simple opposition between two poles, one of which is thought of as positive, the other negative. Consequently men might think that they are perfectly justified in dominating, ruling, and repressing women. The ten years of male initiation are devoted to promoting and exalting the superiority of the positive pole, whereas the handful of female initiate rituals are designed to induce consent to women's subordination and recognition of their inferiority.

This proposition is true, and probably tallies with the way boys and girls view matters at the beginning of their initiation. After all, their language itself is evidence. In Baruya, game becomes feminine once dead. So the masculine denotes movement, life, strength; the feminine their opposites. Woman and the feminine gender connote physical weakness, passiveness, ignorance, lack of intelligence, all of which are essential sources of disorder in social life.

Yet this vision is misleading, or at least inaccurate inasmuch as it reflects but one facet of the truth, a moment in the unfolding of reality during the years of initiation. We need to examine the missing pieces of the puzzle in order to rectify and complete our analysis of the forms and foundations of male domination. However, a perusal of Figure 5, which lists the ideological significations of the bodily substances in Baruya body language, should give some idea of what is missing. What stands out is the duality and essential ambivalence of the most negative pole, namely, menstrual blood, which represents both a mortal danger to man and the welcome sign that women are henceforward fertilizable and ready to give life.

Female powers and the ambivalence of woman

Let us take another look at the example of menstrual blood. Closer scrutiny of Baruya thought shows it not to be a mere negative opposite of sperm but a double reality which also contains an irreducibly positive element. For it is only when it flows and because it flows that previously sterile little girls will tomorrow become women capable of being fertilized. It is this ambivalence that accounts for the strangeness of this blood. Although it springs from an internal wound, it does not bring death to the person who suffers it as do most other wounds. On the other hand, it does represent a mortal danger for the man, who does not suffer this wound. At the same time though, this blood, which opposes the power of the sperm, is also an indispensable con-

63

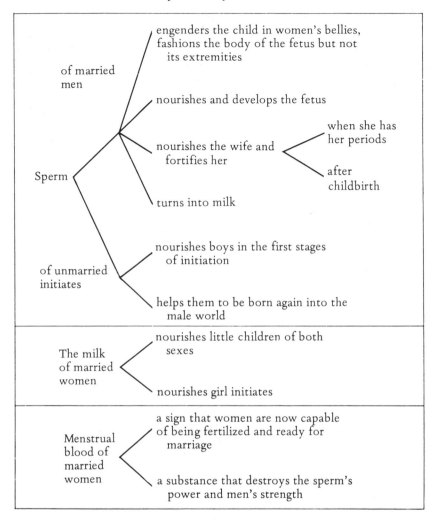

Figure 5. Body language: the material and ideological functions of certain bodily substances

dition of the manifestation of its power in the woman's belly. In this substance, then, she does indeed possess a power that is distinct from that of men and necessary to the reproduction of life. Of course, this power comes not from herself but from Moon; but then men's sperm comes not from them but from Sun and all the trees in the forest whose sap he drinks.

So relations between men and women cannot be reduced to a simple, rigid opposition between a positive and a negative sex, between a power of life that legitimately dominates and controls a power of death. This opposition does not disappear, but it corresponds merely to a superficial level of Baruya thought and to the first stages in the development of initiate knowledge. More deeply, and later on, male/female relations emerge under a somewhat different light, as the opposition between two realities each of which has its limits in the positive characteristics of the other, in the positive characteristics that it itself lacks but that collaborate with those that it does possess in order to produce a result beneficial to both.

Looked at in this light, male domination is no longer a reflection of the superiority of one group that possesses power over another that does not, but rather as the outcome of distinct, complementary, and unequal powers, which ultimately place the men above the women, and, as we shall later see, the great men above all others. But the fact that this domination is imposed upon women who possess real power, not upon women devoid of any, does not make it any the less oppressive and violent. Quite the reverse, as we shall see; the need to justify male domination in the eyes of women with acknowledged power of their own has stimulated an ideological "working through" [*un travail idéel* in the French] in Baruya thought, an effort to evolve a system of ideas and interpretations. There can be no doubt that this process has been dictated by two major concerns, namely, the need to denigrate her power, belittle its importance, and even debase it, and on the other hand the need to control women and shackle them to male power, and subsequently expropriate the women in order to add her power to the men's own and turn it against the women, by converting it into additional means of obtaining their submission. To appropriate someone else's power and turn it against the person in order to enslave, in our culture, is an act of violence.

This ideological working through and this violence against women emerge in the Baruya myths, which "explain" how women invented bows and arrows, and so on, and how men appropriated them. These myths not only express male violence but are themselves acts of genuine violence, ideological and symbolic to be sure, but constantly overspilling the bounds of thought, or at least accompanying it at all times, for this thought is at work not only in the symbolic practices of the initiation rituals but also in the myriad details of everyday life. It is to be found in the path snaking along the hillside below the men's path; in the way a woman squats as she moves about her home; in her habit of never looking a man in the eye when he talks to her; in her reflex of standing aside to let a man pass, or in the habit of serving men first; in all those constant, everyday gestures that serve both to signify male domination and to produce and reproduce the submission of women. Thoughts become gestures and deeds; ideas become bodily reflexes and add to the force of their evidence all the weight of tradition and custom – all these acts of everyday life contain within them a kernel of ideological and symbolic violence that is permanently at work upon the individual, upon all individuals, acting upon their consciousness, within their consciousness, and beyond it. Thus the power of ideas is distinguished from all those visible acts of direct, physical, psychological, and social violence that men perform on a woman (or women) from time to time, or indeed on all women, whenever they feel the need to impose their will. The force of ideas lies in their being shared, in the belief and confidence in the truth of their proposed interpretations of the world. These ideas are acted out in Baruya mythology.

We shall begin with two supernatural beings whose distinct powers combine to make life and sustain the universe, namely, Sun and Moon. Sun is the father of men. He gives light, heat, and strength. Moon brings darkness, cold, and weakness.

In the beginning, Sun and Moon were indistinguishable from the Earth. All was gray. Men, spirits, animals, vegetables lived together and spoke the same language. Men were not like men today, their penises were not pierced and women's vaginas were not opened. The genitals of dogs too were walled up. Then Sun and Moon decided to rise above the Earth and they did so by pushing the sky up above them. Once in the sky, Sun thought he ought to do something for the humans and he ordered Moon to go back down again. Moon went down and stopped midway. Since then, day and night, rainy seasons and hot seasons have alternated. Since then, the animals have separated from men to go and live in the forest, which is where the spirits, now hostile and malevolent toward men, have also gone. The language that everyone used to speak except that between men and dogs, disappeared in the process of separation.

But Sun also remembered that the man and the woman were not pierced. So he cast a flintstone into the fire, and the stone burst and pierced the man and the woman. Since that time they have been able to copulate and multiply. Later, the men, wishing to punish dogs for having spoken ill of them, shot arrows at them which pierced their sex. From that time on, dogs have ceased to speak and instead howl at night. Nowadays, men hunt the animals in the forest with their dogs. Nowadays, if Sun comes too close to Earth, he scorches it and devastates the gardens. If Moon comes too close to us, she engulfs everything in rain and darkness, and the crops then rot.

Thus we may summarize the content of several Sun and Moon myths. In them two supernatural beings with distinct powers separate, then join up again, and by this two-way movement establishing the present order that reigns in the universe. This order depends on a mixture of contraries in the right proportions. Sun and Moon must keep the correct distance from each other and from Earth so that the world may rotate properly and give men all that they need. But the proper mixture of contraries also presupposes respect for their hierarchy. Sun must remain up above, Moon below. More heat than cold is needed, and more light than darkness.

But who are Sun and Moon? To which part of the universe do they belong? For Sun, there can be no doubt. He is on the male side. He is the father of us all. But Moon? On which side does he, or she, stand? That is the problem. The Baruya word for Moon is *lonwe*, a masculine name, and in certain versions of the myths, *lonwe* is described as the younger brother of Sun, helping him in his work, whereas in others Moon is Sun's wife. How are we to account for these different versions of the myths and Moon's opposing iden-

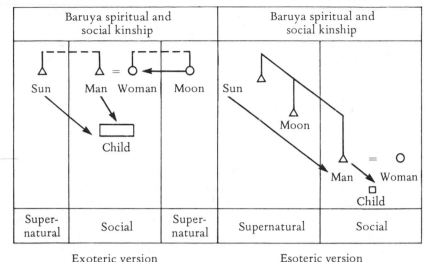

Baruya spiritual and social kinship			Baruya spiritual and social kinship	
Super-natural	Social	Super-natural	Supernatural	Social

Exoteric version   Esoteric version

Figure 6. Baruya spiritual and social kinship

account for these different versions of the myths and Moon's opposing identities? The Baruya never answer this question, and never seem to have asked themselves the question. So it looks as if we shall have to seek an explanation.

Let us now take a closer look at the two versions [Figure 6]. The one that makes Moon Sun's wife is far commoner than the other. Everyone, men and women alike, is familiar with it, whereas the second is known to men alone, and even then not to all men, but to the shamans above all, and to the *kwai-matnie*-men who are in charge of the rituals.

In the exoteric version, Moon is female power. She plays an active role in bringing order to the world, but a subordinate role under Sun's command. The supernatural couple emerges as the paradigm of the relations of complementarity and subordination that the Baruya would like to reign between men and women, once it is acknowledged that each sex possesses distinct and complementary powers.

In the esoteric version, the female element has disappeared from the higher powers that govern the universe. All that remains are male powers, some of which are subordinate to others as younger brothers are to their older brothers. In this version, humans no longer have a supernatural mother. All that is left to them are the fathers of succeeding generations, each of whom wields a distinct form of authority and acts in his own way upon the universe and society. So it is not hard to see that by thus eliminating, through thought and in thought, all trace of a female supernatural power, the male aspect of the

67

universe looms all the larger and in so doing it amplifies conceptually [*idéellement* in the French]; it magnifies ideologically the powers ascribed to men in society. For according to the esoteric version it is a male power, Moon, younger brother of Sun, which lies at the origin of the distinct power of women to become fertilizable when the menstrual blood begins to flow. For is it not Moon that pierces the woman and prepares her for fertilization by man and Sun, and finally makes life in her belly?

In both versions:

Sun and man cooperate to fertilize the woman and develop the child in the woman's belly.
Moon pierces the woman and makes her fertilizable.

As elsewhere, the social reproduction of life among the Baruya calls for cooperation between men and powers higher than themselves; consequently, life is both human and supernatural, the combined product of material and spiritual exchanges between humans and the powers that, in Baruya thought, govern the universe. All Baruya therefore have several fathers at once, belonging to different planes of the universe. But whereas human fathers create social distinctions among children because they belong to different lineages, Sun, the supernatural father, is the father of all, without distinction of sex or social origin.

Let us come back to Moon, though, and to the two versions of its identity. It is out of the question to discard one of these versions in favor of the other. Both express the principle of male domination, but in different degrees. The esoteric version carries further the deep-seated tendency in Baruya society and thought constantly to aggrandize man and his merits and to downgrade woman. Also, it corresponds to the fact that the men are the only ones to perform the rituals that, at the beginning of each initiation, summon forth Sun to communicate his warmth and strength to men, or at the end of ceremonies, call forth Moon to cool down the men now burning with Sun's fire and with the force of the initiations, and to enable them to resume life in the cooler world of women and children. Now, the sacred object to call on Moon has two secret names, one masculine, the other feminine; the secret feminine name of Moon is also the name of a large rock, standing in midriver and split like a woman's sex. One ceremonial morning, the initiates shortly to be betrothed must pass unclothed through the rock; on the other side, they receive the adornments and garments ascribed to their new status.

Although women are acknowledged to be in a privileged relationship to Moon (Moon-wife-of-Sun), they do not possess the sacred objects and magic formulas with which to communicate directly with her. They are thus eternally robbed of the means to represent society at large, men included, in dealings with the feminine powers of the universe or, conversely, of representing feminine powers in society. Just as on earth they are separated from their human ancestors and can neither inherit nor bequeath, so they are separated from their supernatural ancestors and excluded from the use of their powers. It could be that this dual identity ascribed to Moon, his/her masculine public name and feminine secret name, is merely the logical outcome of the male appropriation of female powers, powers that have thus been incorporated into the men's universe and put to their service. At the end of the process, the female powers have been converted into male ones, dressed in the livery of their masters.

To sum up, to deal with the powers of women, the Baruya have adopted two contrary, though in fact convergent approaches (even though they may sometimes appear to contradict each other). The first consists in seizing every opportunity of minimizing the importance of, or even denying, the fertilizing powers that apparently belong only to women. It is by this approach that we ought to construe the idea that the women's milk comes from the men's sperm. If we add to this view the idea that Moon, as Sun's younger brother, is responsible for piercing women and making their menstrual blood flow, thereby making them fertilizable, then women's nursing and fertilizing powers must ultimately all have their origins in male principles.

The social and political import of the idea that milk comes from sperm is perfectly clear, as is the custom to which it gives rise, namely, the obligation for young women to drink sperm in order to develop. This custom cuts short any thought that the women might have had of conceiving the feminine world as independent of the men's world or of masculine elements of the universe. For in the absence of this idea and its accompanying custom, might they not imagine that they had been pierced by a feminine power and that they themselves were responsible for the production of their milk, which they distribute to boys and girls alike (keeping aside a portion for pubescent girl initiates); might they not imagine the existence of a female world entirely outside the control of men? It is possible that women's thoughts may sometimes drift in this direction. For them, to the best of my knowledge, Moon is a woman; and they all agree that the sharing of their milk among women, which is highly important to them, must be concealed from the men and practiced in secret. It seems to me that the women, though sharing the men's theoretical views, tend to select and combine those that are least degrading to them, and to ascribe to themselves more power and importance than men are prepared to let them claim publicly. But the idea, and its attendant custom, that their milk is the product of sperm, prevents them from going too far in this direction. So we can see how an idea and a symbolic custom can represent a force capable of blocking or facilitating the development of a different social personality or a new society.

There is thus some play, some contradiction even, in certain parts of the Baruya's conceptual [*idéel*] and ideological edifice, not through faulty logic, but because of the active tension and opposition that flow from the way in which they have organized and legitimized their social relations.

69

Social hierarchies in Baruya society

There is a body of myths in which their thought adopts the opposite approach to the foregoing, only to arrive at the same result. Instead of seeking to belittle or to deny the importance of female powers, these myths start by asserting that, in the past, women possessed far greater powers than those of men, but that the latter, for perfectly legitimate reasons, appropriated them and turned them against the women, who have now been totally stripped of these powers.

Here are some examples. It is forbidden, on pain of death, for women to see the flutes. These, say the men, are the voices of spirits that converse with them in the forest. It is also forbidden for young initiates to reveal to the women and to noninitiates that it is not spirits that emit these sounds, but instruments made by men, who break them into pieces after the ceremonies. Further, during the initiations, initiates are told the true origins of the flutes, namely:

In the days of the Wandjinia [the men of the earliest times, the dream time], the women one day invented flutes. They played them and drew wonderful sounds from them. The men listened and did not know what made the sounds. One day, a man hid to spy on the women and discovered what was making these melodious sounds. He saw several women, one of whom raised a piece of bamboo to her mouth and drew the sounds that the men had heard. Then the woman hid the bamboo beneath one of the skirts that she had hung in her house, which was a menstrual hut. The women then left. The man drew near, slipped into the hut, searched around, found the flute, and raised it to his lips. He too brought forth the same sounds. Then he put it back and went to tell the other men what he had seen and done. When the woman returned, she took out her flute to play it, but this time the sounds she drew were ugly. So she threw it away, suspecting that the men had touched it. Later, the man came back, found the flute and played it. Lovely sounds came forth, just like the ones that the woman had made. Since then the flutes have been used to help boys grow.

The secret name of flutes as revealed in the telling of this myth to the initiates is *namboula-mala*. *Mala* means combat; *namboula*, frogs and tadpoles. Now, another myth tells how the women existed before the men, that the latter appeared to them in the form of tadpoles, and that the women made *pulpul*s and miniature bows for them; later, these tadpoles metamorphosed into men. Today, the women occasionally go off to fish together for tadpoles, offering their catch to the young boys. According to the Baruya, women shamans turn into frogs at night; they squat shoulder to shoulder along the water's edge by the river that marks the boundaries of Baruya territory to stop the spirits of sleeping children, women, and old folk from straying into enemy territory never to return. Is it any surprise, then, that the men use the word *namboula* to refer to the vagina?

The message of this myth is clear. In the beginning, women were superior to men, but one of the men, violating the fundamental taboo against ever penetrating into the menstrual hut or touching objects soiled with menstrual blood, captured their power and brought it back to the men, who now use it

70

to turn little boys into men. But this power stolen from the women is the very one that their vagina contains, the one given to them by their menstrual blood. The old women know the rough outlines of this myth and relate it to young girls when they have their first period.

Another myth explains that the first women one day invented the bow and arrow. They went out to hunt, but they had no idea how to use the bow and held it back to front. That way, they killed too much game, killing wantonly. In the end, the men grabbed the bow and turned it the right way round. Since that time, they have taken care to kill only what they need, when necessary, and have forbidden women to use bows.

This myth, like the preceding one, attributes to women a kind of irrepressible primal creative urge in a sphere that is, what is more, the very symbol of men, namely, hunting, the field in which the great men and great warriors, the *aoulatta,* are made. But the women's creative urge is disorderly, unbridled, dangerous, and the men were forced to step in to set matters right. This intervention and the violence that it entails are thus justified by the fact that they appear to be the only means of establishing order and a sense of proportion in society and in the universe.

Other myths of the Baruya's origins contain the twofold assertion that women play a creative, feeding role, more so than men, but that the latter are right to deal violently with them.

In those times, men and women ate nothing but wild fruit and plants. Their skin was black and dirty. One day, a man went off into the forest with his wife. On the way, he killed her and buried her corpse. He returned to the village and said that his wife had disappeared. Later, he revisited the scene of the crime and saw that all sorts of plants had sprung from the ground where he had buried the corpse. He tasted their leaves and found that they were good. When he returned to the village, the others said to him: "What have you done to get so fine a skin?" He said nothing. The next day, he went back to the forest and again tasted the plants. His skin became finer and finer. When he reached his village, the others begged him to explain how he had changed his skin. That went on for several days, until one day he ordered the other villagers to follow him. He led them to the tomb where all these plants grew and showed them which ones were good to eat, which might be suitable for cooking [certain bamboos]. Since that time, men have taken to cultivating and eating these plants, and their skin has changed. [The myth was acquired from the Watchake, an Anga tribe visited by the Baruya, and known to certain old Baruya.]

In yet another myth, the head of a woman decapitated by her husband caused, as it rolled away, springs to burst forth, irrigating the salt cane fields (the Baruyas' principal means of trade). These springs still flow today near one of their villages, Waiveu.

All these myths thus confirm the preexistence of a feminine creativity, in terms of time as well as in terms of those things invented which today give to men their superiority, for example, flutes, bows, salt. But these myths also stress how this creativity was capable of stirring up disorder. It could not benefit the community as a whole unless men stepped in; they did so, using

71

violence, theft, and murder. A woman had to die so that the edible plants that sprang from her body could be shared among all humans, and so that they could abandon their wild life as eaters of roots and raw meat.

It is worth noting in passing – and this is a matter of some theoretical interest – that the Baruya do not conceive the differences between man and woman in terms of an opposition between nature and nurture (an opposition to which our own culture tends to ascribe universal significance and regards as hidden beneath various disguises).

For the Baruya, it was woman who invented the conditions of culture, the material means of hunting, of trade, initiation, and so forth. All man did was to complete and perfect what woman had begun, doing as the Sun once did, when it pierced man's sexual organs. If one really had to employ the nature / culture distinction metaphorically, then the Baruya man and woman alike are on the side of culture, but each makes his or her distinct contribution to the transition from nature to culture. Thus in another version of the myth of the man and woman whose sexual organs and anus were walled up, the Sun did not intervene to pierce them; the initiative was an unwitting one on the woman's part:

One day, she stuck the wing bone of a bat into the trunk of a banana tree and left it there. [Today, female shamans and old women wear this bone, as slender and sharp as a needle, through the tip of their nose.] A moment later, the man came back and, without looking where he was going, empaled himself on the bone sticking out of the tree. Mad with pain and rage, he grasped a piece of sharp bamboo and with one blow opened up the woman's sexual organ; he slit it.

Here again, we see the sexes acting upon each other in order to distinguish themselves from, and complete, each other. The woman acts first and indirectly upon the man; then the man acts directly, and violently, on the woman's body in order to complete the transformation. Here again, it took violence to differentiate the sexes and permit them to conjoin. But both sexes played an active part in this differentiation. Each contributed at a different moment, and in different ways, to the transition from a state of nature, in which everything already exists, albeit in a relatively undifferentiated form (in which the differences are somewhat frozen), to a state in which all these differences have become more sharply defined, creating not only the possibility but also the necessity of combining these differences in order to transcend them, by means of positive exchanges (inventions) and negative ones (violence) between the sexes and the parts of the universe. Admittedly, one could view the transition from a state of indistinction, of immobile, exchangeless conjunction (everything was gray, says the myth, when Sun and Moon lived on Earth) to a state in which these differences come into their own and exchange becomes possible, as a transition from nature to culture. But this view would be an abstraction since, for the Baruya, exchange is not peculiar to culture; it exists everywhere in the nature that surrounds them.

72

Further, whereas in our culture nature often connotes the savage as opposed to the civilized, this is not so among the Baruya. For them, man's superiority over woman stems rather from his familiarity, from his at-all-times essential identification with the world of the forest and hunting, whereas woman is confined within the "civilized" world of her gardens, the village, and the forest edge, where she goes to feed her pigs or gather firewood. What in fact makes man superior to woman, for the Baruya, is that from the forest, from the savage part of nature, he draws powers to which woman has – and never has had – access. It is in the forest where man receives from the great trees the sap that eventually becomes his sperm; it is there where he hunts, kills, tries his strength, his endurance, and his mastery of the means of destruction; it is there where he sends his spirit to mingle with the wind, which will bear it away to the Sun; it is there where dwell the souls of dead ancestors, who stand guard over the territory of their children. In a word, it is by adding to the powers of "civilization" (e.g., agriculture) those of life in the "wild" that men establish their superiority over women and legitimize their domination. These distinctions will become clearer when we analyze certain functions performed by the great men among the Baruya. Without wishing to juggle paradoxes unnecessarily, I would say that the reason why women in Baruya society are dominated is that they stand far more on the side of culture than on that of nature. At bottom, the fact of having made agriculture possible – in the world of the imagination, in thought – has not benefited women's status one bit, indeed quite the reverse.

What the Baruya myths reveal to us, then, is not evidence of their forgotten origins, memories of an age when women dominated men, for them a now vanished golden age of matriarchy. Nor do they reveal to us an attempt to compensate in some imaginary world for the condition that is imposed on them in real life, a manner of acknowledging women's superiority (in the world of ideas) even though everything in practice denies and negates any such superiority. The lesson of these myths is quite different. By showing that woman was the source of disorder when still in possession of her powers, by showing that the fact of stripping her of these powers was beneficial to everyone, women included, these myths are a means of convincing all concerned, men and women alike, that things are now as they ought to be, that the order now reigning is the correct one, and that it legitimately, necessarily, implies the exercise of some violence by the men against the women. Indeed, what sensible woman, having heard these myths and the description of the disorders attendant upon women's former powers, could want all this to happen all over again, for her own sake or for that of her children? Surely the lesson of these myths is that it would be better for them to abandon all thought and all hope – supposing these should ever manifest themselves – of taking back from the men the powers stolen from them, that it would be better for them to cooperate as willingly as possible in the production and preservation of male domination, and that the best course is to be a good wife, faithful, hard working, and fertile.

By this analysis, these myths are undeniably the dominant ideas of the dominant sex. The myths interpret this dominance in a way that legitimizes the violence contained within it and seeks to persuade those subject to it to consent to and cooperate in the reproduction of the order that dominates them. The myths are truly acts of violence, even if this violence is neither physical nor directly psychological. They are the creations of thought and they act primarily on thought. However, we should recall those other kinds of segregation in Baruya society that are not confined to the world of thought, namely, the exclusion of women from ownership of the land, from the manufacture and use of the principal means of production, weaponry, and trade, from possession of the means of communicating with the supernatural world, and above all the appropriation by men of their children and the imposition on women of separation from their sons. None of these exclusions, segregations, or subordinations can be described purely in terms of thought, even if they all acquire their official, acknowledged, conscious meaning from thought. We must therefore seek their roots both in thought and outside it. It is inconceivable that so great a diversity of facts and relations should flow from a single cause; we find their roots in a wide variety of simultaneous permutations arranged into a hierarchy that subordinates women to men in a given society, at a given moment in time.

Therefore boys have to be separated from girls, so as to make them see the self-evidence of their superiority over women and to persuade them of the legitimacy of their future domination over them. Their childhood spent among women, their early life in their mothers' arms could never have revealed this superiority to them. Therefore all that this world of women has already deposited in them, incorporated into their personality, all the sensations, images, thoughts, and desires that the young initiates bring with them when they first step inside the *moukaanga,* must be driven out of them, must now be forgotten, and they must learn to see things in a different light, with contempt and even horror. But eliminating what has been acquired from the other sex is not sufficient to turn a boy into a man superior to women. He must prove this superiority through a multitude of trials, both physical and psychological. The married men, the elders of their elders, the last-stage initiates who will soon be leaving the men's house to marry, organize these ordeals: hunger, cold, lack of sleep, harassing marches, jeering, blows, humiliation, the obligation to remain silent, and a host of taboos that are gradually removed as the initiate progresses, as he grows in stature and status, acquiring new rights and obligations. There is no comparison between these trials and taboos and what girls experience in their childhood and adolescence. These trials will prove the legitimacy of the men's domination over the women, over all women, and over women not only to the boys but to the girls as well even though the latter are never invited or permitted properly to match themselves with the men.

The first woman that the young man has to deal with on leaving the men's house will be the young girl he is about to marry, for he only leaves the men's house to marry. By now he will be a little over twenty, and he knows that it is his right and duty to exercise his authority over this woman and over the children she bears him. For her part, the girl is ready to acknowledge his authority, especially if he has already earned a reputation as a brave man in battle and a hard worker, already helping his father and father-in-law without complaint.

The return to the world of women after so many years is an awkward moment for the young man. Fear and contempt for women will mingle with desire, and possibly even fondness if he knows the girl already. The girl, meanwhile, is apprehensive about leaving her family to go and live with a man she may scarcely know at all, and whom she has been told to serve, or else risk stirring up serious trouble and conflict for herself and for the families joined by her marriage. Conflicts can end badly on occasion, in violence and even murder. But the separation of the sexes is definitively over. On their wedding day, the young man stands among his already married coinitiates and the young woman sits amid the women, both of them silent and impassive, as men and women renowned for their oratorical talents come to shout in their faces:

> As for you, your life in the *kwalanga* [men's house] is over;
> And as for you, no more living with your mother;
> This house, built today by the young people your age,
> This house will be your tomb,
> This house is your tomb.

The next day, the men from the husband's lineage will come to build the hearth in the center of the new house, where one of them will light the first fire and where the young bride will soon start to cook, always serving the man first. Things may work out well, but sometimes they turn out badly. When a wife can stand things no longer, deciding to leave her husband despite all the possible dire consequences, she symbolically smashes the hearth by kicking the stones apart and then flees. But many Baruya husbands treat their wives affectionately; many youths fall desperately in love with a girl and eventually marry her; many girls end up marrying the men they wanted. At a very early age, the girl knows which man she will be marrying, and she tries to catch furtive glimpses of him in a garden or in the forest. She giggles at her daring and chatters with her friends about what she has seen. Little by little she gets used to the idea of becoming that man's wife.

But we cannot here go into the multitude of different ways in which people either passively accept or manipulate the social relationships within which

75

they find themselves during the various stages of their existence. Our sole concern has been to analyze the machinery of male and female initiations, and to show how these institutions work together to establish and legitimize the general domination, as a matter of principle, of all men, qua men, over all women, qua women. As we have seen, the Baruya view this domination as a gathering into the men's hands of both male powers and female ones, and the female ones are thus made masculine.

The mechanisms of production of the general subordination of women may be illustrated by two significant facts, one of them public, known to all, and the other secret, known only to the oldest initiates and the married men.

Among the Baruya, once a boy is initiated, all his older sisters stop calling him *gwagwe,* little brother, as was their wont up to then. Henceforward they call him *dakwe,* big brother. The male initiation thus turns all women into their younger brothers' younger sisters and, for political and ideological reasons, produces a downward shift in the positions occupied by the women in geneaologies and relations of kinship.

Still more eloquent is a fact totally unknown to the women and young initiates. At the moment when someone comes to separate the little boys from their mother, and when they are about to enter the men's house for the first time, they are made to step across a painted plank lying on the ground across the doorway and serving as a kind of threshold. This plank was made and painted by the shamans belonging to the Andavakia lineage, the masters of the initiation of the shamans and of the rituals accompanying the birth of children. The little boys, who might show surprise at the apparently more bothersome than useful presence of this plank, are told that it is there to warn possible visitors from neighboring tribes that a ceremony is in progress and that they should continue on their way. Of course, the little boys make do with this explanation, and pursue the question no further. In any case, they are strictly forbidden to ask questions or even to speak of it. Later, they will learn that this plank was the "co-wife" of all the women in the tribe, married or marriageable. It is therefore the symbol of all the women that the men have married or will marry, and it is over their collective body that each man taking part in these ceremonies will step, several hundred times, day and night, each time he enters or leaves the *moukaanga.*

Not all men are entitled to carve this plank and present it to the men of the tribe as a whole as the co-wife of their wives. As already stated, only shamans, and then only those from the Andavakia lineage, may do so. We shall now turn our attention to hierarchies, those that distinguish certain men and raise them above the others. It will quickly become apparent that once again the common, incontrovertible basis is the subordination of women and the domination of men.

PART TWO

The production of great men
Powers inherited, powers merited

4

Male hierarchies

Two sets of hierarchical relations supplement those of male domination, yet flow from them, and for the Baruya they appear to be either the conditions, or even the results, of the performance of male initiation ceremonies (a collective mechanism that imprints each man's social personality, a central element in the collective and individual domination of women by men). The two forms of hierarchy revolve around different social functions, and individuals ultimately distinguish between them according to their ability or inability to perform these functions.

The first hierarchy is the one that marks those responsible for the male initiation rituals from other men. These individuals occupy this function because they have inherited from their ancestors the sacred objects and magic-religious formulas required for the performance of the initiation rites. (Their ancestors had themselves received them directly from Sun and Moon.) The distinction between the masters of the rituals and the rest stems from the particular situation inside the Baruya tribe of those clans and lineages that possess a monopoly of the ritual functions and objects. Behind the status of owner–user of sacred objects emerges a social distinction between those Baruya lineages that cooperate directly in the production of men and those that do not have the right to do so. Furthermore, not all initiate stages are equally important, and consequently an internal hierarchy among the ritual-performing lineages themselves results; each one's rank corresponds to the relative importance of the initiate stage for which each one is responsible.

However, in additon to the hereditary hierarchy of lineages embodied in the various officiants, the enduring social framework of initiate practice, which can only with difficulty be overturned or even modified, the individuals of each generation can express their unequal abilities to perform three essential functions in the reproduction of society, namely, war, hunting, and shamanism. It is in these activities above all that men who are selected and achieve promotion can, in the course of their lifetime, distinguish themselves

79

from the rest (whom the Baruya refer to unflatteringly as *wopaie,* sweet potatoes). What do these functions signify, and how does one become a great warrior, great shaman, or great hunter? Is there an order of precedence among these functions and among the individuals who embody them?

Warriors and shamans do enjoy higher status than the cassowary hunters, but is a great warrior worth more than a great shaman? To the Baruya, this question is practically meaningless. The answer would be that it all depends on who is better placed to ward off the particular danger threatening the group: an attack by enemy warriors, aggression by hostile spirits or enemy witches, or a heavy epidemic that decimates the villages and forces the entire population to flee in search of healthier localities, where it may settle for a while or possibly even permanently. The common basis for the selection of the individuals to perform these socially necessary functions is to be found in the initiate machinery.

The Baruya attach equally great importance to another social function that is essential to the material and social reproduction of Baruya social life. Though the exclusive preserve and product of men, it does not give rise to any special ritual of its own in the course of the tribe's collective initiations. I am referring to the manufacture of salt, a central trading medium through which the Baruya obtain the tools, weapons, means of subsistence, and adornments for which the necessary raw materials are not available on their own territory. Its essential economic function depends on magical powers and techniques that are possessed individually. Unlike ritual knowledge, however, such skills may be passed on to anyone who evinces a taste for this specialist craft. Though this function does not qualify for any special social distinction in the course of the initiation rituals, it does nevertheless raise those who excel in it to a higher status than that of the *wopaie,* the common run of men.

Contrasting with the men's world, where individual differences are both sought after and produced, the world of women appears to be far more homogeneous, much duller. Yet among them too we find female shamans and "warrior" women, women able to stand their ground in the conflicts and vendettas that break out from time to time between Baruya villages and lineages. They are perfectly capable of dealing – often dangerous – blows with their digging sticks, and of taking blows in return. But these women fight against other women, other Baruya women, not against enemies. So in the women's world too we find female shamans and warriors distinguishing themselves, but the importance of this distinction is far narrower than in the case of men. Because women do not hunt, and because they neither make nor trade in salt, we find no female equivalent – not even on a lesser scale – of the status associated with these activities among men. Still, as among the men, there are mechanisms for the selection and promotion of women who are "greater" than the others because they possess shamanic powers or exceptional qualities of bravery, and because they excel in all that counts as meritorious and worthy in a woman, for example, bearing many children, working hard, being obedient to her husband.

By analyzing how the different elements combine, we shall have uncovered a mechanism for the production of great men and great women that profoundly distinguishes Baruya society from societies where big men stand at the top of the social ladder. We shall then investigate the underpinnings of the distinct types of social logic, examples of which are also to be found outside New Guinea, albeit in different forms, that is, in Africa, Asia, and America. We shall confine our discussion to pointers for further research; I shall not be offering any fully supported conclusions. Needless to say, I shall describe, though briefly, the upheavals wrought in traditional Baruya social organization first by European colonization and subsequently by the creation of a nation. The basis of the former social hierarchy was partially destroyed by the white colonialists because they prohibited the exercise of the warrior function, introduced western religious ideologies, substituted other means of exchange and accumulation of wealth for the ancient salt money. We are gradually witnessing the emergence of a new hierarchy out of the ruins. The highest rungs of the new ladder are being occupied by those who have grown rich, those who have gone to school and university, who are qualified to occupy key jobs in the new social structure that is now enveloping and slowly dissolving the older one. This new social structure, the state, is laying the foundations of a nation that, though politically independent, is nevertheless subject to the laws of the western capitalist market economy.

Hereditary status and interlineage hierarchies: the *kwaimatnie-owners*

In each generation all the little boys of a given age, regardless of lineage, enter into the *tsimia,* the great ceremonial house built specially for the occasion, and are initiated together. As we have already seen, the significance of the *tsimia* to the Baruya is perfectly precise. For them, it is the body of the tribe. Its bones are the poles that the men have driven into the ground, each one representing an initiate, its skin is the thatch that covers the roof. Its body symbolizes the political and religious unity of the Baruya, irrespective of kinship group or place of residence. Yet, though celebrated for all, the initiate ceremony is not performed by all, for only the men belonging to certain lineages owning a *kwaimatnie,* a sacred object, have the right to celebrate these rites and to perform this function in the general interest.

What is a *kwaimatnie?* The word is a combination of *kwala,* man, and *yimatnia,* to lift the skin, grow. From the same radical comes the word *nymatnie,* which means fetus, but which also means apprentice or novice shaman. So a *kwaimatnie* is an object that makes boys' skin grow, lengthens their bodies and turns them into men. At the same time, it is a lineage's supernatural means of producing men outside the belly of women. It is charged with men's power to procreate among themselves, acting upon each other and giving birth without end to generation upon generation.

This object produces its effects only if it is used at the right time and in the proper way, and by someone who has the exclusive right to own and handle it and who has received the secret formulas connected with its use. For the Baruya, Sun and Moon had given the *kwaimatnie* to the patrilineal ancestors of their present-day owners, who contain inside them a fragment of the powers of Sun and Moon. This bestowal happened, of course, in days beyond the recall of living memory, in the age of the Wandjinia, the first men, who sometimes appear to people in dreams and whose mighty deeds are related in the myths. Before dying, the owner of a *kwaimatnie* hands it on to his son if the latter is already a grown man, a fourth-stage initiate of *kalave*. If not, he will pass it on to the his younger brother's oldest son, provided he meets the requisite criteria.

The *kwaimatnie* are made of hard material, they are oblong parcels, about twenty centimeters long, wrapped in a strip of bark cloak and tied up with an *ypmoulie,* the headband that men alone wear, made of treebark and painted red, the color of the Sun.

Sometimes a handful of black feathers like the ones that decorate warriors' heads protrude from the packet.

In principle, the guardian of a *kwaimatnie* is not permitted to open it in front of anyone except his son or nephew on the day of transmission. Even then he is not supposed to open it completely, for it contains substances and ingredients placed there by Sun and Moon themselves and charged with such powers that were they to escape they would spread sickness and death all around them. The *kwaimatnie* is kept in a string bag hung from the wall in the guardian's home, in the area reserved for men. Often though, he prefers to keep it in a house specially built next door to the conjugal home, where he sometimes sleeps, either alone or with other men. The specially built house is surrounded by a circle of fear; no one would ever dare to enter it in the absence of the owner or without his express permission. Everyone knows that what is kept inside is capable of killing, mutilating, or transmitting some horrible sickness to the intruder or snooper who dared to step inside.

On two occasions, men in possession of *kwaimatnie* granted me the great privilege of a glimpse of the contents of their magic parcels. Each time, the father was accompanied by the son destined to inherit it at his death, who was also being given his first look at the object. Both times, father and son burst into tears as soon as the father had untied the parcel and parted the wrapping to give us a look at what was inside. For minutes on end, overcome with emotion, they remained speechless. Each time, the father alone touched

82

the *kwaimatnie* with his fingers, but neither the son nor I was allowed to do so.

The first of these men, a man from the Bakia clan, of the Kuopbakia lineage, owned two *kwaimatnie,* one a gift from Sun, the other of Moon. Inside the Moon *kwaimatnie* I saw a jet black polished stone, like certain stones of volcanic origin. This stone, which was both a symbol of and a gift from Moon, was associated with its secret names. Significantly, I was told two names for Moon, two names that the Kuopbakia secretly pronounce when they want its powers to work among humans, one name masculine, the other feminine; the latter corresponds to the name of the rock shaped like an immense vagina, through which the *tchouwanie,* the third-stage initiates, must pass in the course of their initiation. The other, the Sun *kwaimatnie,* was scarcely opened for me at all. I did spy, rolled up in a red *ypmoulie,* some flat nuts, the kind that men used to purify their mouth of female pollution, which, according to the Baruya, act on the roots of the teeth and transmit the Sun's powers down to the penis. These nuts, say the Baruya, are like the eyes of babies. On their surface, on one side, is a kind of iris, which, if "open," is a sign of life. These nuts are also used in hunting magic. I saw too a few dried leaves with magical powers, which had been gathered in the clumps of trees that grow on the former territory of the Baruya, the one from which their ancestors were driven, near Menyamya.

The role of the guardian of these *kwaimatnie* was above all to invite Moon to the end of initiation ceremonies in order to cool their bodies, burning and glowing from the heat and light of Sun, so that the married men could resume life with their wives and children. He also had the power, when the Baruya conquered a patch of their neighbors' territory and wanted to build a hamlet on it, to detect and chase away the enemy spirits that came back to lurk and kill the Baruya. But the commonly accepted view was that this man and his lineage had ceased to play anything but a minor role in the initiations.

The third *kwaimatnie* that I saw belonged to a clan that plays a predominant role in the initiation cycle, namely, the Tchatche clan. It shares with a lineage from another clan the responsibility for separating boys from the world of women and for piercing their noses. This magic packet contained the bones of an eagle – the eagle is a Sun bird – sharpened into spikes for piercing the initiates' noses. These spikes were embedded in down plucked from an eagle's breast, magic leaves, nuts brought from the territory of ancestors, and bird feathers, all wrapped in *ypmoulie.*

Each of these *kwaimatnie* has its own name, known only to the guardian, who utters it to himself when officiating. At this time he also invokes the secret names of Sun and Moon, the names of the different peaks of the mountain where the shamans' spirits gather at night, and those of various sacred lakes, like the one from which the first men emerged in their original form, as tadpoles.

The production of great men

A complete list of circumstances in which the *kwaimatnie*-owners use their powers would correspond to all the different collective and individual transitions through which a man must pass in the course of his initiation. To these were formerly added exceptional moments such as when the men left for battle or on their return from fighting, their weapons and bodies drenched in the blood of their slaughtered enemies. The moments of collective transition correspond to the ceremonies marking the entry into each of the four stages of initiation, already dealt with briefly above. Thus each set of ceremonies represents a period of transition, of leaving one stage and entering into the next, and bears a separate name.

The ceremonies of separating the boys from the world of the women are called *mouka* ("to put through all sorts of trials"), and the new initiates also are called *mouka*. After some time, they become *yiveumbwaye* (from *yiveutta*, bark cloak, those who hide behind their bark cloak for the few years that make up the first stage of initiation). Then, by means of ceremonies during which their noses are pierced with a spike of hard, black wood, *palitta*, they become *palittamounie*, in transition toward the second stage, *kawetnie*. It is in the course of this transition that they abandon their still half-female clothes and are dressed as men. Then, at around fifteen, they enter the third stage, through a series of transitional ceremonies in the course of which they are made *pongwanie*, the name given to a feather from the blackbird of paradise, which is stuck in their hair. At this time their brows are circled with the very symbols of male domination, a hornbill beak perched above an open reed circle, ending in two tusks of a pig. Before setting the hornbill beak on the *pongwanie*'s brow, a still-sturdy old man, an old warrior, passes it between his thighs and then points it at the boys' bellies. It is at this point that they are told that this beak is the image of the man's penis standing over the woman's toothed vagina. They then become *tchouwanie*, third-stage initiates, after the name given to the reed object on their head, symbolizing the woman's sexual organs. When his fiancée has had her first period and when he and she have been through the *tsangitnia* ceremony (chewing salt: a collective initiation ceremony for her and an individual initiation for him), the *tchouwanie* moves on toward the last stage, the *munginie* stage, through a series of ceremonies in which he becomes *kalave*, receiving a white parrot's feather to wear on his head, as do all married men. The boy then becomes a *munginie*. From then on, his initiation continues individually, each time his wife bears him a child; he is led to the foot of the wild pandanus (screw pine), symbol of all men, which dominates the ceremonial site in his village, in order to purify him of female pollution and pray to the Sun.

If it is correct to regard the transitional periods as stages, then the male initiation cycle contains not four stages as described above but eight:

mouka (transition),
yiveumbwaye (three years),

84

Male hierarchies

palittamounie (transition),
kawetnie,
pongwanie (transition),
tchouwanie,
kalave (transition),
munginie.

One remains a *munginie* until one's fourth child is born. The series of eight stages and individual ceremonies is represented in Figure 7.

Not all these ritual moments are equally important in the eyes of the Baruya, even if each one must be gone through in order to go on to the following one. Two moments appear to stand out, conferring upon the lineages and men responsible for them a status superior to the rest. The first, that of the break with the world of women, is performed by two lineages belonging to the Tchatche and Baruya clans, sometimes with the assistance of the Lalaounie and Ndelie. The second is the passage from *kawetnie* to *tchouwanie*. These are the high points of Baruya initiate life, compared with which the other passages appear to be somewhat simpler. The same goes for the rites to be performed at the birth of each child; each succeeding birth gradually enhances the father's status until he "truly" becomes a man, that is the father of at least four children.

What immediately strikes one about Figure 8 is that, with one significant exception, it contains all the names of the Baruya clans that came to seek refuge at Marouaka some two or three centuries ago, after having been driven from their territory and their former place of residence, Bravegareubaramandeuc, the village of the Baragaye, as the present-day Baruya then called themselves. So responsibility for the initiations lies in the hands of the conquering clans, with a single exception, the Ndelie, the indigenous clan that had once given shelter to the Baruya refugees and then helped them to conquer the lands of the Andje tribe to which they themselves had belonged. To reward the Ndelie for their betrayal and their invaluable help, the principal clan of the new tribe (which then took the name of Baruya, the name of the clan now responsible for the pongwanie ceremonies) gave them one of its *kwaimatnie* and entrusted it with the task of initiating the *palittamounie*, of ensuring the transition from the first to the second stage.

The distinction between the lineages that possess *kwaimatnie* and those that do not thus turned out to be a fundamental, political one between the conquering clans and the native clans subsequently incorporated into the Baruya tribe. The instruments of the tribe's political and ideological unity are thus concentrated in the hands of the former conquerors and their oldest allies. It is precisely to the Baruya's ownership of these *kwaimatnie*, which they brought with them from Bravegareubaramandeuc, that they ascribe their victory and superiority over the native groups in the Marawaka and Wonenara valleys, the Andje, the Usarumpia, the Yuwarrounatche, and the Goulutche, whom they have gradually dispossessed of part of their hunting

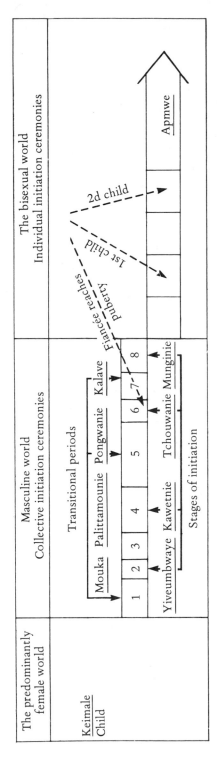

Figure 7. The stages of collective and individual initiation

Collective initiation ceremonies (transitional)				
Transitional stages	1 Mouka	3 Palittamounie	5 Pongwanie	7 Kalave
Clans and lineages responsible	Tchatche + Baruya (Wombouye) + chamanes andavakia	Ndelie + Baruya (Kwarrandariar)	Baruya (Kwarrandariar)	Bakia + Nunguye
Clans and lineages that provide assistance	Lalounie + Ndelie (Endatnie)	Tchatche	Ndelie (Endatnie)	Yuwandalie

Individual initiation ceremonies		
Circumstances	Fiancee reaches puberty	Birth of children
Clans and lineages responsible	Andavakia (Inamwe's lineage) +	Bakia (Boulimmambakia)

Figure 8. The *kwaimatnie*-owning clans and lineages (the lineages are indicated in parentheses)

grounds and gardens. At each initiation the guardians of the *kwaimatnie* sense that they are communicating to the young Baruya boys the might of their great warriors, and with it the military and social superiority that their ancestors claimed to have received directly from Sun and Moon, whose sons the Baruya claim to be.

But the Baruya's group consciousness of their superiority over their neighbors goes still much further. They state quite boldly that the natives whom they conquered were living practically like savages, that they were using rudimentary, ineffective bows, that they were incapable even of making stone and wooden war clubs. They used to make small quantities of a crude sort of salt, but most important, they had no idea how to build *tsimia,* and their boys used to live in men's houses practically as small as the women's houses. The Baruya claim, moreover, that the reason why neighboring tribes now build large men's houses and *tsimia* is that they have copied the Baruya, either stealing some of their secrets or discovering them thanks to the generosity of the Baruya who, in the past, have frequently initiated the sons of their neighbors when at peace with them. In a word, the conquering Baruya like to present themselves as civilizers as well as invaders.

What do the natives, now driven out of the territories and for the most part resolutely hostile to their new neighbors, think of this version of events? I have asked them this question on many occasions. All agree that the Baruya possessed superior weapons and military techniques at the time of their arrival, and that they owed their victories to their more powerful magic, and above all to the fact that their initiation ceremonies were far more elaborate than their own. All local groups with the exception of the Ndelie, who have thrown in their lot with the Baruya and have adopted their version of history lock, stock, and barrel, deny, however, the claim that before the arrival of the Baruya they either did not initiate their sons or contented themselves with brief ceremonies. In the matter of salt making, they claim that it was they who had possessed the most developed techniques and magic. These native accounts throw the Baruya's claims to grandeur and originality into perspective; I suspect that they come closer to the truth. Anthropologists and linguists who have studied some of the Anga groups have now shown that their mythology and symbology too gave pride of place to Sun and Moon, and that among them too various forms of male domination suggest several stages of initiation.

It is therefore practically certain that the local groups incorporated into the Baruya tribe also possessed *kwaimatnie,* but that they must have given up using them of their own accord when they went over to the Baruya. I was even given formal proof of this self-dispossession by a descendant of a native lineage whose ancestor, after having exchanged wives with the Baruya, decided to betray his tribe, the Yuwarrounatche, and go to live with his brothers-in-law. This was indeed the price he had to pay to hold on to part of his lands when the Baruya subsequently burned one of his tribe's villages and seized some of its territory. This event happened a few generations ago, in the late nineteenth century, when the Baruya, having penetrated the Wonenara Valley, were bent on continuing their expansion to the detriment of its former inhabitants. The Baruya had nothing but contempt for them, and considered that they had sprung from excrement defecated in the bush by cassowary birds.

Now Arindjane, the representative of one of the lineages that had chosen to live with the Baruya, told me in secret that far from having sprung from cassowary droppings, his ancestors were born of the fire in the sky, the lightning that had one day struck the forest and caused his ancestors to spring out of the earth. He told me that his ancestors too had owned a *kwaimatnie,* which they had buried in a bush at a secret spot at the moment of parting, some to flee before the invading Baruya, others to join forces with them. A tree had been planted at this spot to enable someone to find it later. So the distinction between the lineages with *kwaimatnie* and those without really corresponds with the political and ideological subordination of the conquered local groups to their conquerors. It represents a kind of social framework for the tribe – its core, its internal unity and strength – and it projects the past into the present day. In essence, this framework is rooted in the past and reflects the existing correlation of power, and the conquered local groups at least within the *kwaimatnie*-owning lineages cannot contest it. Strains and protests, however, do arise among the stocks that have no part in safeguarding and using their own lineage's *kwaimatnie*. There was even a case, before the white men encountered the Baruya, of a stock belonging to the Kwarrandariar (the lineage that owns the most powerful *kwaimatnie,* the one that makes *tchouwanie*) one day displaying a *kwaimatnie* consisting of strange, unfamiliar objects and claiming that it too could initiate the *tchouwanie*. It failed and experienced ridicule when, after the white man's arrival, it realized that these mysterious objects were none other than a trouser belt, bottles, and corks, presumably secretly sold to this stock by tribes already in contact with the whites.

In 1979, another incident flared up, this time between two stocks belonging to the Wombouye lineage, the lineage of the Baruya responsible for piercing boys' noses after their separation from the female world. These stocks had separated three generations ago as a result of a murder and the ensuing vendetta. The once vanquished tribe, now strong in men and rich in land conquered from enemy tribes, decided to exhibit a *kwaimatnie* bought in Manyamya in exchange for some salt bars, and started to pierce the noses of *mouka* in the place of the rival stock that had performed this task until then. In at least one respect it was entitled to do so; both stocks were descended from a single ancestor who had owned a *kwaimatnie*. But at the same time, it was asked to explain why it could not exhibit the ancestral *kwaimatnie* and had been obliged to buy one from a master of rituals of the Menyamya tribe, descended from the same groups as the ancient Baruya conquerors. It claimed that its old *kwaimatnie* had become worn out from having pierced so many generations of noses and had thus become useless and needed to be replaced.

In 1980, more serious still and, as all agreed, without precedent, a young Boulimmambakia (the lineage traditionally in possession of the *kwaimatnie* used in the puberty and birth ceremonies) claimed to be able to initiate the *tchouwanie* – the very heart of the entire Baruya initiate machine – in the place of the Baruya clansman normally responsible for this function. All he did was to bring shame upon himself, and no one followed him; but the incident does plainly show that, even today, when the white man's peace and national independence have done away with the possibility of becoming a great warrior, the ownership and use of a *kwaimatnie* continue to confer high status and to represent an important issue.

Whatever the case may be, these present-day disputes confirm the deep-seated belief of all Baruya, men and women, young and old, that it is their *kwaimatnie* that give them their strength and superiority over all their enemies, and that the *kwaimatnie*-owners alone are capable of transmitting this strength to the men when they celebrate their initiation rites. But how does this transmission occur in practical terms? What does one have to do to "lift up" the skins of boys and make them grow more quickly into men? How does one go about turning boys brought from the world of women into men?

Concretely, transmission occurs by means of direct contact between the *kwaimatnie* and the initiate's body. At the beginning of the ceremonies, and then on frequent occasions in the course of them, initiates from the different stages line up, standing shoulder to shoulder. The master of the ritual then suddenly appears at the mountaintop, and brandishing his *kwaimatnie* over his head, rushes down the side with his assistants. When he reaches the first initiate in the row, he strikes him violently in the chest with the base of the *kwaimatnie,* once to the right, once to the left, while uttering the secret name of the Sun to himself. He repeats these gestures with each of the initiates in turn. Then with his hands he squeezes weak points in the initiates' bodies, their leg joints and their arm joints, and ends by sharply stretching their arms above their heads in order to lengthen them and to make their bodies grow, to lift up their skin. To mark the change brought about in their bodies, the change of skin, he daubs them with red or yellow clay, which makes them glow and embellishes them.

Next, he adorns each of them with feathers, wickerwork, or cowrie necklaces – in other words, the insignia that will henceforward indicate the initiate's place among the four initiation stages – after which he adjusts the adornments on each initiate's brow, chest, and arms. Lastly, he gives each a mouthful of magic food that he has prepared himself and that contains a sauce consisting of chewed salt, intended to cool the liver, the seat of strength. Into this salt he has secretly mixed some dried magic leaves that he had gathered before the ceremonies at Bravegareubaramandeuc, a few days' walk from his village. This now deserted site was formerly the village of the Baruya's ancestors. All the Baruya *kwaimatnie* are supposed to have come from this sacred site, and before each initiation the various ritual masters travel there to gather the magic leaves that they require. Later, the initiates will receive more solid sustenance in the shape of taros and sweet potatoes sliced in two, into which the officiant will have once again slipped a few crumbs of magic leaves. As he picks up each taro to hand to the initiate, he presses his *kwaimatnie* against him.

It would be a mistake to view the touching of the initiates' bodies merely as symbolic gestures. They are that indeed, but not in the sense of simply symbolizing a reality that exists elsewhere and is merely suggested by these signs. For the Baruya, the fact of pulling on the arms or pressing the weak points of the limbs, of giving secret food to eat and tying the *ypmoulie,* red

90

like the Sun, about the brow – these gestures are not symbolic in that sense of the term; they really do pass the powers of the *kwaimatnie* into the initiates' bodies, turning the officiant into the mediator between men and the superhuman powers that govern the universe. The ritual actions on the bodies of the initiates are generally performed in silence, but they are followed by long, vehement speeches, which are delivered to the initiates by men renowned for their oratorical talents or, at moments of exceptional importance, by the *kwaimatnie*-owner himself.

Thus at the climax of the *tchouwanie* ceremony, Ypmeie, the most important of the *kwaimatnie*-men, after having placed the hornbill beak and circle of pigs' teeth (the symbols of male domination) on the heads of the initiates, then delivers a speech to them, explaining the significance of his gesture. He goes on to enumerate their future duties toward their elders, their future wives, children, the old, enemies, other people's property, the glory of the Baruya, and so on. In other words, he rehearses the political and ethical standards of the Baruya, the mighty deeds of the past, and threatens them with dire retribution – death – should they ever take it into their heads to reveal to women what they have seen, heard, and undergone in the course of their initiations. But he also promises them success and general esteem if they behave as they ought. In this way, the power of the Sun and the Moon are poured into their thoughts, and the institutions of the Baruya, which draw their strength, effectiveness, and, needless to say, their legitimacy, from this power, are imprinted into their bodies.

The guardians of the *kwaimatnie* are not only mediators of the Sun and the Moon and men. They also possess the power to divine the future of each initiate; but this power lasts only for the duration of the ceremonies, as long as they hold the *kwaimatnie* in their hands and the Sun communicates its powers through them. This limitation distinguishes their power of clairvoyance from that of the shamans, who have in themselves the power to know the past or the near future not only of initiates but of all men and women at any time in their lives; the *kwaimatnie*-men exercise their gift of clairvoyance at nighttime or dawn only on certain of the most important days in initiation ceremonies.

At dawn, accompanied by his assistants, the officiant comes with little bells in his left hand to scare away the evil spirits, and gently wakens the initiates, many of whom are only pretending to sleep. The gentleness and the precautions are most important, as the spirits leave the sleepers' bodies at night to travel through space and roam the mountainsides and forests; a sudden awakening might condemn a sleeper's spirit still abroad to eternal wandering.

Now these spirits sometimes bring back signs such as fragments of eagle feathers, or splinters of the kind of wood used to make arrows, from their nocturnal travels, and the *kwaimatnie*-man seeks these out, meticulously inspecting each initiate's bed after having quietly waked him. Any such sign, once found, is carefully kept and interpreted by the man in charge of the rituals as the sign that the initiate in question is destined to become an *aoulatta* (a great warrior), a *koulaka* (a shaman), or a cassowary hunter. He then informs the initiate's father and brother, together with the great shamans. For these minute fragments of feather, wood, or plant are sometimes placed beneath the sleeper's bed or in his hand by the spirits of the forest or ancestors lurking around the men's house.

Reactions to these messages are not unmitigated, and the Baruya know perfectly well that only the future can tell if things will come to pass as foretold. What is certain is that a boy ceases to behave in quite the same way once the others, and he himself, start to imagine that he is going to become a shaman or a warrior. Subjectively and socially, he comes under pressure to act accordingly, to do as is expected of him. Sometimes, however, the supernatural message leaves no doubt whatever. Early one morning, a cassowary's tail feather is discovered stuck in one of the *tsimia* poles. Ritual masters and shamans consult among themselves and conclude that an initiate is destined to be a great shaman, for this object could have been planted there only by the spirits that assist the shamans in their work. And should anyone suggest, as I did, that perhaps some human hand had performed this deed under cover of night, one is met by a chorus of shocked protest.

But it sometimes happens that a *kwaimatnie*-man sees a sign of imminent death or grave illness threatening one of the initiates. To discover this sign, he comes at night with flaming bamboo torches, which he waves up and down each initiate's chest and belly. Sometimes, through the flames, he "sees" a dark obscure mass in the initiate's body, this mass is the boy's liver, riddled with disease, already darkened by death. He says nothing, but later he discreetly confides this news to the shamans, who make arrangements for the initiate to attend one of their forthcoming cures so as to try to save him.

Last and above all, the *kwaimatnie*-men are responsible for stage-managing all the rites in their charge. It is no small matter to select the appropriate place and time for the performance of these rites, to place the different groups of initiates, to get the hundreds of married men to urge their wives to make new clothes and adornments, and to gather up the food necessary for the celebration of these ceremonies.

It is hardly surprising, then, that the *kwaimatnie*-man, as stage manager, mediator between men and gods, soothsayer, is looked up to with respect and gratitude for his contribution to the community. This respect is due more to his functions and to the powers of the *kwaimatnie*, however, than to himself, especially if he inherited the *kwaimatnie* while still young and began to exercise his functions a little early. But in addition to this respect, he enjoys several other advantages. In the general interest, people see to it that he finds a wife easily so that he can have sons and hand the *kwaimatnie* and ritual knowledge on to them. If he has no sister to exchange, there will always be a lineage to propose a wife, and he will return the compliment in the following generation by exchanging one of his own daughters. The *kwaimatnie*-man must observe the general rules, but he has the privilege of not having to look for a wife. Unlike ordinary mortals, he is offered one. This is an advantage, for quite often a Baruya is unable to find a wife outside his clan and is obliged, to his great shame, to marry one of his classificatory sisters, that is, a girl from his own lineage. Now, according to tradition, the owner of the *kwaimatnie* belonging to the Kwarrandariar lineage of the Baruya clan used to be offered wives by three or four lineages from other clans. Traditionally, therefore, he had three or four wives.

Above all though, the *kwaimatnie*-men were not permitted to stand in the front line in wars between the Baruya and their neighbors for fear that they may be killed in battle before having had time to hand on their knowledge to their sons or nephews. And the *kwaimatnie*-men from the Kwarrandariar lineage of the Baruya clan, who were responsible for the *tchouwanie* initiations, were not allowed to go to trade the salt that they had made with neighboring tribes. They were regarded as *tsimaye,* the poles of the *tsimia.* The entire politicoreligious machinery of the tribe, the reproduction of its ideological and spiritual unity, would have been endangered by their premature deaths.

However, the *kwaimatnie*-men did not have the power to impose their will in areas outside the initiation ceremonies, for example, war. Their prestige, though real enough, was not convertible into general political power; still less did it entitle them to demand material or other advantages in exchange for their services. On the contrary, the *kwaimatnie*-owners constantly repeat that their sole concern is to satisfy the demands of Baruya mothers and fathers eager to see their sons become men as quickly as possible. Indeed, in the middle of ceremonies, orators frequently come up to the initiates to remind them of all that they owe to those who have worked hard to provide the *pulpul*s, adornments, and vast quantities of food necessary for the celebrations. In this way, they draw attention to the way all lineages and generations work together for the common good.

The *kwaimatnie*-owner and his assistant, who carries out all sorts of little tasks to help him perform his function, are permanently accompanied by three or four brothers and cousins, on hand as a continual reminder that the *kwaimatnie* belongs to the lineage as a whole, in the same way as land or hunting territories do. Each *kwaimatnie*-owning lineage knows full well that it alone would be incapable of turning Baruya boys into men, and that all the other *kwaimatnie* need to be brought into play in order to complete the task. This is common knowledge among the Baruya. Everyone knows as well that no individual or lineage can avoid cooperating with the others: materially, by from time to time offering a patch of its forest to all the other lineages in order to clear their huge collective taro gardens; socially, by exchanging its women; politically and ideologically, by allowing everyone to benefit from the powers of its *kwaimatnie*. Thus, alongside inherited status, which acts as a kind of stable framework for the Baruya tribe, there is a huge area open to individual talent, including war, hunting, shamanism, economic activities, and so on, in which some people are destined to excel, namely, those whose exceptional destiny the *kwaimatnie*-men frequently claim to have seen long beforehand.

Therefore one can see why ownership of a *kwaimatnie* brings prestige to the name of the man in whose hands it has been placed and to the clan that he represents. It means that he and his clan are the guardians and guarantors of the social and cosmic order; that the reproduction of these two orders rests (to be sure partly, but permanently) on their shoulders. Through their possession of these sacred objects, they stand as the link between man and the gods, the living and the dead, between their present-day lands and the territory of their ancestors. When the guardian raises the object above his head and inwardly utters its name, all these invisible forces course through his body and, by his gestures, into the bodies and spirits of the youths before him.

For the *kwaimatnie*-men are first and foremost the guardians and guarantors of men's general domination over women. It is they who establish it both socially and ritually, and who legitimize it ideologically. For – and here I must reveal a fundamental fact hinted at in all of the foregoing, a fact that goes to the heart of social power among the Baruya – *all the kwaimatnie exist in pairs, and operate as a couple; one is male, the other female, and the more powerful of the two is always the female kwaimatnie*. It is the "hottest," most effective of the two, and only the master of the rituals, the guardian of the *kwaimatnie*, can hold it in his hands. The other, the male *kwaimatnie*, is left to brothers and cousins, to the others from his lineage who help him in his ritual functions and repeat after him the magic gestures practiced on the initiates' bodies. What these *kwaimatnie* contain buried deep within them is the entire social and cosmic power, all the power of men, which flows from the fusion and synthesis of masculine and feminine. But this synthesis only exists, and this power only goes to work, when the feminine has been torn from the women and added, shackled, to the masculine, to the power of men – in a word, made masculine.

The lesson is always the same. In order to dominate, the masculine (the men) must contain the power of the feminine, and to do so, it must first seize that power by expropriating it from the women in whom it originally resides. In somewhat the same way in our own society, the wealth of some is the wealth that has been expropriated from others who produced it.

So the message is clear. In order to dominate, it is not enough for men to be themselves; they must also turn the power of the women into an attribute of their own power, into a male attribute in other words. When the most prestigious of the Baruya ritual masters, Ypmeie, the guardian of the *kwai-*

matnie belonging to the Baruya clan, revealed to me that his *kwaimatnie* were in fact two, the more powerful being the woman, he also gave me their name, for there was but one: Kanaamakwe, the secret name given to the Sun. Because of this revelation I believe that the esoteric version of the identity of Sun and Moon coincides profoundly with the social and ideological practice of Baruya men. By claiming that Moon is not Sun's wife but his brother, the esoteric version more clearly expresses the essence of male power, which ultimately resides in the absorption of the female into the male, the trans-mutation of the submissive feminine (Moon-wife) into the subordinate mas-culine (Moon-younger-brother-of-Sun).

Equally clearly, we can see why possession of the *kwaimatnie* not only establishes male domination but also legitimizes it. The *kwaimatnie* are evi-dence of an order that transcends the world of men, living or dead, and the social order as well. They bear witness to a cosmic order established in the past for the good of mankind, the benefits of which the living merely reap today. Consequently, it behooves them to do everything in their power to cooperate in ensuring its survival throughout eternity. Nothing could better illustrate the legitimate, sacred character of the male initiations and of the general subordination of women instituted by these ceremonies than the myth of the origins of the most powerful Baruya *kwaimatnie*, those belonging to the Baruya clan itself. This myth was told to me in 1970 by Yarouemaye, the new master of the *tchouwanie* rituals, a young man who had replaced his uncle, the prestigious Ypmeie, after the latter's death.

In the olden times, all the men lived in the same place, at a spot near the sea. One day, the men parted and our ancestor, the ancestor of our own lineage, the Kwarran-dariar, the Baruya Kwarrandariar, the Kwarrandariar of the Baruya clan, rose up into the air and flew to the spot where we thereafter lived, Bravegareubaramandeuc, not far from Menyamya.

Our ancestor was called Djivaamakwe, and Djivaamakwe had flown through the air along a path red as fire. This path was like a bridge that the Wandjinia (the spirit-men of the earliest time, the dream time) had built for Djivaamakwe and for the *kwaimatnie* that the Sun had given to our ancestor before he took off. The Sun is the man of the middle. He sees all and everything at once. Djivaamakwe had received three *kwaimatnie*, three *moukamaye* [*maye*, flowers; *mouka*, young initiates]. When he touched the earth, the Wandjinia, the spirit-men, revealed to him the name Ka-naamakwe, the secret name of the Sun. They also revealed to him the name of the spot and the name he was to give to the men he would find there: the Baragaye, the Baruya. Baruya is the name of an insect with black-spotted red wings, which the members of the Baruya clan are not permitted to kill. These wings are like the red path that led Djivaamakwe to Bravegareubaramandeuc.

His men were there. He gave them their [clan] names, Andavakia, Nunguye, and so on. Then he instituted the male initiations. He explained that a boy had to become *mouka*, then *palittamounie*, then *tchouwanie*, and so on, and he gave them all tasks to perform, rituals to accomplish, and made them build a *tsimia*. Then he said to them: "I am the central pole of this house, the *tsimie*. You are beneath me. I am the first, and for all of you now your first name will henceforward be mine, Baruya."

The others, the Andavakia, the Nunguye, and so on, did not protest when he raised his name, the name of the Kwarrandariar Baruya, and lowered their names, Andavakia, Nunguye, and so on. They had little *kwaimatnie*. He said that he was *tsimie,* the central pole and the others said to him: "Your two names are Baruya-Tsimia." He said to them: "Now try your *kwaimatne.* Try to make them do what I told you to do during the ceremonies."

They said to him: "We are your warriors. We cannot allow you to be killed by the enemies. You shall not go to make war. We shall go and you shall remain among us." For from the moment Djivaamakwe touched ground at Bravegareubaramandeuc, there were many wars and wars "for nothing." Formerly, when the men had not yet parted, there were no wars. It was because of war, endless wars, that Yarouemaye, the son of Djivaamakwe, had to flee Bravegareubaramandeuc and come to take refuge in Marouaka. But he brought with him the *kwaimatnie,* the gift of the Sun.

At Marouaka, our ancestors changed their name. The Ndelie gave them hospitality and settled them at Kwarrandariar. Since that time, we are the Kwarrandariar Baruya. Then the Ndelie helped us to defeat the Andje and to seize their territory and, to thank them, our ancestor at that time, who was also called Djivaamakwe, grandson of the previous one, gave to the Ndelie a third of the *kwaimatnie* given by the Sun and gave them functions in the initiations. This is why we now only have two. And Djivaamakwe, he too, stood before the defeated enemy, before the Andje, and dressed the young men and placed the insignias on their heads. Then he said: "Those shall be *aoulatta,* great warriors; those shall be shamans." He saw and marked those who were to be great men.

This account is perfectly explicit as regards the functions and status of the *kwaimatnie*-owners. Evidently, the *kwaimatnie* not merely institutes male domination and communicates to future warriors the force of the Sun and of the great warriors of the past, but is also capable of discerning the future great warriors in each generation who are destined to replace their predecessors. It is capable of picking out those who are to become the rampart of the tribe as a whole, those whose names are destined to grow in glory: the *aoulatta,* (the great warriors), the *koulaka* (the shamans) whose status is not inherited but merited, shown and demonstrated. Now it should be clear why, for the Baruya, only the masters of the Sun *kwaimatnie* have the right to place the hornbill beak and circle the pigs' teeth, which symbolize the young men's status as men and warriors, on their heads and to remove them. Their own fathers are not entitled to do so, proof, if such were needed, that the initiations represent a higher social order than that of relations of kinship. It is the order of masculine solidarity as well as the order of the political and ideological unity of the tribe as a whole.

Warriors, shamans, cassowary hunters: status for the taking

Like any terse formula, the heading calls for some comment in order to clear up certain misunderstandings that are bound to flow from its conciseness. In actual fact, the status for the taking is not that of warrior, shaman, or hunter, but those of great warrior, great shaman, and great hunter.

Male hierarchies

Every Baruya is a warrior, hunter, and horticulturist. The initiations and the community life that the Baruya impose on boys for a period of over ten years are precisely designed to turn each of them into a man competent in all three areas. It is worth adding that, though war and hunting are reserved for men and valued as attributes of their virility, women play an extremely important role in gardening.

War is – or rather was – an essential and permanent feature of the life of the Baruya and their neighbors. Hunting too is a permanent activity; although it scarcely plays any part in the Baruya's subsistence, it contributes to the production and reproduction of their social relations. For instance, a man is obliged to offer game each time one of his daughters or sisters has her first period, each time his wife gives birth, and each time the initiates complete a cycle of ceremonies to mark their entrance into a new stage of initiation.

Game circulates constantly from men to women and initiates to compensate them for the suffering and hardships that these two social groups endure in their development and for the sake of their development. The principal object for ritual gifts, game is also what permits men to survive in the forest in time of war or on trading expeditions. Game, say the Baruya, is the men's sweet potato. For hunting offers the men an opportunity of emancipating themselves from the women for a while; they do without the fruit of their labor in the garden which requires the combined efforts of both sexes, each enjoying a right to his or her share in whatever is grown there. The women neither are allowed to hunt nor do they know how to do so.

One final point to be cleared up is that, though all men are hunters, very few become cassowary hunters. The cassowary is very different from the other varieties of game, the opossum, wild pig, wallaby (a small forest variety of kangaroo), birds, and so on. It cannot fly, and so [to the Baruya] it is not a bird; yet it has wings. Unlike other wild animals, it is killed not by being pierced by an arrow, for the Baruya are reluctant to shed its blood; they prefer to strangle it. We need to know what the cassowary signifies for the Baruya so as to understand the reasons behind this manner of hunting it and the status of its hunters. For it is the possession of spiritual powers, not mere technique that makes a man who knows how to hunt a hunter of cassowary, and makes him rather similar to the shaman, with whom he is sometimes associated.

As for shamanism, it is important to make a certain number of things clear from the outset. Unlike war and hunting, this activity is open both to men and to women. Admittedly, the women occupy a position subordinate to that of men in shamanistic practices, but they nevertheless find here the opportunity of distinguishing themselves individually, and this possibility is readily acknowledged by all.

Shamanism consists of a variety of magic techniques designed either to cure or to kill and relying on the aid of spiritual powers. For all Baruya, the possession of such powers is regarded as perfectly normal even as everything that surrounds them – stones, water, trees, animals, insects, light, and so on – possesses one or more spirits, each the source of certain powers. These spiritual powers suddenly appear to a man or woman as he rounds a bend along a path in the reflection of a leaf, a splash of water, the shadow of an opossum vanishing into the branches, the persistence with which some insect follows you around. At each such meeting, a spirit, a power, a *koulaka* is captured and added to those that one already possesses within oneself. Nothing ever happens without magic among the Baruya, be it warfare, hunting, farming, pig raising; and powers, once captured by an individual, are added to all the inherited magic powers belonging to his/her family (*yanga boulaka*, magic words), shared with paternal or maternal kin, and handed down from father to son (gardening) or from mother to daughter (pig breeding).

Koulaka (magic power) is also the Baruya term used to refer to shamans. What distinguishes shamans from other men and women is that they alone have the ability to put their spiritual powers to other people's service and to struggle victoriously against aggression by enemy shamans. The dividing line between warfare and shamanism, which we rather rigidly set earlier on, blurs somewhat here. For the Baruya wage two kinds of warfare, military warfare and a war of spirits. That they have ceased the former and laid down their arms does not necessarily mean the end of the latter. The shamans continue the struggle with their invisible weapons. The women have no part in this spiritual warfare, and their exclusion restores the male monopoly of warfare inside the field of shamanism and confirms, albeit in a different form, the men's superiority.

One further point; though one finds quite a few shamans among the Baruya – three or four men, and one or two women per village – one encounters very few great shamans, and all are men.

War, hunting, shamanism, these are the spheres in which status is undeniably there for the taking, although the opportunities vary greatly according to whether one is a man or a woman, a member of the Tchatche or Kavalie group, and so forth. Whereas the men have many opportunities of distinguishing themselves, the women have few, even before individuals come into the picture. Opportunities are offered or withheld by the social relations, institutions, and culture, which necessarily exist before individual development and initiative.

Does the word *initiative* mean the same thing to the Baruya as it often does to us, namely, an action undertaken by an individual in order to stand out from the crowd? If certain kinds of status can be acquired, who then does so: those who have the as-it-were innate capacity, those who are capable of doing so? The Baruya envisage the problem of innate or acquired in ideological terms, their sole practical data being their own everyday collective observations of the individual's behavior in the ordinary and extraordinary circumstances of his or her life. But is there a culture in which the problem is not initially conceived in ideological terms, or is there a culture in possession of substantially more reliable material?

5

The discovery of great men

When, in the middle of the *pongwanie* ceremony, the *kwaimatnie*-man points out to the assembly one of the future *tchouwanie,* standing silently with his head bowed among others of his age, and when, in the grip of the powers of the *kwaimatnie,* he proclaims that this young man will one day be a great warrior, shaman, or cassowary hunter, he is revealing to the community the existence of a force already propelling this boy toward his destiny, even though neither he nor the others had guessed it, still less willed it. At any rate that revelation is what happens in public during the male initiations. But what goes on behind the scenes? What happened before the curtain went up?

I have already explained that after the boys have left their mothers to become *mouka,* the *kwaimatnie*-man – a Tchatche or a Wombouye by rotation – runs the ritual accompanying the separation from the world of women and looks carefully, on several occasions, for signs that may give some hint as to each youngster's future. He rarely finds any, and when he does, they are never all that clear. Nor does he announce the fact publicly, merely mentioning the matter discreetly to the shamans and to the boy's father and uncles. We must remember that, although the boy is only about ten at the time and has spent his entire life with the women, he nevertheless spends more and more time with boys his age, catching rats, hunting in the bush, or scrapping with his peers at the village outskirts. Therefore the adults already have had occasion to observe his conduct. For the next five or six years, he is under constant watch, criticized, reprimanded, encouraged, and praised by his elders, who take the place of his mother and father in training him and form their opinions of him. They watch him hunt, shoot with a bow and arrow in competitions, react to the death of one of his brothers or his father killed in battle, put up with the physical and psychological bullying that goes on during the initiation cycle.

All this information and the various judgments to which it gives rise form the basis of a social evaluation of each individual's abilities, these opinions

100

are public property, as it were, and are thus available to the man in charge of the rituals when the time comes to pick out one or more youths from the crowd and proclaim their destinies. So what this prediction actually reveals is to a large extent an a posteriori judgment; needless to say, the youngster will be thus further stimulated to do what is expected of him. A process of self-persuasion is thus set in motion, or reinforced, and is profoundly though unconsciously rooted in the ideas that underpin the interpretation of individual destiny that all Baruya share.

The understanding of individuals among different generations with different experiences thus furnishes one explanation of why the ritual master's prediction frequently comes pretty close to the actual outcome. But it is not the only explanation, for prediction is both harder and easier than it appears. It needs to take into account not only individual psychological factors but also the social position that each person inherits through his lineage, a position in connection with military and shamanistic activities. As we have already seen, for example, the Baruya do not expect their *kwaimatnie*-men to be great warriors. Their function excludes them. Nor are they expected to become shamans, great or less great, even though this role is not impossible.

The twin need to multiply the number of great warriors while keeping the *kwaimatnie*-men out of war has entailed a division of all the tribe's clans and lineages between two poles, each of which is occupied by two clans, the Nunguye and the Bakia on the periphery and the Ndelie and the Baruya in the center, as the Baruya themselves put it. The first two are regarded as warrior clans par excellence, always ready to grapple with the enemy in order to protect the rest of the tribe, and especially the *kwaimatnie*-men from the Baruya and Ndelie clans. Yet there is no real opposition between warrior clans and *kwaimatnie* clans, as proven by the fact that the Bakia and the Nunguye also have *kwaimatnie* of their own; but these are *kwaimatnie* of the night, those used in ceremonies that take place behind the walls of the *tsimia*, or on dimly moonlit nights in the center of the village, away from the eyes of women and children. The *kwaimatnie*-men of the Baruya and Ndelie clans, on the other hand, are the masters of rituals performed in broad daylight, in full view of the Sun and under its protection. Two other lineages take their place alongside the Baruya and the Ndelie, namely, the Inamwe, belonging to the Andavakia clan, and Boulimmambakia, of the Bakia clan. Both own a *kwaimatnie* for childbirth and male puberty rites. All the other clans are spread between these two poles, some closer to the Bakia, such as the Tchatche, by the virtue of their warriors and their martial magic; others closer to the Baruya, such as the Yuwandelie, renowned for their great shamans.

Reality is still more complex and reveals that these two poles are not the stable framework of a fixed, hereditary system of lineage-based statuses, but two forces of attraction for the performance of two functions that all clans are not only supposed to, but can, perform equally well. For instance, the Bakia, which is the foremost warrior clan, also has a lineage renowned for its shamans, the Kuopbakia, whereas the Yuwandalie, who have a reputation for their shamans, also have a lineage well known for its warriors.

Whereas at first sight one gets the impression that the positions of the various clans relative to war and shamanism are entirely dependent on heredity, it turns out in fact that, externally, all clans are divided into a certain number of lineages more or less exclusively concerned with one or another of these functions. The fixed points in this otherwise fluid situation remain the positions of each clan in the performance of male initiations (according to whether they are included in them or, a fortiori, whether they have no part in them).

From birth then, each man finds himself, by virtue of his name, which instantly announces his lineage, under social and psychological pressure to sustain and reproduce the position of his lineage within the tribe. Therefore, unconsciously and consciously, he comes to display either his warlike disposition or spiritual powers, if we assume he possesses either, depending on the lineage into which he was born.

Regardless of lineage or clan, all Baruya are convinced that the tribe can hope to survive and reproduce itself only if there is a healthy proportion or mixture of great warriors and great shamans both within each clan and among all the clans taken together. This is the second aspect, the second series (sociological, this time) of data well known to the man in charge of the *tchouwanie* rituals and helps to shape his vision when, in the light and power of the Sun, he suddenly "sees" the function that the given young man will ultimately perform in his lineage and in the tribe. For his message to be both credible and acceptable, what he sees must coincide not only with the social evaluation of an individual's abilities but also with the social demands that each clan and lineage places on its members: the need to reproduce the lineage's position within the tribe as a whole and to ensure respect not only for its living members and its glorious dead, but also for its lands, pigs, and hunting territories.

We may therefore surmise that this vision of the future, which is as clear to the man in charge of the rituals as to all those around him, who are merely the silent witnesses, is the product of a frame of mind that is much less submissive to suprahuman forces than appears to be the case on the great public stage of the initiation ceremonies. This well-informed and apparently passive vision in fact turns out rather to be a kind of intelligent (public) choice, which emerges from the synthesis of a great number of social and psychological factors and seeks to provide the best possible response to the expectations of the tribe in general and of each lineage in particular.

Yet, despite the ritual-master's visions, at sixteen years of age a future warrior has still not killed an enemy, a future shaman has still not healed anyone, and a future cassowary hunter has still to lay his traps nor has he seen in his dreams a cassowary caught by the neck in one of them. Final proof is still lacking, and may indeed never come. Failure will merely demonstrate that the enemies have shamans, or at least one shaman, as powerful as the best of the Baruya. Consequently in his speech the man responsible for these visions acknowledges the possibility of failure since he frequently warns the crowd that "time will tell" and the Baruya react with some skepticism to the proclamations, preferring, as we ourselves say, "to wait and see." For a warrior who kills no one, a shaman who never heals anyone, or a hunter who finds his traps empty or broken ultimately suffers far deeper humiliation than someone who has never been mentioned in this context and yet who one day might become a hero through having performed some unexpected feat.

Such is the social and psychological background against which some at least will achieve the statuses "for the taking." I have tried to reconstitute the complex web of conditions that propels some rather than others to the forefront. Let us now take a look at the great men once they have proven themselves and achieved recognition. What have they actually done, and what is their status?

The *aoulatta:* the great warrior

We shall begin by taking a look at the functions and the importance of warfare among the Baruya. Their history speaks for itself, since it is the tale of the expansion of a group of refugees from the Menyamya region to the detriment of the Andjc and Usarumpia tribes that used to inhabit the Marouaka Valley. These refugees were a remnant of the Baragaye tribe, which had been split asunder after a murderous quarrel between two hostile factions. According to the Baruya, the pretext for this event was the humiliation suffered by an orphan in the men's house of his village. No one looked after him, and he was given nothing to eat. One day, he set out for the neighboring village, Bravegareubaramandeuc, where he had cousins, and complained to them about the way he was treated. One night, they, accompanied by other initiates from their village, slipped into the youngster's *tsimia* and killed all the occupants. The blood flowed upon the ground like a lake of *marita* [pandanus cone; from the pidgin *marita,* pandanus] juice. Next morning, the fathers of the victims discovered the massacre and swore revenge. They said nothing, biding their time, making a secret agreement with an enemy tribe, the Tapache, whom they entrusted with the task of massacring the inhabitants of Bravegareubaramandeuc. One day, when part of the population was out hunting in the forest, the Tapache sprang forward and exterminated the remaining men, women, and children. The village was razed to the ground. It is on this now deserted site that the *kwamatnie*-men come in search of the magic plants that they require for the initiations.

Most of the hunters, accompanied by a few women and children, managed to flee and sought asylum in all directions, some with the Tchavalie, others among the Kokwaye, two friendly tribes. Yet others formed a new group, the Yoyue, whom the Baruya still look upon as kin, or cross cousins.

Later, certain of the Baruya who had taken refuge among the Tchavalie and the Kokwaye, presumably feeling a little cramped, decided to move still farther on. They left behind them all those who did not wish to follow them (and whose descendants are now full members of these two tribes). After a few days and nights of walking in silence, they reached one of the high points of the valley of Marouaka, expecting to be killed by the natives. In fact, they were given a warm welcome by the Ndelie, a lineage of the Andje tribe, who later helped them to take over the territory belonging to the other lineages of their tribe, thus reproducing the treachery – this time to the benefit of the Baruya.

According to Andje tradition, before this event the group called Mouontdalie had been in the process of expanding, and had already displaced the Yagoulaganje, which had in turn invaded the territory of the Tapache, the very tribe that was to massacre the Baruya's ancestors. This movement was to continue, with the Baruya taking over the territory of the Andje and the Usarumpia, who drove their neighbors out in turn, and so on.

So recourse to armed violence was a customary, continuing process among the Anga tribes in settling their group conflicts. Internal vendettas and external wars periodically broke out and served as pretexts for further violence, breaking up ancient tribes united the day before, and forming new ones the next day out of the remains of the earlier tribes, which joined forces in order to survive and cope with their environment. Without discussing the causes of these conflicts in detail, we note that on each occasion they resulted in a redistribution of land, hunting territories, and groves of pandanus trees planted by the ancestors of the defeated groups. What was in fact preserved, lost, or extended whenever a piece of land changed hands, depending on the outcome of the battle, was the material basis of life itself. Periodically, land became the essential issue in war, and we can readily imagine that conflicts would gather in intensity and frequency among groups beginning to feel the pinch, as each sought to increase its territory at its neighbor's expense.

For the Baruya, the result of the vast centuries-long movement of expansion among certain Anga groups was that they found themselves at the center of an extensive network of oppositions and alliances with their neighbors. This network revolved around two poles, as it were. On the one hand, they had permanent enemies, the Andje, whom they had driven from their territory and who represented the fixed negative pole in their intertribal relations. On the other hand, they maintained permanent relations of friendship and

Permanent warfare

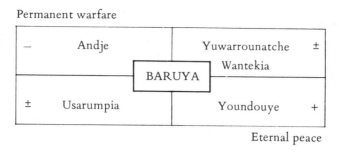

Figure 9. Politicomilitary relations between Baruya and neighboring tribes

economic, and sometimes even military, cooperation, with the Youndouye, a tribe not belonging to the Anga culture, even though it did incorporate the descendants of an Anga group who had preferred to leave the Wonenara Valley when, at the end of the last century, it was invaded by the Baruya.

Between these two opposing poles, we find all the tribes immediately adjacent to the Baruya, all of which belonged to the Anga culture, and which were all, at one time or another, either allies or enemies of the Baruya.

It is in this overall social context and long-term historical perspective that we must examine the role and status of the Baruya great warrior, the *aoulatta*. *Aoulatta* refers to three things in the Baruya language: a type of arrow ending in four slender tips, used to kill certain birds; a variety of pandanus whose trunk is covered by so many long, hard, and thorny leaves that it is difficult to climb it; and certain warriors, the greatest among them, who directly grapple with the enemy hand to hand, wielding their clubs. The term also sometimes refers to a sharpshooting archer, capable of holding off an enemy attack singlehanded simply by virtue of the accuracy and rapidity of his firing rate, protected by a narrower shield than the one used by other warriors, as he nimbly sidesteps the shower of arrows raining down on him or striking his shield. But above all, the *aoulatta* is, or was, the man who advances alone toward the enemy lines, followed by a handful of assistants known as his "dogs," and who engages in single combat with any warrior prepared to match his skill and strength.

Few men were prepared to do that, and for the most part the Baruya's idea of warfare was for the mass of warriors, who were skilled archers, to stand some way off from the enemy and to send off a volley of arrows, or else to lay carefully organized ambushes and launch surprise attacks involving no great danger. The *aoulatta*, on the other hand, took all the risks, and his stature grew every time he smashed an adversary's skull. He would plunge his club into the enemy's blood and raise it above his head, crying, "*Wi-wi,*" the victory cry, the signal that an enemy had fallen. His name would spread

105

far and wide among enemies and allies alike, and he naturally became a prime target in subsequent ambushes.

Needless to say, in Baruya eyes, his prowess was not solely because of his bravery, physical abilities, or his extraordinary virtuosity in battle. The *aoulatta* is described as being driven by a murderous force, by a magical power that goes before him and enables him to detect the presence of an enemy, to anticipate his moves, and even pin him down in a spot where it is easier to kill him. Indeed, the surviving great warriors, whom I had occasion to meet after twenty years of enforced peace, were not among the most imposing men in the tribe in terms of size.

The *keuleuka,* the skull-breaking stone war club and the *aoulatta's* favorite weapon, is also endowed with magic powers. The Baruya do not make the weapons and claim that they are the work of benevolent spirits, who gave them to their ancestors. Ever since, they have been lovingly preserved and handed down from generation to generation, to those thought most worthy to bear them. One of these weapons, moreover, is brandished at the end of the male initiations, when the *tchouwanie* are lectured on the might of the Baruya and their glorious history.

The high point in Baruya warfare thus came when their *aoulatta* came face to face with those of their enemies, when the heroes met in single combat. The *djilika,* the *aoulatta's* "dogs," stood some distance behind him, ready to rush forward to give him cover after his adversary had fallen but was not yet slain. The *aoulatta* would then try, if the enraged enemies left him time, to drag the corpse back behind his own lines. There, he would cut off his right hand, the hand that shoots and kills, and daub his body in the victim's blood. Sometimes he also cut off his arms and legs, which he then cooked and ate in order to appropriate the strengths and powers of the vanquished enemy. This posthumous homage was reserved for the *aoulatta,* and the ordinary warrior or rank-and-file soldier was not entitled to such treatment.

On their return to the village, amid victory chants, the warriors would expose the hand like a trophy, palm upward nailed to a plank displaying a number of arrows and surmounted by a red *ypmoulie* and a yellow headband, like the ones the men wear on their brow, and spread fanlike; to crown the display, they would place the victor's war club.

Needless to say, the memory of the *aoulatta's* deeds is kept alive in the form of tales and songs which have come down through the mists of time. They relate mighty deeds and glorious names such as Bwatchouiwe, a young Andavakia who, while still only a *kawetnie,* instead of fleeing like the others before the Andje warriors who had surrounded his village, grasped a war club abandoned by one of his elders and, in company with Bakitchatche, another legendary hero, hurled himself onto the enemy. In the face of such bravery and seeing that the two boys had already killed one of their men, the enemy retreated and took to their heels. After the war, Bwatchouiwe and

Bakitchatche were sent to the Kokwaye, who were about to initiate their *tchouwanie,* and, having already killed a man, they were made *tchouwanie* without further ado, ahead of all their coinitiates.

For the Baruya, such deeds cannot be accounted for without the intervention of supernatural powers. They say that, one day, when the Baruya who wanted to take the Andje from behind found themselves arrested by an unbridgeable abyss, the spirit of Langaoundje, an *aoulatta* from the Bakia clan, changed himself into a sharp-toothed variety of opossum and gnawed the base of a tree which fell across the ravine. The Baruya crossed the miracle-bridge, took their enemy from behind, and slaughtered them.

As for Bakitchatche, he reappears in all the great battles of the Baruya. We find him everywhere, fighting against the Andje, against the Usarumpia, as well as against the Wantekia, Yuwarrounatche, and so forth. Yet it seems he must have been dead at least a century at that point. After his death, his descendants cut off his fingers and kept them with loving care, and they still had them in their possession in 1960 when the white men arrived. These relics disappeared a few months later when one of the first Australian outpost commanders burned down the village of the Tchatche. The flames also consumed the two flint stones that the Nunguye had always used to rekindle the primordial fire inside the *tsimia* on the occasion of each initiation.

What the *aoulatta* had to gain is clear then, namely, prestige, a name for himself, glory, and admiration. Did he also derive any wealth or power from it? Wealth, certainly not. An *aoulatta,* say the Baruya, is a man with few wives, few children, spending most of his time keeping watch over the enemy, laying ambushes for him, attacking him or escaping his clutches, and he usually leaves his descendants very little newly cleared land. The Bakia clan provides clear evidence, for although they are the warrior clan par excellence, and its warriors had been among its most energetic conquerors, they now own little land in the Wonenara Valley. According to the Baruya, at that time land was not all that important, but because of the growth of population it is now important to produce cash crops in addition to providing for one's subsistence.

But that is not the main reason. It is to be found in the relation that used to exist, in the precolonial era, between warfare and the economy, that is, mainly gardening. It goes without saying that truces were concluded at the appropriate moment, when the forest was being cleared and the gardens were harvested. This arrangement suited everyone. War kept a lot of men busy watching the enemy, protecting the women on their way to and from the gardens, guarding the village and the men's house against surprise attack. To cope with this situation and support the warriors in the pursuit of their task, certain hard-working and skilled farmers decided to remain behind, devoting their strength to cultivating fine, large gardens and sharing their produce with the others. Far from earning contempt in the eyes of the Baruya, they were called by two names that speak volumes for the importance attached to their function, namely, *tannaka* and *tsimie*.

Tannaka means protrusion, a hold by which to climb a rock face or a tree trunk. *Tsimie* refers to the central pole in certain buildings such as the great ceremonial house which is indeed called *tsimia* (the house that "supports" the Baruya tribe). The *aoulatta* protect the *tannaka,* just as the roof of the ceremonial house shelters the initiates and can only stay up by resting on the pole that supports it in the center. Every village had one or two such men on whom everyone could rely. Needless to say, given the forces of production, the techniques and the division of labor as it then existed among the Baruya, the *tannaka* needed help in order to perform his task, and first of all the work of his wives. They had to be hard working like himself. But whereas a special word designates the man, the Baruya merely speak of such women as *draginie:* tough, not afraid of drudgery. "With us," say the Baruya, "we single out and 'distinguish' only the man, not the woman." But even the help of several wives was not enough, and the *tannaka* used to call in his sisters, sisters-in-law, distant kin, and neighbors' wives, a common practice among the Baruya when laying out large gardens. The youths living in the *kwa-langa,* who did not accompany their fathers and brothers to war, used to help him clear the forest and put up fences around his gardens. So he thus gathered around himself a labor force of women and youngsters, who joined their efforts to his in support of the war.

In times of peace, during the initiations, the *tannaka* made his sugarcane, sweet potato, and taro gardens available to all. He was not alone in doing so, but he always gave more than the others. Each time the Baruya held a meeting in his village to decide on war or initiations, to put an end to a vendetta threatening to drag on too long or endanger the unity of the tribe, he would have his wives prepare a few fillets of sweet potatoes and sugar cane for serving at the end of the meeting. For, among the Baruya, any meeting or other group activity always ended with a meal taken together. This description of the *tannaka* and his relations with the *aoulatta* explains why the Baruya were sometimes, for the sake of war and initiations, prepared to work harder and expand outward. Therefore it looks as if, for the Baruya, the role of economic activity in their social life was to create temporary surpluses to meet the needs of warfare or initiations, which they regarded as indispensable to the common good.

Their attitudes toward material production or "economic" matters thus seem to have left little room for the pursuit of personal enrichment. The *tannaka* does not work for himself alone, nor even for his descendants, even though he will be leaving them a greater expanse of cleared land; he produces in order to redistribute. However, the contexts in which he redistributes do not permit him to rise alone above the others, but only to do so in company with others who are just as indispensable as he is, namely, the great warriors. Ultimately, this position is what distinguishes him from the big man, with whom there are many resemblances in the sense that both concentrate a considerable amount of labor force around themselves and produce in order to redistribute. But the big man, with his many wives, pigs, gifts, and debts, rises alone above the crowd, as if he achieved the greatness of the *aoulatta* while essentially playing the *tannaka,* but for his own benefit. As a result, a big man's name, like that of an *aoulatta,* quickly spreads beyond the borders of his own tribe.

So, if *aoulatta* and *tannaka* do not accumulate wealth in addition to their prestige, do they at least accumulate power? Do they exercise any authority over the other members of the tribe? The *tannaka* could have, if he wished, cooled warlike passions by referring in public to the crops needing to be harvested in the gardens; but that statement would have been news to no one, for everyone, particularly the women, were usually aware of what needed to be done. If he wanted to bring people around to his viewpoint, he would have had to have been a good public speaker, a *kououndje,* a man capable of making fine speeches not for the sake of oratory but in order to find solutions to problems. But whatever his oratorical gifts, the *tannaka,* with his reputation for wisdom and devotion to the common weal, was always listened to with respect.

For the *aoulatta,* things were rather different. In time of war, his authority was unquestioned. In peacetime, his function disappeared, but his prestige remained, as did the gratitude of the rest of the tribe toward him. Furthermore, and more prosaically, he was just as fearsome physically in peacetime as in time of war. He was surrounded with respect, and he and his supporters were listened to. So great was his authority on occasion that he could intervene in conflicts between brothers or cousins threatening to kill each other over a woman, a garden, or a pandanus tree. Although such conflicts were generally the exclusive business of the kinship groups concerned and the others waited for something serious to happen before intervening, the *aoulatta* could step in beforehand, separate the adversaries, order them to make their peace and stop creating a disturbance. He thus rose above the obligations and limitations of kinship so that the wider interest might prevail. He used his potential for violence and his prestige not for war or in the struggle against external enemies but for the sake of peace, in the struggle against mischief-makers within the tribe. Therefore he derived his authority both from his bravery and from the fear that it inspired, and thus converted his prestige into social power. But there were limits to this power and it was dangerous to overstep them.

There were many cases of *aoulatta* who lost all sense of proportion and, confident in their fighting abilities, gradually gave themselves up to the pleasures of despotism.[1] They killed their neighbors' pigs, forced their wives to make love with them and hit them if they refused, ridiculed their husbands and mocked their reproaches or threats. Once an *aoulatta*, an Andavakia called Andaineu, killed a woman who resisted him by impaling her on a garden fence; another time, he punished a woman who had stolen a piglet of his by cutting off her fingers and slicing her cheeks from the lips, before beating her to death and throwing her body into the river. Then admiration and trust turned to secret loathing and fear. Many Baruya began to hope that some enemy would rid them of their great man, and their wish finally came true. He was struck in the eye by an arrow and returned home to die. His body was exposed on a platform as was the custom for great warriors, but people felt that this arrow must have killed him because his misdeeds had gradually robbed him of his magic powers and his fighting strength.

Sometimes the Baruya did not wait for their enemies to mete out justice by chance in some battle. They carefully arranged the tyrant's murder, supplying the enemy with all the information necessary as to when and where to surprise him in order to be sure of killing him. Needless to say, the plotters acted in the greatest secrecy, and were still at the future victim's side, smiling and joking, a few hours before the murder. At the critical moment, they always had a cast-iron alibi. For even if by this treachery they did succeed in delivering many people, duplicity ought normally to be avenged by the death of the traitor, and it was up to the victim's brothers and brothers-in-law to execute the sentence.

The punishment for despotism, therefore, was the tyrant's death. This policy was meant as a clear reminder to all that, for the Baruya, differences between individuals are only permitted and desirable insofar as they work for the common good. Each initiation ceremony indeed conveyed the lesson to be strong, but to use strength to serve others.

Whatever an *aoulatta*'s prestige might have been, there was little chance of his sons inheriting it. The great warrior's son was usually an ordinary man, a "sweet potato." Yet the *aoulatta*'s magic powers did not disappear with his death. They were reincarnated, but just as likely in a nephew, brother, or grandson as in a son. So there was no automatic mechanism liable to result in the foundation of a dynasty. Quite simply, the fact of having had an *aoulatta* among one's ancestors made it reasonable for descendants to hope that another *aoulatta* might arise in this lineage to distinguish himself. This hope once more raises the question of the meaning of the "visions" of the *kwaimatnie*-man and that of the facts capable of influencing their content. It

---

[1] This analysis coincides with the discussion of "despotism" among big men in New Guinea: Paula Brown, "From Anarchy to Satrapy," *American Anthropologist* 65 (1963): 1–15; Richard Salisbury, "Despotism and Australian Administration in the New Guinea Highlands," *American Anthropologist* 66 (1964): 225–39; and Andrew Strathern, "Despots and Directors in the New Guinea Highlands," *Man* 1 (1) (1966): 356–67.

is perfectly conceivable that the "discovery" of a future great warrior must have been far less foreseeable than that of a future shaman, given that shamanistic powers tended to be inherited from father to son, and even to daughter. Before going on to analyze shamanism, we note some additional remarks concerning warfare, highlighting the intimate bonds that exist in war, the male initiations, and the institution of men's general domination over women.

Among the Baruya, war was suspended in two cases, namely, at the time when the big taro gardens needed to be cleared, and at the time when *tchouwanie* were to be initiated – in other words when reproducing the material basis of life and when reproducing the basis of the social order. Furthermore, during war, the Baruya would spare an enemy caught in the forest if he was able to prove that he had been there for one of the following reasons: that his wife had just given birth and he had come to hunt to offer her the ritual booty presented at birth; or else, that he had come to cut poles to hold up his sugarcane plantation.

Planting sugarcane means planting the very symbol of man, his penis. Therefore this activity is viewed as the men's ritual and political horticulture, as it were; by producing fine sugarcane gardens they thereby produce one of the symbols of male domination because a sugarcane garden is divided into two parts. In the middle, supported by long hardwood stakes, stand the tall, straight canes whose juice is exclusively reserved for the men; the varieties that the women are allowed to consume, often without a stake to hold them up, droop around the side.

Consequently the fact that war between men is suspended whenever one of them goes off to honor his obligations to women, or to reproduce the symbol itself of male strength and superiority, is perfectly eloquent. To be sure, the male initiations in each tribe, in each generation, turn out their contingents of warriors destined to kill each other; but they also serve to breed among them a sense of unity and community that transcends their mortal confrontations and tribal frontiers, making them aware of their common superiority over women and their common solidarity against them.

One final point may perhaps rectify the frequently misleading picture of the great warrior conveyed in Melanesian ethnography. There is a tendency to depict him as a kind of bloodthirsty killer, a maniac with "bloodshot eyes," deaf to advice and ready at any moment to break a truce or peace agreement by murder or provocation, instantly fanning the flames of war and bringing him back onto the battlefield in the hopes of adding further exploits to his renown. A Baruya *aoulatta* was absolutely forbidden, however, to kill an enemy in time of peace. Not that the Baruya were above stirring up their own provocations. Indeed there was never any real peace among the tribes, merely truces, which one or the other broke whenever it felt ready to take up arms. Simply, for the Baruya, war could only be decided on by an assembly of all the men from all of the tribes' villages. These assemblies, *mala ko-uounie* (*mala,* war; *kouounie,* speech, harangue), used to take place in the morning outside a *kwalanga.* The women, sitting below the men's area, on the other side of the barrier but within earshot, also volunteered their opinion. Once they had decided to resume hostilities and had made enough arrows, shields, and clubs, the Baruya arranged a series of provocations to serve as a pretext for the fighting. They would send some unimportant man to steal or kill one of the enemy's pigs, or perhaps to rape one of their women in a garden. After two or three incidents of this kind, the enemy would swear vengeance, threatening the Baruya and insulting them. The pretext was thus found. The troops were assembled and took to the warpath, *aoulatta* in the lead. But it was never up to an *aoulatta* alone to decide on war on behalf of the others.

The *koulaka:* the shaman

With shamanism we enter a world very different in appearance from the initiations or warlike activities already analyzed. This field of activity is open to women as well as men; it is the only area of social practice in which both the sexes rigorously perform the same essential task, namely, warding off death, driving out sickness, in a word, protecting life. Although there is a certain core of shamanistic practices common to both sexes, some are restricted to men, and here too male domination rears its head in many different forms.

A second feature that distinguishes shamanism from all other activities is its requirement of special training. This training is crowned by a public ceremony called the *koulakita,* during which novices are installed. The process of training, initiation, and public installation reproduces the pattern of male and female initiations, though it differs because it concerns only a minority of individuals, and in this case they are of both sexes.

The function of the shaman tends to be confined to certain lineages because magical powers can be inherited. Despite this tendency new *koulaka,* both men and women, are constantly emerging in one or another of the lineages. All that is necessary is for them to give proof of their magic powers.

Although the recruitment of shamans is open, there is a constant tendency toward reducing the number. Shamanism revolves around one of the lineages belonging to the Andavakia clan, which, from generation to generation has supplied the leading shamans, those responsible for the *koulakita* ceremonies initiating their peers. It is as if this lineage possessed a special *kwaimatnie,* whereas in fact a *kwaimatnie* has nothing to do with it. As we have seen, the *kwaitmatnie* are objects that possess supernatural powers of their own, which pass into individuals through the agency of the men who inherited the objects along with the functions of their ancestors. Without the sacred object, the *kwaimatnie*-man is nothing. The *koulaka*'s power, on the other hand, lies in his own spirit and in his glance. In addition to his personal power, the Andavakia shaman is deeply learned in the myths and has knowledge of the supernatural powers that influence the universe and form its invisible medium.

The prime task of both male and female shamans is to fight sickness and death. Not all sickness – injuries, bones broken accidentally, diseases of the bone, colds, bronchitis, and breathlessness are outside their sphere of competence and are dealt with by traditional medicine and pharmacology, whose remedies are common knowledge. The shamans fight internal sickness, the invisible ills and epidemics that strike the population from time to time, taking many lives in a few days. The Baruya believe that death can come without even giving a sign, a symptom, or an illness to herald it, if their spirits, which leave their bodies each night, are unable to return to them before sunrise. So the shamans' constant job, their unseen task, is to stand guard at the frontiers of Baruya territory and send back the spirits of those Baruya that try to get across, for beyond lie enemy shamans waiting to kill them or devour them.

Again with a view to protecting human life, the shamans interpret negative events that strike the Baruya either individually (sickness) or collectively (a landslide that swallows up a hunting party, for example). They also seek to detect epidemics heading in their direction in good time so as to divert them toward neighboring tribes. Having treated and cured a sickness, they prevent its return by prohibiting the consumption of certain foods identified as responsible for the illness.

These functions are common to shamans of both sexes; others however are reserved to men only, and some even are the exclusive preserve of men belonging to certain lineages. Male shamans play a part in military expeditions. They prepare the warriors for battle by communicating a magic power to their arrows, by performing a rite in the vicinity of the men's house. But they also wage, either individually or collectively, a spiritual, invisible war of their own against the enemy; it is the famous unending war, unbroken either by truce or oaths of peace sworn by warriors. Last, the Andavakia clan's shamans deal with events that the Baruya view as disturbances or threats against the cosmic order, such as eclipses of the sun or moon; they are believed to have the power to rekindle the Sun and make the Moon be born again.

These are the provinces of the *koulaka*. In order to delineate their limits we must first ascertain the links between shamanism and sorcery in Baruya thought. The Baruya distinguish two types of sorcery, one of which they call *lakia*, the other *gritnie*. A man or a woman practices *lakia* sorcery when casting a spell publicly, or at least without making any effort to hide the fact. In 1979, for instance, after the murder of one of his nieces, Panandjuyac,

Gwataye announced that he was going to cast a spell on the taro gardens belonging to all the other lineages in order to make them suffer with him. At the girl's second funeral, when he came to clean her tomb in company with the rest of his family, Gwataye undid his spell. He was able to cast this kind of spell because his lineage is reputed to possess the most powerful magic for making taros grow and for always having the finest gardens; the power of this magic is heard by the taro plants, which thereafter either grow faster and better (positive magic: *yangaboulata*) or else wither and die (*lakia*). *Lakia* sorcery is the negative application of a presupposed positive magic, and it attacks not people so much as the things that they own. Nor is it directed against anyone in particular, which is why it can be practiced in broad daylight and even publicly proclaimed.

Gritnie is the secret sorcery, directed against people rather than things. It can however be publicly announced on occasion, as when directed against some unknown guilty person. On learning that he is threatened, this person will make good the wrong he has done, or may even publicly denounce himself. Usually though, this type of sorcery is directed against a known troublemaker, by gathering up morsels of leftover food and little shreds of *pulpul* that have fallen to the ground, and by casting magic spells on him to compass the person's death.

The shaman has no power over these two types of sorcery, which exclusively concern the Baruya. Only the person who casts the spell can undo it. It sometimes happens, in the course of a cure, that a *koulaka* discovers that a patient is a victim of *gritnie*. In that case, he immediately abandons the treatment, declaring that there is nothing he can do for the sick person.

But shamanism is also used against neighbors. Baruya shamans are constantly sending their spirits to patrol beyond their tribal frontiers in order to surprise enemies, preferably their shamans, to devour the liver and kill them by means of some more or less mysterious and swift illness. From time to time, during war or when resentment begins to accumulate beneath outward signs of friendship, or as peace begins to break down, the shamans organize a collective ceremony in which they concentrate the powers of ordinary men and women (whose powers by themselves would have no effect). After adding these powers to their own, they hurl them toward the enemy in the hope that this formidable spiritual force will precipitate some catastrophe, such as a landslide or the snapping of a bridge as troops pass over it. Against the non-Baruya peoples, shamanism works as black magic, whereas for members of the tribe, it takes the form of a protective white magic, providing defense against enemy shamans. The Baruya have a name for collective black magic: *koulaka wareuna*. *Wareuna* means to concentrate; *koulaka* means magical powers.

Being witches themselves, the shamans could use their baneful powers against members of their own tribe. But this practice is totally forbidden.

114

They regard themselves, and they are regarded, as being in the service of the community. Still, everyone knows that they can involuntarily make people sick or in certain circumstances even kill people in their entourage. The *kou-lakita* is one example. Their spirits roam above the territory in broad daylight, and they sometimes enter the body of a Baruya and devour his or her liver. Women and children are particularly vulnerable to this kind of involuntary aggression, which is less a matter of sorcery proper than of what the Anglo-Saxons call withchcraft, an evil activity, taking the form of a power of death that emanates from some individual independently of his or her will.

It fairly frequently happens that a *koulaka* flouts the prohibition on using his maleficent powers against the Baruya and employs them directly to his own advantage. For instance, in 1980, a young but already famous *koulaka* was accused of having caused a woman to die in childbirth; this woman had publicly insulted and struck him two years earlier because he had only allotted her a small parcel of poor, infertile land in one of his gardens. The dead woman's brother threatened to cut off his head if ever they met. He preferred to flee and went to take refuge with his family in the village of his maternal cousins. So it does sometimes happen that a shaman acts unethically and intentionally kills his neighbor. Indeed stories abound of *koulaka* suspected of killing each other by means of sorcery, and one of them achieves a reputation that arouses jealousy among his colleagues. But their official function is to protect against sickness and death, and to furnish public interpretations of the causes of accidents that occur in the lives of individuals and groups.

How do they perform this function? They do so in two manners, one on a daily basis, continuously, invisibly, in secrecy and unknown to the public, the other in public, visibly, discontinuously, in the form of individual or collective curative sessions; these ceremonies have distinct names, *kwalie* and *nare*.

As we have already seen, whenever a Baruya goes to sleep, his spirit leaves his body and roams throughout the tribe's territory. When the spirit returns to the body, the sleeper awakens as he was when he fell asleep. Consequently one should never waken someone brutally, for if his spirit has not yet returned to his body he may continue to live a normal life in appearance, but without his spirit he will be vulnerable to sickness, accident, and death. All the Baruya share these ideas, just as it is common knowledge that, whenever a shaman sleeps, his spirit, instead of wandering at random, goes to inspect what is going on around him, detecting dangers threatening another spirit, warding them off, and so on. But ordinary mortals do not know that each night the spirits of men and women shamans gather together at the frontiers of Baruya territory, at a spot where the waters of the rivers converge before flowing on into enemy territory. Now it is important to realize that waterways are roads and pathways for the spirits, and that the dead follow them. At the confluence of the waters, the spirits of the male shamans turn into birds and go to settle on the top of an invisible barrier, at the foot of which squat the spirits of female shamans, who have meanwhile turned into frogs. The bird spirits then fly off and, after having inspected every inch of the tribe's territory, gather together in open caves at the top of the highest mountain, Apmourarie. The female shamans are not capable of metamorphosing into birds; once they have turned themselves into frogs they stay close to the water.

Thus the *koulaka* spend their nights. Their spirits stand sentry, constantly observing Baruya spirits that have lost their way or try to cross the magic barrier. If they do manage to get across, they risk death, either at the hands of enemy shamans or by falling victim to the dead who live beneath the earth, in a world into which the spirits of the living can sometimes fall, borne there by the water. The shamans' surveillance and protection, their permanent battle against sickness wins them much gratitude and respect from both sexes, even though most Baruya know nothing of their nocturnal metamorphoses or the practical details of their combat.

Therefore the first of the shaman's powers is to send his double each night to serve other people directly, to do a useful, responsible job of work, rather than to wander aimlessly along the paths of night. The shamans neither demand nor receive anything in return for this permanent, though unseen, good work. This is not so, on the other hand, when they are called in for consultation and organize a ritual to drive out a sickness, whether alone (*kwalie*) or collectively (*nare*).

A *kwalie* is a ceremony to drive out sickness performed on a sick person at his explicit request either by a male or by a female shaman called in by the patient or by one of his relatives. The shaman visits the patient, examines him, then goes home. There, he falls into a dream, and his spirit seeks to identify the sickness. Depending upon the inspiration of his dream, the shaman will decide either to act alone (or with the help of his wife, if she too is a shaman), that is, to perform a *kwalie* or, if the case is very serious, to call on the assistance of colleagues, male and female, to perform a collective cure known as *nare*. This ceremony takes place in a family home, in other words a place where both sexes may assemble. But if there are reports among neighbors of an epidemic with many victims, the male shamans will assemble all the men in the village at the *kwalanga* and perform a *nare* to protect them; the next day, or the day after, they celebrate a *nare* in a family house, where all, men and women, can gather together and where the women shamans can join forces to officiate.

Shamanistic cures always follow the same pattern, using various means (chanting, silence, powerful inhalations of green tobacco smoke) to establish communication between the *koulaka* and the supernatural world; for this communication is not spontaneous, as it is during sleep each night, but deliberate and made possible by a trancelike state which frees the spirit from the

116

body. Little by little, after having smoked several pipefuls of green tobacco, the shamans' breathing quickens and their spirits leave their bodies uttering little whistling cries, as certain birds do. The spirits then all rush off in search of the patient's spirit. Sometimes they discover it just as a forest spirit, *yimaka*, is about to drag it off into its own world and to death. They deliver it, bring it back, and reintroduce it into the patient. They then carefully inspect his body, for their gift of clairvoyance allows them to discover the magic objects that evil spirits may have placed there – arrows in the liver, for example. Once they have located the object, they mysteriously extract it with the aid of leaves rolled into cones, which they apply to the patient's body and twist in their hands, while clearing their throats and whistling. At length, they tear the object from the body, swiftly wrap it up in the leaves and slip the magic packet into their bark cloak. Then they cool the audience by sprinkling them with some water contained in bamboo poles, which they finally hurl through the roof, breaking the thatch, in the direction of their enemies, in order to cast out the disease at the latter's expense.

Thus there is an immediate connection between warfare and shamanism. For if healing is all about extracting poisons and sickness from people's bodies in order to send them in their neighbors' direction, then all acts of healing are simultaneously acts of aggression, an attempt to undermine the neighbors' health and well-being. What is more, since they share the Baruya's ideas on sicknesses and their causes, any sudden and unaccountable death in the neighboring tribe or among the Baruya may serve as a pretext for war. Conversely though, both for the Baruya and for their neighbors, their view of sickness also sets limits to war. For it would be senseless to kill all one's enemies and create a void around one. In any war, the victor is obliged to spare some of his enemies if only to be able to dispatch in their direction the disease liable to afflict himself. This theory of sickness strikes me as a remarkable feature of New Guinea ethnography, for it reveals the existence of social forces that, though rooted in their imaginary world, nevertheless display a high degree of pragmatic prudence by circumscribing any desire to exterminate one's enemies down to the last man. This prudence, needless to say, was dictated not by ideological imperatives alone. The need to maintain trade relations with neighbors made it expedient not to kill them all off, even if one did cast a greedy eye over their land. Consequently it was not rare to see the victorious Baruya going some years later to fetch their defeated enemies, who had taken precarious refuge with other groups, and resettling them on part of the land that they had abandoned in their flight.

The official reason for this compromise was the sudden spate of mysterious deaths among the Baruya, which were surely caused by the sorcery of enemy shamans, or alternatively, by the fact that the victorious Baruya now found it impossible to drive away the diseases that were threatening them and to send them to afflict their enemies, who had taken refuge too far away; indeed the two reasons could perfectly well coexist. Needless to say, the shamans provided this interpretation of collective misfortunes that befell the Baruya at the appropriate moment; in the same way, having completed an individual or collective cure, they would reveal to the patient the cause of his illness, and present to him, nestling in the packet of leaves that they had just pressed to his belly, an object that, so they claimed, they had just extracted from his body: a dried insect, a sliver of glass, and so forth. Usually, the shamans publicly explained that, if the victim was sick, it was because he had deliberately or involuntarily transgressed some taboo. For example, when Meyendjavanoumwac fell seriously sick, her husband, Dedaiwe, called in an eminent *koulaka*, Panandjeemaye. After examining the woman, the *koulaka* dreamed that Dedaiwe's dog had killed an opossum on the Buigamieu Mountain, where a spirit dwells. Now, this opossum was none other than the spirit of the mountain, which had revenged itself on Dedaiwe's wife. The husband confirmed this account, or at least said that he had indeed killed a *bwaraka* [opossum-like marsupial] in the forest of Buigamieu, and had shared it with his wife. Panandjeemaye then went to work, organized a *kwalie,* and finally managed to extract a red stone from Meyendjavanoumwac's body, the arrow that the mountain's *yimaka* had shot into her body. The shaman's interpretation of these negative events or misfortunes thus reconfirms the laws of the group, serves as a reminder of the taboos that must not be transgressed, and thereby reinforces them in the individual and collective consciousness. Not only is he on the side of order against disorder, protecting the social and cosmic order against individual misconduct, but he also changes disorder into order, negative into positive.

Having analyzed the shaman's functions, techniques, and social role, we must ask: How does a Baruya become a *koulaka?*

To become a shaman, an individual must accumulate within himself powers (*koulaka*) that are in fact spiritual realities, the power of the spirits that belong to things that surround us. For example, one day a man passes close to a banana tree whose broad glossy leaves are rustling in the wind and reflecting the sun's rays like mirrors. He is distracted by the motion of the tree, and his eyes are dazzled by the sparkling light playing on the leaves. On his return home he feels unwell and is suddenly overcome with dizziness, collapses, and falls asleep. On awakening he feels better, recalls what has happened, and realizes that the spirit of this banana tree is inside him, and that equally part of his spirit is now imprisoned inside the tree, united with the spirit, with the power concealed within it. Sometimes so many powers accumulate within a single man or woman that his or her eyes start to shine with a special glow; only experienced *koulaka* have the gift of discerning this glow, and they usually do in the course of the public shamanistic healing ceremonies. The *kwamaitnie*-man responsible for the *tchouwanie* initiations also has this gift, but only episodically, when, with the sacred object in his hand, he perceives the destiny of each initiate. But he does not possess the power of clairvoyance in himself; the *koulaka,* however, are capable of doing so, recognizing the power in each other at any time. Men or women thus become shamans before realizing it, and they only become aware of the fact when an existing shaman discovers it for them.

Self-awareness, then, comes through someone else's awareness of oneself. But this external recognition is not enough; or at least, it is not definitive so long as the newly discovered *koulaka* has yet to learn his trade, has yet to prove himself and, above all, has yet to be publicly installed in the course of the *koulakita.* Even then, nothing is definite. He must still furnish ultimate proof by healing a patient in front of his peers, and by doing so during the collective healing ceremonies that follow the *koulakita.* He may fail. The Baruya cite names; so-and-so failed, such-and-such is good for nothing now, having become afraid to dance around the fire, and so on. So the difference between the *aoulatta* and the *koulaka* is clear. The *aoulatta* kills, and by this act he is recognized as an *aoulatta.* The *koulaka* starts by being acknowledged as a *koulaka,* and then tries his healing arts afterward. But, like the *aoulatta,* he only gains true recognition when he has proven himself properly, by healing a patient. Thus we can form an opinion of the shaman's potential social power, since he alone is in a position to recruit new members destined to perform his essential function. Here, though, as with the *kwa- matnie*-man, the divining process is guided by what everyone knows about the relations among lineages and clans, by the requirement that certain of these supply a greater number of shamans than others. Although one cannot suspect the *koulaka* of deliberately and permanently manipulating the signs, one can nevertheless assert that they necessarily and confidently "see" and "discover" a future shaman in a lineage that already has a lot of shamans and expects more.

We have shown how a future shaman can acquire a new power. A dying shaman can also hand down all his powers to his son without the latter realizing it. All he has to do is hand them on in his last glance. According to the Baruya, it has even happened that a shaman, knowing that he is about to die in the absence of his son, can look at his wife in a certain way and make her the unwitting recipient of his powers. Later, when she next sees her son, these powers will then leave her to enter him through her glance. Nor will he know anything about it and, once again, it will be the shamans who will discover what has happened and certify that the dead shaman's powers have well and truly been passed on.

Consequently, as pointed out at the beginning of this chapter, although shamanism is in principle ever open to new recruits, there is a constant tendency for its recruitment base to grow narrower and the function hereditary. Indeed it is a hereditary function in the Andavakia lineage. The justification for the supremacy of the Andavakia, who are responsbile for the initiation of shamans, is that they are the possessors of sacred lore. They know the original myths of man, woman, and life; they know why the rites prescribe this or that gesture, whereas the other Baruya simply know what they are supposed to do. They know why the shamans wear an eagle's feather on their heads, why they are supposed to snap their fingers and whistle in certain ceremonies. In addition to this sacred learning, the Andavakia also possess a sort of equivalent of the *kwaimatnie*. It is a dummy made from lumps of banana tree and *walala* (a wild bush growing in the forest) whenever shamans are initiated. This object represents a cassowary – the wild woman – and carries on its back a sort of display board into which eagle feathers have been stuck, and the *koulaka* master then places it in the hair of the new shamans once he has "discovered" them.

Yet despite these factors of superiority, Andavakia shamans still have to be recognized by the others and installed in the course of a *koulakita*, which can only take place in the presence of all the shamans. Furthermore, the *koulaka* are not entitled to place on the heads of the novices the insignia of their new status. This honor falls to the man in charge of the *tchouwanie* initiations, who possesses the most powerful *kwaimatnie*, that of the Baruya clan. The system thus displays a marked tendency to self-recruitment without ever actually reaching that situation. Its other overriding characteristic is being rooted and ultimately founded in male domination, and this fact represents the limit to its internal tendency to become an autonomous field, a society within society. It is no accident that, having mentioned the existence of female shamans throughout our analysis here, we have nevertheless spoken mainly of men. The reason is that even in the sole area of public activity open to women, male domination immediately reasserts itself, just as it is present elsewhere in society, providing the basis upon which the social order rests.

We have already seen in passing some of the signs of the reproduction of this domination in shamanistic practice, and the time has now come to assemble them. As we have already seen, women are not entitled to take part in the *nare,* which is held in preparation for war and takes place in the *kwalanga;* nor, needless to say, do they attend the ceremonies performed to confer magical powers on the warriors' weapons. Women are unable to counteract cosmic disturbances (eclipses of the Sun and Moon). In the course of collective healing ceremonies held in one or another of the houses in the village, the female shamans come into the picture only after their male colleagues, standing around the hearth, have conducted the principal phases of the battle against the spirits. When the women do intervene, they do so seated or squatting on the floor of the house, as they too extract from the bodies of those around them fragments of objects that, in Baruya eyes, are so many arrows fired into them by the *yimaka.*

Another essential aspect of the reproduction of male superiority in shamanism is the way in which the *koulaka* initiation ceremonies proceed. They start with a series of rites lasting several weeks, which take place either in the men's house in the presence of all the men, or alternatively in the heart of the forest, in the presence of the male shamans alone. The female shamans are excluded from these rites, as is the rest of the population. After the *koulaka* masters have turned out a new generation of male shamans, the female shamans' installation ceremonies can begin. They last only a single night and day; at nighttime, they take place in one of the houses in the village, and are conducted throughout by the *koulaka* masters, who have just initiated the new shamans.

Therefore it is the men who discover and consecrate the female shamans. The ritual surrounding this consecration is significant in itself. After having been discovered by the ritual master, who can tell from their eyes whether or not they are shamans, each woman is allocated a sponsor among the male shamans, who will help her to collect and imprison within herself the spirit-powers that will make her into a shaman. Each male sponsor stands next to his "god-daughter"; he stretches a red *ypmoulie* (the men's headband) between his own head and the crown of the young woman's head, this *ypmoulie* having been given to him by the postulant's husband. He then takes an arrow, also given to him by the husband, and slips it into the woman's right hand, while she stands with her head bowed. Thus she has in her hand the arrow, which is the symbol of man, and is linked by a fiery path to a male shaman, who dominates her. The latter starts rolling the headband slowly downward from his brow toward the woman. When the strip is completely rolled up, he "unties it" from the woman and gives it to her in a gesture signifying that powers have passed into her by him and through him, that they have entered her spirit in which they will henceforward be imprisoned.

The next day, the male shamans take the female shamans, old and new, to a small man-made lake which they have dug out for them, and show the novices how to resuscitate frogs and water insects. The experienced female shamans then repeat the demonstration.

A few days after the male and female initiation ceremonies, the male shamans leave in a procession to go from village to village, from men's house to men's house, to treat the young initiates and men. After that, they set out again in the opposite direction, this time accompanied by the female shamans, stopping not at the men's houses, which are inaccessible to the women, but in the ordinary village houses, those where the families dwell and which the Baruya call *balanga,* women's houses. They treat the women and children, though not forgetting the men too. It is then, and then only, that the new female shamans are given the opportunity of demonstrating their powers in public. The "priority" that men repeatedly enjoy is the permanent expression of their assumed superiority over women.

Ideologically speaking, the female shamans' inferior status is legitimized by the fact that they are not capable of turning into birds and soaring above the Baruya territory up to the highest of the mountain peaks. They remain earthbound, close to the water, incapable of halting spirits "too strong" for them, those of men or young women, or alternatively those of patients about to die, which are much too weak for them to be able to revive. They succeed in healing only the least serious cases and the less sturdy humans. They are most at home in the *kwalie,* the individual cures of benign cases. However, as we shall see at the end of this analysis, this explanation of women's inferiority represents merely an initial interpretive level, concealing a contradictory one, since once again the second level of interpretation reveals that the men's superiority springs from their appropriation of the women's powers.

As everyone acknowledges, some male shamans have a minor stature compared with certain female shamans; in other words, one does encounter great shamans belonging to the female sex. But by their very nature they can never hope to equal or even approach the powers, the renown, and status of the male great shamans, for unlike them they can never participate directly in the battles of magic with the enemy in time of war.

The *koulaka*'s status is visible in his distinctive adornment: an eagle's feather on the head, an eagle's bone through the nose for men, a large black feather from a cassowary's wing stuck through the tip of the nose for women (women are forbidden to wear feather adornments). The shaman inserts hair he has saved from patients into this bone. But his powers are also concentrated in this bone, where the spirit comes to perch when returning to the body after one of its nocturnal voyages.

Shamans are expected to behave with gravity, to maintain a calm, aloof bearing in public, and to speak little but wisely. They (both men and women) are highly influential. The male shamans' houses stand a little apart, on the edge of the village, and no one would dare to enter without their permission. It is believed that snakes teem about their hearths, ready to leap at the face of anyone so bold or reckless as to enter in the owners' absence. But although feared, they also enjoy the gratitude and loyalty of those they have treated and healed. Nor can a *koulaka* ever refuse to come when called, and he (she) is expected to do everything in his or her power to heal the patient and save his life. If he or she is suspected of negligence, the accusation is made public and leaves a blot on the shaman's reputation. Indeed, matters sometimes take a turn for the worse and the shaman can find that he or she is involved in a brawl or victim of acts of sorcery caused by people with some complaint to make. At one moment in the course of the *koulaka* initiation ceremony, the novices are gathered around a rotting tree stump and told that this is an old woman, already half-dead, stinking of urine and coughing endlessly. Someone says: "Let's move on, she's dead, she stinks." Immediately a shaman steps in and says: "No, look, we can save her, I'm going to try." And he adds: "Treat everyone in need, don't be afraid of disease and the sick."

Most people are satisfied with the treatment they receive from the shamans and reward them with gifts: salt, money, a slice of meat whenever they kill a pig; or they perform services for them. Unlike the *kwamatnie*-man and the aoulatta, the *koulaka* is rewarded for his services; or at least his services quite explicitly demand payment in return, in the form of a redistribution of material goods. This is not to say that he can become wealthy in this way, for none of these gifts consists of land or work. Quite simply, he lives comfortably and enjoys certain privileges. A village is delighted to take in a *koulaka* who expresses the wish to come and live there, and one or another of the lineages living in this village will offer him a wife. From that moment on, according to the principles of Baruya land tenure, he may use the lands of his affines, although without ever becoming a landowner. Or, if he is already married, the lineages in the village will allow him to clear gardens on their land.

Therefore, although the function and status of male and female shamans alike rest upon inherited or acquired powers, the existence of these powers can never in themselves confer this function or status on an individual. These powers need to be recognized by other shamans and, as a result, like the warrior function, the shamanistic function is redistributed among individuals according to their abilities, and among lineages and clans according to their respective positions in the production and reproduction of the ritual and political order of the society. Shamanism is thus firmly rooted in the underlying structure of society, in the hierarchy of the sexes, which it produces and reproduces in specific forms, even though in this sphere the existence of female powers and their appropriation by men is most clearly apparent and openly acknowledged.

For the secret behind the power of the male shamans is twofold. It has two origins which are revealed to the new *koulaka* in two stages. In the course of a series of secret rituals which take place in daylight in the heart of the forest, at the bottom of a sheer ravine, the novices are led to the foot of a huge tree that grows tall and straight up into the sky. There, the master of the rituals has already cut a number of gashes high up the tree trunk, having first built and subsequently removed a platform for the purpose. The eagle bones that all *koulaka,* old and new, wear in their noses, are passed one by one through the sap oozing from these gashes in the tree trunk; the ritual master inserts the bones into the gashes and the thick white sap quickly blocks the two extremities. The spirits, the powers of the shamans, are henceforward locked up in these bones. Then someone plucks a few hairs from the tuft remaining on the the otherwise shaven pate of each *koulaka,* and these are passed from hand to hand until they reach the master of the rituals, perched five or six meters above the ground. The master carefully inserts them into the sap flowing from the gashes. Henceforward, the tree will continue to grow and to communicate its strength to the shamans; it will protect them and serve as mediator between them and the Sun. For the ceremony ends with a prayer to the Sun. All the shamans then snap their fingers, whistle, and thus send their breaths and their spirits to the treetop, whence the wind will bear them away to the Sun.

The second secret ritual, which reveals the other origin of the male shaman's power, takes place in the semidarkness of the *kwalanga,* in the sight of all the men; but it consists of a series of gestures whose meaning is not commented on or made clear to the onlookers.

All of a sudden, when all the shamans, old and new, are dancing and whirling about the fire, the old shamans lean toward the blaze and appear to gather something that they immediately bury in a long bamboo pole held in one hand. No word is uttered, there is no chanting, and yet the gesture is crucial. Here is the meaning as revealed to me by the master of the shamans' initiation.

What the shamans suddenly grasp from the fire is the power to heal, which is given to them by Venus, the morning and evening star, the Sun's constant companion, ever preceding or following it across the sky. Now, who is Venus for the Baruya? Here is the myth that relates its origin:

In the days of our ancestors, an enormous pig, an animal that was thought to be a gigantic pig, came and returned each night to devastate a taro garden belonging to the Baruya near Kaapmounie [a spot near the village of Marawaka]. On seeing what had happened, the men would say each morning: "But what is this pig that comes to eat the taros in our gardens? Even when we are holding our ceremonies for the birth of a child, he comes and wrecks our gardens!"

So men built a house in the garden and two of them were appointed to spend the night on sentry duty. While they were sitting quietly in the house, they heard a noise near the garden fence and said to themselves: "That's our pig, he's near the fence." And indeed, the pig cleared the fence and landed with a loud bump. When they heard the noise, the two men said: "The pig has just jumped over the fence." They left the shelter, went toward the fence, crossed to the other side, and started running along it to stop the pig from getting out. They called to the other men: "Hurry up, bring bamboo poles to make torches! Bring your bows and arrows! Come along, hurry up, everybody come!" Everyone came and stood near the fence. Dawn came, and in the middle of the garden they saw a gigantic python. It was he who had eaten all their food. So they surrounded it and killed it with arrows. The women carried it away and gathered the taros and vegetables while the men cut wood. They built a fire to heat the stones for the oven and sliced the python. Then they put it into the oven to cook. Later, they opened the oven and shared out the meat and taros. They began by eating the taros and vegetables, which had soaked in the meat's tasty juice. They shared out the other morsels among the women, who put them into their bags and went off home to sleep. Next morning, one of the women awoke very early and thought to herself: "Last night, I didn't eat any meat. I'm going to eat some now, with a sweet potato." She went to fetch some from her bag, but there was no meat in her bag. "Who's been stealing?" and she began to sing: "The meat has disappeared, the meat is gone, watch out!" The other women heard her, looked in their bags to check, and found that their meat too had disappeared.

What had happened was that, during the night, all the lumps of meat had flown out of their bags and returned to the site of the oven, and there they had reformed themselves into a gigantic snake, which was still sleeping the next morning. Soon people who were looking for their meat arrived; they saw the snake and were terrified.

They drew near to it, looked at it, and said: "What do you want of us? What can we give you? Do you want sweet potatoes and taros?" The snake did not move. "Do you want some salt?" The snake remained motionless. "Would you like some shells or cowries?" Still the snake did not move but remained there, its head hanging to the ground. Finally, they asked it: "Would you like us to give you a woman?" At these words, the snake reared up, and that meant "Yes." It bowed its neck, yawned, then looked toward the sky. "In which direction will you be leaving us?" It looked once more up into the sky. Then they cut some wood for burning, to light a fire and make smoke. They took a gigantic stone and put it on the fire. It quickly grew yellow from the heat. They wrapped it carefully in leaves and put it in a string bag.

Then they led out a woman, heavily adorned. The snake motioned her to pass ahead of him, but she said, "No no, that's not my direction. You go ahead and show me the way." She took the bag in which the stone had been placed, and slung it over her back, ready to go.

The snake went ahead, and they began to climb up the column of smoke rising above the fire. Once in the sky, they found themselves near a big house, and the snake said to the woman: "You go in first." She replied: "No, it's your house. Open the door and go ahead." He did so, while the woman remained standing outside. While the snake was moving about inside, she took the big stone from her bag, unwrapped it without touching it, and blocked the door with it. She then started down the column of smoke as quickly as she could, but halfway down, she was turned into Venus, the morning and evening star.

Meanwhile, the snake was wandering around inside the house, thinking: "She'll be coming soon, I'm going to watch her come in." He slithered to the door and bumped his nose against the stone; he burned himself terribly. He cried out: "Mum, mum"; that was the sound of thunder. Now, whenever people hear thunder, they know that it's the python snake crying out in pain.[2]

Venus originated as a Baruyan woman offered by men to the python snake, that is, to the god of thunder. By her courage and self-sacrifice she saved her people, who had been terrorized by the sight of this supernatural monster.

Once again, the formula for the men's power is twofold. In addition to their own powers, to their links with the Sun through the intermediary of the trees in the wild forest, the wind, and the eagle, they have added the powers of fire from the star of Venus, whose course follows in the footsteps of the Sun (twilight) or else precedes it (dawn) across the sky. The male shaman's superiority arises from the formula itself of male domination, from the way in which men manage to combine their own powers with those of the women,

[2] The story was told by Bwarimak on 17 March 1967. Richard Lloyd has published the fullest version of this myth, together with other Baruya myths, in *Legends from Papua New Guinea*, ed. K. A. McElhanon, Ukarumpa (Papua New Guinea), Summer Institute of Linguistics, 1974, pp. 54–68.

appropriating the latter for their own use. By thus appropriating the female powers, the male shamans can reproduce themselves qua shamans in the absence of female shamans, whereas the female shamans cannot reproduce themselves without the male ones. This process gives full expression to the fundamental ideological structure and deep-seated desire of all Baruya men.

But the female power, which the men appropriate for themselves, is the outcome of a woman's act of self-sacrifice for her people and perhaps, the reason why the female shamans receive two male attributes par excellence to symbolize their higher status among women as a whole, they are given the *ypmoulie*, the red headband (red being the color of the Sun, the image of the path taken in mythical times by the *kwaimatnie,* those sacred objects that guarantee the order of the cosmos and male domination) and the arrow, the symbol of war and of the battles that men wage against all the forces hostile to mankind.

The function and status of cassowary hunters illustrate the same symbolism of male domination, but it is the violence that men permanently perform on women that moves to the center of the stage. Though symbolic, this violence is unambiguously displayed.

The *kayareumala:* the cassowary hunter

Cassowary hunting occupies a place all its own among the various forms of hunting practiced by the Baruya. It is peculiar because of the nature of the game hunted, the technique used in hunting, and the social status that attaches to the lucky hunter. It stands midway between war and shamanism, and makes a particularly explicit contribution to the production and exaltation of men's domination over women, yet it is deeply rooted in this domination.

Kayareumala refers both to cassowary hunting and to the hunter. *Mala* signifies making war, killing. *Kayarie* is the name given to the cassowary. The variety that lives on Baruya territory, *Casuarius Bennettii,* is distinguished from the New Guinea lowland variety (*Casuarius casuarius*) by its plumage and smaller size. The cassowary is a powerful animal that usually lives alone in the heart of the forest. In the very hot weather, it plunges even more deeply into the forest, climbing ever higher, up to as much as 2,500 meters (into the spongy moss forest stratum), where the air is cooler. It is a dangerous animal, with a powerful beak and paws armed with a slender rear spur, which can cause serious injury to anyone too slow to skip clear. Because it runs so fast, it is practically impossible to bring it down with an arrow. Even when injured, it is capable of scuttling away before the hunter can bend his bow for a second arrow. The only effective way to kill it is to trap it. All Baruya know how to make traps and use them to catch a wide variety of game, including wallabies, opossums, quails, and even wild pigs.

The discovery of great men

There are two types of cassowary trap, one concealed in the ground, near a tree regularly visited by the cassowary to eat its fruit, the other slung between two trees along a path regularly taken by a cassowary, at a spot where the path becomes very narrow. As it enters this bottleneck, the cassowary springs the trap and is hanged by the neck. It strangles itself to death as it struggles to escape, whereas with the other technique it is the hunter who kills it by clubbing it to death. In both cases, he must take care not to shed blood.

In strictly technical terms, either of these two types of trapping is within the capabilities of any Baruya hunter. They all know the habits of cassowaries, their favorite food, and their telltale tracks. From childhood, they learn to track them, build a trap, and hide it. Yet only a few men actually dare to set cassowary traps and announce the fact. Why?

The reason lies in the mental, conceptual [*idéel* in the French] universe of the Baruya, in the way they view and interpret nature. For them, the cassowary is not, nor could it be, a bird, since it is incapable of flying and does not perch on tree branches. It is a land animal like the mammals and a biped like man. To this unique animal, they attribute an essence akin to that of women and, despite empirical evidence, consider all cassowaries to be female. Needless to say, the Baruya are perfectly capable of distinguishing male and female in all the different species of birds around them, and they also know that there are male as well as female cassowaries. But this empirical knowledge would appear to be suspended, repressed, inoperative once they talk about cassowaries. They distinguish them by age, size, and the color of their plumage. The young, with their light plumage, are called *bwarandac,* little girl. The "little girls" then grow and, when almost adult, become *tsindraye,* pubescent girls. The adults are called "women" or "old women," depending on their age. So the cassowaries fundamentally belong to the world of women and are so to speak the coinitiates of women, their classmates. At the same time though, they possess supernatural powers. The story goes that one day Puidatneu, a great cassowary hunter, dreamed that he had caught a very large "old woman"; immediately, violent winds began to blow and the "thunder snake" started to growl.

Therefore cassowary hunting at once acquires the significance of a struggle with the feminine world, of a contest that ends up providing particularly spectacular evidence of men's superiority over women. Consequently it demands special precautions and methods, involving dancing, dreams, and clairvoyance, making it somewhat akin to shamanism.

In the rainy season, the cassowary hunters set out in search of a variety of hallucinogenic mushroom. Once they have found it and have carefully marked the spot, they return to inform the other men in the village. They all then gather in the men's house and start to chant. The young initiates are sent off into the bush to cut down the branches of certain species of tree, which are then used to decorate the interior walls of the *kwalanga.* The men then go off to where the mushrooms are and, as their chanting rises to a pitch, they gather the mushrooms and point them in the direction of the men's house. At that moment it often happens that one of the cassowary hunters, sitting among the other men and mingling his voice with theirs, starts to tremble, possessed by the spirit of a cassowary. Then come the men with the mushrooms. The bodies of all those taking part are painted with ochre-colored clay (*noumwaka*), and their arms and head are decorated with magic leaves. Little pieces of mushroom are then handed out to everyone and are eaten raw. Some people soon fall into a kind of trance, and their bodies are seized with violent trembling. They are held up as they foam at the mouth, possessed by the spirit of a cassowary. Later on, the men who are possessed will make cassowary masks, put them on and dance, mimicking the bird as it looks for food among the trees. They hop about, shaking the long necks of the masks and uttering the animal's small cry. (These masks are the only realistic aesthetic objects found among the Baruya, who generally prefer a more abstract symbolism.) It is these same dancers who, when the rainy season comes around, go off to build cassowary traps. They are allowed to lay them wherever they like, without having to ask permission from the lineage that owns the area of forest selected. This fact distinguishes cassowary hunting from all other forms of hunting, for in general it is strictly forbidden to lay traps on other people's land unless explicit permission has been obtained.

Later, in the early part of the dry season, one of the hunters will have a dream one night, announcing that a "woman" has been caught in the trap. Here is a summary of one of the dreams related by Pandjaaouye, a young hunter who had caught only two cassowaries at the time of writing:

I dreamed that I was in the forest and that I was looking at a rotting tree trunk. I tried to lift it. It was heavy but I managed to raise it up and put it on my shoulder. I went off and suddenly came upon a small clearing and a woman dressed like a *tsindraye* [young pubescent initiate] was busy cleaning the grass in order to prepare a patch of land. I dropped the rotten trunk and started to cut down branches of *ilamboukounanie* [a plant whose leaves are used to decorate the ground around the house where the first-stage initiates live or around the *kwalanga* during the initiation of shamans] which I planted all around the *mumu* [oven pit]. At that moment, I awoke; my head was burning and I began to tremble, tremble. I was possessed [*yikeulaka*, the term also used to describe the way shamans are possessed]. Then I thought about what had happened to me and then I knew that a woman had been caught in my trap.

The next day, he went to Tsimouac, on the territory of the Boulimmam-bakia, where his trap was. He spied the stretched rope from far off. He drew near. The cassowary was dead, strangled. He plucked the feathers from its wings (which are like stumps); the second-stage initiates, the *kawetnie*, use them as insignias, and the female shamans put them through their noses. He then wrapped the beast in pandanus leaves and placed the package in a tree-top, out of the reach of wild animals, and returned to the men's house. There,

128

he told the young *kawetnie* and *tchouwanie:* "An old woman is lying out there in the forest; you ought to go out and fetch her." They understood, went into the forest, found the animal, and plucked it at the foot of a large tree that bears the same name as the trance referred to above, *yikeulaka.* They then decorated the spot with *ilamboukounanie* leaves, the same as those that Pandjaaouye, the cassowary hunter, had planted in his dream. At length, having plucked the body and wrapped it up, they left it at the top of a young male pandanus (the symbol of men) and went back to the men's house.

Two days later, they returned to the forest and prepared a big oven pit. They cooked the meat with *tsamaye,* a huge tuber (*Pueraria lobata*), which is an old New Guinea plant eaten in time of famine. It is impossible to cook a cassowary's innards or flesh directly on the fire, for the stench would kill the men outright. They have to be cooked in an oven; then the oven is opened, and the meat is shared in small slices, together with the *tsamaye.* The hunter and the shamans do not partake of this meal. They are strictly forbidden to do so, as they would lose all their powers. Nor are the *yiveumbwaye* (the first-stage initiates who are still in transition between the world of women and the world of men) allowed to do so. The rest of the meat is then taken back to the *kwalanga,* where it is shared by the men of all ages who had not gone out into the bush. Everyone paints his body with yellow clay, *yetcheaka,* and they all spend the night there, singing, delaying their return to the world of women.

The men keep what has been going on to themselves. But the women can guess from the traces of paint on their husbands' bodies. Women are totally forbidden to eat cassowary meat, for it would be as if they were eating themselves.

One can imagine the renown that a great cassowary hunter can hope to win. The names of the hunters are known to all, and everyone knows who the best one in the tribe is, although his preeminence lasts only as long as someone else has not done better and captured still more cassowaries. However, their reputation does not depend only on the number of cassowaries caught, since each of the hunters' victories provides further evidence of men's superiority over women, and thus stands as a victory over the world of women, exalting and strengthening men's solidarity in the face of the dangers and pollution of the feminine world. For it goes without saying that a cassowary hunter owes his success also to total abstinence from sex with his wife or wives during the hunting season.

The cassowary then is a savage woman, familiar with the forest spirits and supernatural powers, but she is defeated by the powers of a man, who captures her spirit and bends it to his law. The cassowary is a savage woman in another sense, as the image of a woman who lies in wait in the forest to provoke a man into making love to her, or lies in wait for young initiates and married men to steal some of their sperm. So it is understandable that the

129

kwaimatnie master should carefully inspect the initiates' bedding during the men's initiation ceremonies in search of signs marking a boy or adolescent as a future cassowary hunter. It is understandable that, when the women draw near to the great initiation house to throw the bales of straw up to the men standing on the roofs, certain cassowary hunters fall into a trance and collapse, so that the men standing next to them have great difficulty holding them up. The female spirit of the cassowary that lives in them quickens at the approach of these hundreds of women, and it invades their spirit and submerges it. By this possession, their cassowary hunting powers are both reaffirmed and reinforced.

However, the status of the cassowary hunter is always inferior to that of the *aoulatta* or the great shaman. Unlike these two functions, which tend to be mutually exclusive, anyone can hunt the cassowary while also assuming other functions. Davaiwe, now the greatest cassowary hunter in the tribe, was already a young and brilliant *aoulatta* in 1960, when the white men arrived, his career having been interrupted by the imposition of peace. Inamwe, the greatest shaman in the tribe, who died in 1977, was also a highly honored cassowary hunter. Others, however, are exclusively *kayareumala*, as was Mikeunai, who died in 1974; he was generally regarded as a "sweet potoato" man, leading a rather undistinguished life outside the cassowary hunting season. So cassowary hunting alone is not enough to confer high status upon a man, but it does enhance the reputation of those already renowned as great warriors or great shamans.

Here ends my analysis of those functions that are explicitly developed in the course of the male initiation ceremonies and conferred upon those who assume a publicly distinctive status, made manifest by such outward signs as insignias and adornments. However, the list of functions that men may acquire does not end there. There is one that plays a key role in the material and economic life of the Baruya, conferring special status and renown on those who perform it, even though the initiations make no particular reference to it and devote no special ceremony to it. This function is the manufacture of salt.

The *tsaimaye:* the salt maker

The Baruya were well known beyond their own frontiers because of their salt before the white man's arrival. In the region of Mumeng, for example, which no Baruya had ever visited personally, the local tribes greatly appreciated this product, which reached them, carefully packaged, from the Bakia, a tribe which they knew spoke an Anga language similar to their fearsome neighbors, the Watchake or the Katsiong, and which lived far away on the other side of the mountain chain that dominates the Markham River Valley.

It was one of these bars of salt, and a smattering of similar details that, in

1951, aroused the curiosity of a young Australian officer, Jim Sinclair, who had just been appointed to Mumeng. He immediately decided to mount an expedition to discover the famous Bakia. After some weeks of fruitless wandering over some very rough terrain indeed, he and his column finally reached the valley of Wonenara. There, he was surprised to find, in the midst of this tribe hitherto unvisited by any white man, a large number of men with steel implements in their hands. He was also surprised at the sight of their vast salt cane fields, stretching across the floor of the valley, strewn with buildings which, he was told, were salt kilns. He wrote an admiring description of them in his travel diary.[3]

Sinclair never discovered that the Baruya had agreed among themselves to attack the column and kill him with his soldiers in order to appropriate their powers and that they had discarded this plan after watching a shooting demonstration. They then tried to persuade him to help them kill some enemies whose village, surrounded by a war palisade, was defying them from the other side of the valley. Jim Sinclair declined the invitation and left as he had come after five days' stay. Because of their salt, the Baruya thus joined the mainstream of world history, at least the history of that part of the world that is subject to the West.

What is this salt? How do the Baruya produce it?[4] It is potassium, not sodium salt, made from the ashes of tall cane (*Coix gigantea*, Koenig ex Rob., commonly called Job's tears), and is grown on vast terraces cleared and irrigated by small streams. Each year, the canes, which grow to a height of several meters, are cut, dried, then thrown onto a heap for burning. The ashes are then sheltered from wind and rain by a roof, while the *tsaimaye* (from *tsala*, salt and *maye*, flower) has made a filter with the aid of long gourds, dried and emptied, which he places on top of a pandanus leaf. He fills them with the ashes and then pours water taken from the river over them. The water picks up saline elements as it passes through the filters. The saline solution drips onto the pandanus leaf, and is then gathered into bamboo poles and carried to a kiln, four to five meters long. This kiln belongs to the salt maker. He is the only man entitled to use it. He pours the salt-laden water into molds of refractory clay dug into the bottom of the kiln. For five days and five nights, the *tsaimaye* keeps watch over his fire, removing impurities from the film of salt that crystallizes on the surface of the water as it evaporates, tamping down the gradually accumulating salt. He will finish up with a bar of crystallized salt weighing approximately two kilos. Depending on the size of his kiln, he can produce between twelve and fifteen bars per

---

[3]This diary is unpublished, but Jim Sinclair kindly allowed me to consult it. He himself has published an account of his discovery of the Bakia in *Behind the Ranges* (Melbourne: Melbourne University Press, 1966), esp. chap. 4.
[4]Maurice Godelier, "La monnaie de sel des Baruya de Nouvelle-Guinée," *L'Homme* 9 (2) (1969):5–37.

firing. During these few days and nights, the salt maker lives apart from his wife, and must abstain from all sexual relations with her. His customers' salt would turn to water, lose weight, and be worthless for trade. No woman has the right, moreover, to approach either him or his kiln while he is at work. Then the salt is removed from its mold, and the owner of the canes, with the aid of his brothers and brothers-in-law, comes to wrap up the bars with bark thongs to protect them against blows, rain, dirt, and so on during transport. The bars are then brought to their owner who shares them: one or two to the maker for his services, the others to be divided among his wives, brothers, and brothers-in-law. He retains three or four for himself, keeping them dry above the fireplace in his house.

The first operations – cutting, drying, burning the cane, and filtering the ashes – are carried out by the cane cutter. He is helped by his wives, sisters, sisters-in-law, brothers, brothers-in-law, but such crucial operations as watching the fire, preparing molds, evaporation, crystallization, or cleaning the salt are performed by the specialist, who works either alone or with an apprentice, if he is prepared to teach his craft to a younger man.

Needless to say, his first task is to build his kiln, which is made of earth and refractory stone, together with salted, dried, and baked mud. It is heavy work, and the technique is a delicate one, although to my mind it merely represents the most sophisticated expression of the Baruya art of building domestic ovens. Indeed the Baruya are all craftsmen to some extent. They make their own bracelets and ornamental flatware for their own use; so they are all skilled with their hands. Consequently specialized craftsmanship represents no material break with the techniques in use in everyday life. It simply demands greater virtuosity. In addition, the *tsaimaye* like everyone else is obliged to farm and hunt and so on in order to live. To be sure, he is in possession of the technical and magical secrets necessary to make his salt. When he sets to work, he utters a formula, a *yanga boulata,* and his work, like hunting, shamanism, or war, cuts him off from everyday life by virtue of the sexual taboos imposed on him, by the separation from the world of women, which is essential if he is to perform his task correctly. But the Baruya are in the habit of submitting to this kind of taboo everytime they do something out of the ordinary. So it is not this restriction that makes a *tsaimaye* different from other men or from the great men. The difference, apart from his virtuosity and his knowledge of secret magic, lies in the fact that, to become *tsaimaye,* all one need do is to ask an experienced maker and persuade him to share his knowledge. His fame depends on the "weight" of the salt.

The acquisition of salt-making magic, like the magic handed down within each lineage for making sweet potatoes grow or raising pigs, involves no kind of possession or personality-splitting; it is handed down individually

132

and consciously to anyone who expresses an interest in the subject, be he the son, a distant nephew, or just one of the *tsaimaye*'s neighbors. This feature distinguishes it fundamentally from the function of cassowary hunter, shaman, or great warrior.

What do the Baruya do with their salt? They use it both for ceremonial consumption and as a medium of trade. It is not, like our cooking salt, an everyday staple, for two reasons. One is perfectly material, and stems from their own empirical observation; namely, that if they eat too much of their salt, they fall sick. For potassium is even saltier than sodium, and, if consumed to excess, acts as a violent poison. The other is ideological. The Baruya believe that salt has the power to cool the liver, which is the seat of strength in human beings. For this reason, it is kept for the exceptional circumstances that mark a turning point in the life of an individual or group, such as the girls' puberty ceremony, the initiates' meals, the meal eaten by a woman after childbirth, for whom the game caught by her husband, brothers and brothers-in-law is cooked.

But salt is also the Baruya's principal medium of trade, and well before the arrival of the whites, they treated it as a kind of money. They used it to obtain from neighboring tribes all that was materially necessary to the reproduction of their social life but could not be found on their own territory. They were obliged to import their means of production (stone adzes), their weapons (war clubs, black palmwood to make bows), their symbolic means of production (feathers of birds of paradise, shells from the coast, magic nuts, bark cloaks made by tribes living in the warm, lower valleys where the mulberry bushes grow).

Therefore they do not exchange salt for superfluous goods, but for the things that they need. Their trading demonstrates, as I pointed out at the beginning of this book, how misleading is the notion that the so-called primitive societies are self-sufficient. Each tribe produces and is obliged to produce for purposes of trade. It is therefore part of a regional economy which serves as the material and social support for the reproduction of each particular tribe. This reciprocal dependence has one major political consequence already encountered above, namely, the limitation that it places on war.

Therefore the salt maker occupies a crucial position in the Baruya economy, and his work confers upon him a de facto status that raises him above ordinary men. Paradoxically though, to a Westerner's eyes at least, there is no spectacular reference to this highly important economic function in the major expression of Baruya ideology, namely, the male initiations. Even though women do contribute to the work of growing the cane and receive salt bars, which they may use to buy bark cloaks from the foreigners who visit the Baruya from time to time to exchange goods, salt making itself remains an exclusively masculine task, one more in a long list, further adding to women's material, political, and symbolic dependence. Still, the fact that men concede to women the right to use this product as they wish makes salt making somewhat akin to farming.

Consequently, although reproducing and reconfirming the gulf between the sexes, the production of salt should be classed with horticultural production and domestic handicrafts, both of which require female cooperation. Despite its ritual use and importance, salt would appear to stand midway between ritual game and sweet potatoes. Therefore the *tsaimaye*'s activities help to distinguish him from other men, but carry with them none of the characteristics that would qualify for ideological distinction. There are no distinctive signs to draw the salt maker to everyone's attention as he enters the world of men and the *kwaimatnie*-man inspects his bedding in the *moukaanga* or the *tsimia*. In this respect, the *tsaimaye* resembles the *tannaka*, the great gardener, whose merits all recognize, but who remains undistinguished by any supernatural sign.

The need for "trade" is not absent from the male initiations, but this theme occupies a minor place in the ceremonies. It is only at their very end that a Youndouye, a man belonging to a neighboring tribe, but with different language and culture, with whom the Baruya formerly signed a treaty of eternal peace and trade, arrives fully armed, bedecked in his costume and his tribal insignias, which are quite distinct from those of the Baruya. This man stands motionless facing the ranks of the initiates while the men in charge of the rituals, who have for weeks been preaching the virtues of strength and war, now remind their listeners that an exception must be made on behalf of those wearing this costume and speaking this language. They also point out that because of this costume and language it is forbidden to exchange women with the tribe. Trade and friendship, without becoming kin or enemies, is the correct standard of conduct. That comment is all that the Baruya have to say about trade from an ideological standpoint during their initiations.

Some economic considerations

In the Baruya economy, the logic of production for the market is fundamentally subordinate to that of horticulture and domestic handicrafts. Their production is destined primarily for the satisfaction of their own needs, which are limited. The Baruya never produce for the sake of accumulation. They expand their production only to meet the needs of exceptional consumption connected with special circumstances.

Furthermore, garden land, hunting territory, and salt-growing land are roughly equally divided among the clans. Admittedly, tensions and vendettas have led to the breakup of many lineage segments which, having preferred to live apart from their clan, have thus lost their land rights. But they have found refuge with allied lineages which have since shared their resources with them. Needless to say, the new relationship places them in a situation of dependence, but the obligations that arise from the exchange of women and of kinship are such that the dependence does not breed exploitation, but rather generates an even more intense form of economic, political, and military cooperation than that demanded by the norm. Since all clans and lineages periodically undergo crises that culminate either in the departure of certain of their members or alternatively the arrival of affines, in the long run these opposing movements tend to rebalance the distribution of resources among lineages and clans, little by little forcing those in difficulty to seek a mutually advantageous solution.

Until the arrival of the white man, the whole of Baruya social life depended on acknowledgment of the fact that individuals and kinship groups depended on each other for survival. To the Baruya way of thinking, reciprocal dependence was more important than their autonomy.

For readers interested in the theoretical analysis of economic systems, the Baruya offer a clear illustration of the fact that it takes particular circumstances for market-oriented production to prevail over nonmarket production. Production, whether market-oriented or not, concerns itself with accumulation; accumulation yields only unequal distribution of some product; the autonomy of production units leads to mutual dependence; and, finally, marketable commodities represent the prime form of wealth and market-oriented production the general form of material production. It was just such a change that Australia's colonization of New Guinea has imposed on all of the tribes.

6

General view of Baruya social hierarchies

In covering the field I had set out to explore, namely, the various forms of social hierarchy that existed among the Baruya before the white man's arrival, before the emergence of a colonial order, I could have given more details concerning the place of men and women in the various forms of material activity, or in the male and female initiation ceremonies. It is highly frustrating to have to sacrifice material here, but the reader should bear in mind that it would take a whole volume to describe these ceremonies, some of which last several weeks or even months. Ian Dunlop and I have shot eighteen hours of film on the *mouka* initiation, the moment when the young are separated from their mothers, and nine hours of film on the ceremonies surrounding the three other stages.

To have included all this material would have upset the balance of this book, the chief purpose of which is to analyze in depth all the different aspects of Baruya society in the light of the social relations that seem to me to play a major role, namely, relations between the sexes. My aim turned out to be twofold inasmuch as the very process of analyzing all the different key aspects, material and conceptual [*idéel* in the French], and in all the different contexts imposed on individuals by the Baruya way of life, lays bare the mechanisms whereby male domination is established and made legitimate and leads to the discovery of other social hierarchies. These hierarchies derive from this domination and plunge their roots into it, while revealing how men are distinguished from other men and women from other women.

Let us therefore take one final look at the three kinds of social hierarchy in precolonial Baruya society. We shall then examine the problems of male domination and the production of great men from a more theoretical viewpoint.

The first form of social hierarchy is the general relation of male domination over women. As a matter of principle, all men, whoever they may be, dominate all women, whoever they may be:

men

women

For the first relation to be fully operative and socially legitimized, men and women must undergo a series of initiation rites, whose objects and formulas are controlled by the men. From this relation flows a further distinction and hierarchy, but this time among the men themselves, between the *kwaimatnie*-men and the rest:

men with *kwaimatnie*

men without *kwaitmatnie*

This distinction is neither merely nor essentially a distinction between individuals, but one between the Baruya clans that took refuge at Marouaka (which includes the local clan of the Andje tribe, their accomplice in the conquest of the hosts' land), and those clans made up of segments of native lineages incorporated and absorbed by the conquerers. Thus the distinction between men with *kwaimatnie* and men without *kwaimatnie* coincides with a political hierarchy:

conquering clans + native clan, accomplice

native clans subsequently incorporated

But things in reality arc still a little more complex since by virtue of the powers inherited from their ancestors and received directly from Sun and Moon the *kwaimatnie*-men are not merely the guarantors of male domination but also the "discoverers" of those destined to excel in functions of general interest, that is, war, shamanism, cassowary hunting, all of which, in their different ways, produce and reproduce men's superiority over women. Shamans themselves cannot place the insignias of their functions on their own head in the course of their initiation, and therefore the one who does so, the *kwaimatnie*-man, enjoys responsibility for the entire arena of competition and encouragement of individual differences among men as well as among women. The *kwaimatnie*-man acts as a kind of pivot for the social order in general. The relation between the *kwaimatnie*-man and the non–*kwaimatnie*-owning man is thus simultaneously a relation between the living and the dead, between humans and the supernatural powers.

ancestors   +   Sun–Moon

living   humans

The relation between the *kwaimatnie*-men and the others, as shown in Figure 10, is the prime condition of the discovery and the promotion of great men, of those singled out in the initiation ceremonies, that is, the great warriors, shamans, and cassowary hunters.

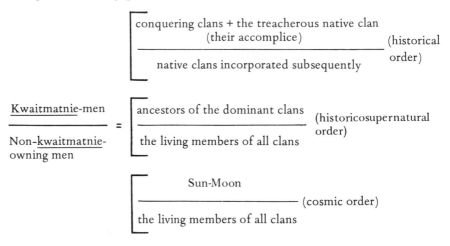

Figure 10. The prime condition of the discovery and the promotion of great men

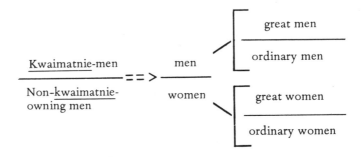

Figure 11. The establishment of domination

The *kwaimatnie*-men stand at the junction of the two main axes of the Baruya social hierarchy, between the sexes on the one hand, and within each sex on the other. They are instrumental in the establishment and accomplishment of male domination, just as they are the indirect condition of the promotion of the great men (see Figure 11).

Therefore the *kwaimatnie*-men are also great men. Moreover, because they have the most important function they must be kept hidden from the enemy, concealed and protected within the heart of the tribe. They are great, yet each one's name must under no circumstances pass the frontiers of his territory and spread abroad like the names of an *aoulatta* or that of a big man in other New Guinea tribes.

Shamans too, by virtue of their function, are condemned to the same dis-

138

General view of Baruya social hierarchies

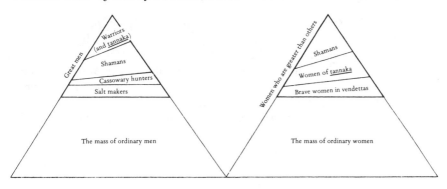

Figure 12. Activities open to initiative and talent

cretion and secrecy vis-à-vis neighboring tribes, friendly or enemy. Both they and the *kwaimatnie*-men place their magic powers at the disposal of the community as a whole and must therefore not reveal them to the gaze of outsiders. In contrast the great warriors essentially prove themselves in the face of outsiders.

Consequently it is difficult to represent the different characters and the different functions performed by the great men in the form of a descending hierarchy. I shall nevertheless attempt to represent the scope of activities open to individual initiative and talent by means of diagrams (see Figure 12). These diagrams obviously leave no room for the *kwamatnie*-man, since his is an hereditary function, although it is up to him personally as to whether his prestige waxes or wanes. The diagrams do not show that, for the Baruya, the conduct of war, the success of warriors great or small, implies the active, irreplaceable intervention of the shamans, of their own magic powers, as well as of those belonging to the tribe as a whole, which they project onto the enemy. Nor do they show that the masters of the shamanistic initiations belong to a single lineage, generation after generation, and in this respect their status is akin of that of the *kwamatnie*-man.

Therefore it would be thoroughly misleading to represent the great warrior as the great man in Baruya society, dominating all the others. One could imagine that a man who combined the powers of the *aoulatta* with those of the *koulaka* would enjoy the accumulated prestige and authority of great warrior and great shaman. Tradition does supply the names of a handful of individuals endowed with the two powers. One called Kwagiriana, who died around 1960, belonged to the Yuwandalie clan, one of the three clans, together with the Andavakia and the Boulimmambakia, that supplies the greatest number of, and the greatest, shamans to the tribe. But by taking a closer look at his career and asking those who knew him to interpret his career, I learned that Kwagiriana started out as a *koulaka,* applying the techniques of the shaman and the cassowary hunter to warfare, and gradually turned into an *aoulatta.* At night he would see in his dreams the spot where his enemies would be the next day. His spirit would then go off to immobilize them and, the following day, he would go to the spot in company with a number of warriors whom he had told of his vision, and there he would indeed find their enemies. They surrounded them and Kwagiriana would be the first to advance on them in order to kill them. But, say my informants, he then ceased to "circle the fire," that is, to take part in cures, and became a full-blown *aoulatta,* though of a rather special type owing to his gifts of clairvoyance, which he now put to work in his function as warrior.

Fundamentally, however, there is no accumulation of the warrior and shaman functions in Baruya thought, whereas a warrior or a shaman may perfectly well be a cassowary hunter or salt maker at the same time. The impossibility of accumulating the two great functions is clearly expressed in the fact that the *kwaimatnie*-men never find (in other words must not find, must not even look for) signs in an initiate's bedding or in his clenched fist, indicating that he will become both *aoulatta* and *koulaka.* If they find an eagle's feather, the sign of the shaman, they cannot, must not, find the piece of *pitpit* from which arrows are made and which herald the future great warrior.

In the eyes of foreigners, though, the man whose name is well known, who represents the Baruya in the eyes of all, friend or foe, is naturally the battlefield hero, the *aoulatta,* the great warrior. He is the only one who can conceivably be compared to the big man found in many Melanesian societies, to that hero of other battles, fought out by means of gifts and counter-gifts. But the comparison is a lame one, since it covers only certain aspects. The societies of great men and those of big men differ vastly in terms of their structures and overall logic. We shall be coming back to this point, for its theoretical importance goes well beyond the interpretation of Melanesian societies alone.

First, we shall take one last overall look at the situation of women in Baruya society, for it is fairly clear that, for the Baruya, although some women are greater than others, there are no really "great women," none so great as the great men, and none even truly comparable to them.

The greatest women are the female shamans; but female shamans cannot initiate other women, as male shamans can initiate other men. The *tannaka*'s wife has no name to distinguish her from other women; she is said to be particularly hard working (*draginie*), just as women able to fight with their digging sticks are referred to as warlike (*aoulatta*). But the wives of the *tannaka* are always overshadowed by their husbands, and the *aoulatta*'s wife only steps out of her everyday routine on the occasion of set-tos between all the men of two given lineages and their affines, or in vendettas between the inhabitants of two villages following a suicide or murder.

140

7

The nature of man/woman relations among the Baruya

Violence and consent, resistance and repression

I shall attempt to outline a general view of relations between men and women as these must have been in Baruya society's last years of sovereign, autonomous existence, that is, in the years leading to 1951, when the first white man arrived.

As we have seen, Baruya men enjoyed a whole series of monopolies or key functions, which guaranteed them, either collectively or individually, permanent practical and theoretical superiority over women in material, political, cultural, conceptual [idéel], and symbolic matters. Although I have already given details of this series of monopolies and key positions, it is worth itemizing them once again. Men own the land and the natural resources associated with a territory consisting of forests, rivers, savanna, cultivated and fallow land. Men make the tools, their own as well as the women's. They monopolize hunting, war, "foreign trade," the sacred objects and musical instruments, and, consequently, communication with the ancestors and the benign supernatural powers.

In addition, the men occupy key positions in the agricultural production process, since it is their job to clear the forest and open it up to the production of the principal means of human subsistence, namely, agricultural produce. They divert waterways to irrigate or drain the gardens, dig terraces to hold back or distribute the water, build barriers to protect the food-growing area from damage by wild and domestic pigs. They gather most of the materials used to build houses, shelters, fences, and so on, and they carry out the construction work.

Yet another key position is their exclusive responsibility for the final, most delicate, and most important operations in the salt-making process, salt being an essential means of exchange for the Baruya, enabling them to overcome the limitations of their local resources.

In the field of shamanism, the men combine both the monopoly of the (re)production of shamans, male and female, and, in healing, the first place,

141

ahead of women. In the workings of relations of kinship and in the social mechanism of the reproduction of life, they act as "representatives" of kinship groups, lineages and clans, and take the lead in the conclusion of alliances with these groups. Women do have the right to reject the alliances proposed, or rather imposed on them, for, as we have seen, one may turn down another family's proposal that she promise her daughter to their son, and a girl can, when she has her first period, break a marriage promise of many years' standing, in order to escape marriage to a man she does not like. In such cases, though, it was not the principle of being exchanged in order to procure a wife for their brother that these women were rejecting, but rather the particular exchange in which they were being asked to take part. Before 1960, no woman, apparently, would have dreamed of contesting the principle of an exchange designed to ensure the physical and political continuity both of her own kinship group and of the group to which she was given in marriage. In practical and psychological terms as well, this principle implied an act of personal subordination and submission, which is what was expected of a woman. Obviously, insofar as the young men concerned were frequently not consulted in the exchange of women, they too had no choice but to bow to their elders' wishes. But the men did not circulate between groups; their children belonged to them and to their lineage; in Baruya thought, marriage is first and foremost a direct exchange of women (*ginamare*) between groups, not an exchange of men.

The division of labor and occupations, and the values attaching to them meant that men on the whole lived a more colorful, more dangerous, and more exciting life than the women, a more worthwhile life in their eyes. As for the women, they had a virtual monopoly over pig breeding, whose meat plays an essential role in establishing and maintaining alliances, good neighborly relations, mutual help, and so on. They had the monopoly of their own initiations, and of course they alone brought new children into the world, in an area socially forbidden to men. In the few weeks following childbirth, they had the power of life and death over their child. If they accepted it, they kept it, otherwise they killed it and buried it beneath the shelter in which they had given birth. We shall be returning to this highly important aspect of Baruya society, but it is worth pointing out straightaway that the women did not hesitate to emphasize this right of life or death, and most of them had killed at least one of their children. They were familiar with the use of plants for abortion, but they tended to shy away from such use as painful and often ineffectual and preferred to dispose of their children at birth. Even if the child was stillborn or died of natural causes in its first few days of life, when a woman returns home and tells her husband, he immediately suspects her of having killed it, and even of having killed it because it was a boy.

In a word, socially cut off from the principal factor of production (the earth) and from the principal means of destruction and repression (weapons);

excluded from knowledge of the most sacred lore; kept out of, or granted only a minor position in discussions and decisions relating either to the general interests of the tribe or to their own personal fate; endlessly exhorted to do everything in their power to contribute to the reproduction by the order by which they are dominated; appreciated when they work unstintingly; and they remain faithful, docile and cooperative – are not Baruya women what we in our culture would call a dominated, oppressed, and exploited class?

By class, I mean quite simply what we have called class in the West ever since defined by the founders of political economy, François Quesnay and Adam Smith, namely, social groups characterized by their specific place in the process of production and redistribution of the material conditions of existence, in the process of production of the material "wealth" necessary to the reproduction of their society. This definition has remained unchanged, from Quesnay to Lenin, via Ricardo and Marx. What has changed has been the theoreticians' views on the nature of material "wealth" and on the identity of the classes that "produce" it (landowners, capitalists, workers – to confine ourselves to the three traditional classes of our bourgeois, industrial societies).

At first glance, relations between the sexes among the Baruya come very close to bearing out this definition of class relations. Do not men control, and often monopolize, both collectively and individually, the material means of existence, of governing, and of thought and action? Is this control more than enough to turn them collectively into a sort of dominant class, oppressing and exploiting another class, that is, the women? In fact it is not, for one additional, primordial condition remains unfulfilled, namely, that men, all men, must have ceased to be direct producers, confining themselves exclusively to the functions of management and control over the various labor processes, and supervising their execution by the women. This situation does not prevail, since all men, even the greatest among them, contribute to the production of the material conditions of the existence of everyone, women and men alike, although occupying positions quite distinct from those occupied by women.

Things are very different in societies in which women are exchanged for a certain number of pigs, live or dead, and shells. As it is generally the women who contribute most work to the production of pigs by their labor, the direct control and intensive use of their labor become crucial social issues. As we shall see in the big men societies in New Guinea, the number of wives depends on the number of pigs one can exchange for them, and the number of pigs on the number of women one is capable of looking after. In these societies, relations of exploitation of one sex by another do develop, whereas forms of oppression associated with the direct exchange of women disappear. Women gain in personal autonomy, but their economic enslavement is greater too.

143

The production of great men

By material conditions of existence I mean the material means that permit individuals physically to subsist as well as those that enable them socially to exist and thereby permit the material reproduction of the social relations that enable them to exist as they do.

For classes to arise it is first necessary for distinct social groups consisting of both men *and* women, occupying specific positions in the production process (kinship groups, clans, for example) to be dispossessed of the material conditions of their existence and thus collectively made to depend on other kinship groups for their material reproduction. "In exchange" for these conditions of existence, they hand over part of their labor power and their product, and submit, politically and ideologically, to those who "provide them with their living."

For classes to emerge, there must be an evolution in which the solidarity of men against women vanishes from the forefront of the social scene and takes a backseat, occupying a position subordinate to the production and reproduction of the other social solidarities. We shall be returning to these problems in the conclusion of this book.

From a strictly theoretical point of view, the relations between men and women in the Baruya society are not class relations even if they bear many resemblances. Nevertheless, in actual practice, women do have in common with a dominated class that they are separated from the ownership of the principal means of production, destruction, and government, and that this separation is interpreted, in Baruya thought, as the consequence of a radical expropriation by the men of the creative powers that had formerly belonged to the women, and of which the men have legitimately dispossessed them.

We have already seen how, for the Baruya, the men's superiority stemmed from their success in accumulating and combining two sorts of power, namely, those possessed by the men, qua men, and those which, in far off times, they had expropriated from the women, and which, in men's eyes, had sprung from an original creativity superior to their own. Nothing could better illustrate the men's dual power than their interpretation of the origin of the musical instruments that they use during the boys' initiations, which the women are strictly forbidden to see, just as the men are prohibited from revealing anything about them to the women. These instruments are the bull-roarers and the flutes.

The bull-roarers are long, narrow, slender pieces of wood, tapered at both ends, which are attached to a length of string and twirled as fast as possible about the head. They produce a strange sound like nothing to be heard in the jungle or in any place inhabited by humans, nothing like animal calls, cracking sounds, thunder, or voices. It is a sort of rumbling that grows ever more strident, arising from the depths of the forest, and then stops suddenly, rather like our factory sirens, which suddenly cover all the sounds of city life and then stop after a few seconds. The first bull-roarer, so the story goes, was found by a man who had climbed to the top of a tree to lop off its branches, the way the Baruya do when clearing the forest in order to open up a new garden. All of a sudden, something came and planted itself in the highest branch of the tree before the astonished man's eyes. He cut off the branch and recovered the object, one of whose ends was pierced; a piece of string had been tied through the eyelet. He guessed that this must be an arrow fired by the *yimaka,* the forest spirits, but he could not discover how to use it. So he tried whirling it, holding onto the string. As he did so, he made such a noise that all the men who had come to take a closer look at his object grew frightened and asked him to stop. He did so, but he said that what this arrow had brought them was the voice of the spirits, and that the men should sound it when initiating the *mouka.*

This "arrow" is the source of the men's fighting powers, their powers of death and destruction. It is the *kwaimatnie* of all the men, as it were, a sacred object that belongs to no lineage in particular, which distinguishes it from all the other *kwaimatnie.* The bull-roarers are played when sponsors of the *mouka* take in their mouths sap from a tree and place it in the mouths of the young initiates. At this point, the initiates are ignorant of the cause of the dreadful sound. Later on, in the course of the same ceremonies, the *mouka* are served morsels of cooked opossum liver on the tip of a bull-roarer used as a fork; the initiates, unaware of the true nature of this fork, see it as nothing more than a sharp stick, useful for spearing lumps of meat. How could they guess that the fighting powers given to men by the *yimaka* are at that moment being communicated to them through this bull-roarer, and that it will strengthen the powers of those who will become *aoulatta?*

As for the flutes, these are simple narrow-diameter bamboo tubes, closed at the bottom and open at the top. The sound which never varies is drawn from them by pressing the opening to the lower lip and blowing. The men often play in pairs, one blowing a high note, the other a low one from their flutes. These rudimentary instruments are a far cry from the highly elaborate ones with their holes down the side found in other parts of inland New Guinea. We already know the significance of the Baruya flute; its very name links it to the vagina and to the tadpoles from which the first men sprang. Therefore the flute is the symbol of the women's power to give birth and to "grow" children. In one sense, it is the woman's sex, though here purified of all those mortal dangers that it represents for men and society. It is the women's power of life, separated from their power of death.

We should take care not to interpret this separation as implying the disjoining of two contents and two distinct powers. It is rather the separation of two aspects of one and the same power, although it assumes two opposing aspects as long as it is vested in the woman's body. The flute is the woman's creative and procreative power at last made fully positive — that is, once she has been dispossessed of it. Only when these female powers have become an additional part of the male substance can they become wholly positive and enter fully into the service of the social and cosmic order.

Thus the classless Baruya, by asserting that it is necessary (and therefore legitimate) to separate the procreators from their procreative powers and from their fruit (that is, their children, and especially their male children), have in a way constructed in their mental world all the conceptual [*idéel*] elements of class exploitation and of its legitimization. For we all know that the wealth of the masters of Rome was produced by their slaves, who were totally deprived of and separated from that wealth; and that the power and wealth of the feudal lord depended on the number of subjects under him and on the toil of his peasants.

There is one essential difference between the formula of class exploitation and the Baruya formula of sex domination. In the former, the producers are socially and materially separated from the conditions of production, just as an essential part of the products is concretely expropriated from the producers. In the latter, women are separated from their procreative powers by thought and in thought alone. But the way in which they are separated from certain of their products, namely, their male children on a given day, when men come to fetch them to reprocreate them and turn them into men, is perfectly concrete and real. Essentially, then, the transformation, the new procreation is not imaginary, since it is intended to turn these boys into men, who will one day concretely occupy the leading positions in the relations of production, in relations of kinship, in trade, in warfare, in a word in the administration of things and the government of people. At the heart of the issue is the denial of the importance of women in the process of the reproduction of life in the enforced separation of sons from their mothers. Baruya thought is accordingly obliged, in the imaginary world, to dispossess women of their creative powers and to transfer these to men.

Historically speaking, Baruya women probably invented neither bows nor flutes. What these myths are actually saying is that, for the Baruya, the powers entailed in the creation of culture (bows, cultivated plants, musical instruments) are bound up with the powers of procreation, of the reproduction of life; in order to establish society properly on a firm basis, women must be subordinated to men in the process of the reproduction of life, and relations of kinship must be subordinated to the production and preservation of male superiority and solidarity. Over and beyond women's subordination to men can be seen a quite different type of subordination, namely, that of certain kinds of social relation to others; this subordination, at bottom, has nothing whatever to do with "personal" relations among individuals or groups, since it involves relations between relations within a hierarchy, within a specific logic of society.

We should therefore try to uncover the unintentional reasons that have turned relations of kinship and the position of women in these relations into a major social issue. We should try to discover the reasons that have made it necessary to subordinate the production of these relations of kinship to other forms of activity and other spheres of concrete activity (warfare, hunting, or trade, for example) in which men (though for other reasons) also happen to occupy the foremost positions. It should be clear by now that, contrary to all theoretical, scientific, or mythical reductionism, there is no single foundation for men's domination of women, but several bases rather, whose variable nature and relations are the sources of the profusion of forms that male domination has taken in the course of history; these forms will gradually become clearer. Needless to say, a case study – even that of the Baruya![1] – is plainly inadequate to uncover the unintentional reasons and account for the multiplicity of forms.

It is worth warning, in passing, against a misconception common in Western culture, especially among the self-proclaimed "empiricist" thinkers. When we speak of relations of kinship among the Baruya, we are naturally referring to the rules and forms of descent and alliance, to patterns of marriage. These are the specific and universal functions of kinship. One marries in order to have children; one allies oneself in order to have descendants belonging to one or more kinship groups which are determined according to whether descent is unilineal or not. But among the Baruya, as in many societies, relations of kinship also operate internally as relations of production. Through them, a human group appropriates natural resources, organizes its material operations on nature and the labor processes, and shares the fruits of its labor. So when reproducing the relations of kinship one is also reproducing the social framework of production. Here, then, the distinction between kinship and relations of production is an analytic one only; in practical terms, it only corresponds to something that is socially real in a handful of societies (among them the industrial societies). Consequently, reproducing children to take the place of their elders is both to prolong the physical existence of particular social groups, namely, kinship groups, and to reproduce the primary condition that will enable each of these groups to preserve its rights over a certain quantity of land and resources, labor power, and produce. But of course, this condition, though necessary, is not sufficient; "something more" is necessary to safeguard the rights over the human and material resources necessary to the reproduction of social life in the face of the many and varied situations of population growth and decline, in the face of internecine warfare, tribal warfare, natural calamities, and so on. This

---

[1] For several years now, I have been working on an essay on the forms and foundations of male domination, in which I analyze these questions, relying for the most part on anthropological data gathered in some fifty or so societies. I have broken off this project in order to write the present book, which is based on my own ethnographical material and has enabled me to develop my abstract reasoning as far as possible, that is, closer to the practical realities known to me at first hand.

147

"something more" is what has led to the subordination of kinship relations to other social relations more fully dominated by men.

Among the Baruya, therefore, the fundamental social issue is the general subordination of women in relations of kinship. This subordination goes hand in hand with a two-way process in which female reproductive powers are denied and belittled, while the role of men in the reproduction of life is amplified and overvalued. It is symptomatic that Baruya men reject the idea of male sterility (*yangananga*). In a childless couple, it is always the wife who is accused of sterility. Yet it sometimes happens that a man has several wives, none of whom ever conceives. It sometimes happens, moreover, that this man inherits the widow of one his brothers, to whom she has already borne five or six children, but that his new wife fails to conceive after her remarriage. I have often talked over such cases with the Baruya, but still they cannot bring themselves to believe that men too can be sterile. As long as a man has sperm, he is fertile. What is more, the Baruya believe that men have only relatively limited quantities of sperm, and that they should therefore spread it around with some moderation. They suspect the women of trying to extract as much out of them as possible in order to weaken them and dominate them. Is not the cassowary the image of woman lurking in the forest to commit sexual aggression on initiates and married men?

Suspicion, denigration, denial, dispossession, expropriation by means of theft, murder, or imaginary forms of violence – perpetually reproducing itself at the heart of Baruya thought and symbolic practice lies a formidable barrage of conceptual [*idéel*] and ideological violence aimed at women.

Though committed in thought and by thought, this violence joins with other, less conceptual [*idéel*], that is, physical, forms of violence, humiliation, insults, and other kinds of psychological violence, and social violence as well, such as the kind of violence that consists in forcing a woman to marry a man against her wishes, or in separating her from her sons. However, these various kinds of violence break out on relatively rare occasions in the life of a woman, such as marital quarrels or male initiations, or in forced marriage. It is one thing to have a fight with one's husband over some specific matter; but it is quite another to be separated from one's son in the general interest. Conceptual [*idéel*] violence, on the other hand, lies permanently at the heart of the Baruya's entire social organization, in every aspect of their practice; what makes it so efficient is that, as the ideas arise, they are self-legitimizing and justify all the forms of physical, psychological, and other violence. Such violence steps beyond the bounds of thought yet forever refers back to it for recognition that it is part of the very "order" of things. For men's greatest strength lies not in the exercise of violence but in women's consent to their domination; and this consent can only exist if both sexes share the same conceptions, which here legitimize male domination.

We have already observed the sharing of these conceptions at work in the

148

female initiations. Their initiations do not stand in opposition to the men's ceremonies. Rather they represent their complement, their extension into the consciousness and practice of women. Needless to say, as we have already shown, there is some leeway in the uses made of these conceptions, and the exoteric version of Sun and Moon, in which the latter is the former's wife, confers on women a more important position in the world than does the esoteric version, according to which Moon is Sun's younger brother and pierces women's sex with a stick.

Violence and consent are the two key factors of male domination. To this we must add a third, that is, women are divided among themselves in their dealings with men. The prime example is the jealousy that sometimes rages between a man's wives, which may lead to blows, or even murder. The Baruya try to avert trouble by marrying the two women of their choice on the same day and in the same ceremony. That way both can be called "first wife" and stand on an equal footing. But often this arrangement is not enough to avoid rancor or jealousy, and should the husband appear to favor one over the other, fights and quarrels are liable to flare up time and time again. I have often seen a wife reproaching her co-wife for having stayed at home to make love to their husband, upbraiding her, showering her with obscene insults, accusing her of laziness, of neglecting the children, and so on, all in the presence of the husband, who waits for the anger to blow over, laughing at the insults as long as they are not aimed at himself. The neighbors gather round, commenting on the affair, while the kids go on playing, getting in everyone's way. Sometimes things take a turn for the worse. One of the wives grabs a machete or her digging stick and strikes her opponent. Blood flows, and people start to shriek. The husband then steps in. The onlookers loudly take sides. Sometimes one wife will bring such pressure to bear on her husband that he ends up parting with the other wife, giving her to one of his brothers or to a patrilateral parallel cousin.

We must not suppose that women consent at all times and in every way to male domination. Once a woman is married, this domination is manifested first and foremost in the everyday presence of a husband. Some husbands are good to their wives, but society tends rather to encourage indifference in public. Domestic fights are frequent.

Forms of female resistance and rebellion

The first and simplest form is for a wife to "forget" to prepare her husband's meal or to forget to set aside some food for him. Given the division of labor (he is forbidden to gather and cook his food for himself), the husband is forced to have himself discreetly invited by a sister or female cousin. Alternatively, a wife may visit her family too often or too long, taking the children with her and neglecting her husband, gardens, and pigs. Sometimes she expressly refuses to cultivate certain plots of land cleared for her by her husband, leaving them to become overgrown again. She may neglect to feed the pigs, which get lost in the forest, die, or revert to their wild state.

But there are more serious ways of resisitng. She may refuse to make love, for instance, shouting and commenting on her husband, knowing that all the neighbors can hear, so close together and thin-walled are the huts. Sometimes the insults are so intimate and obscene that the husband is driven to commit suicide out of shame. Worse still, a wife may use sorcery against her husband by taking shreds of his pulpul or leftovers from his meals in order to cast a spell on him. The most dangerous of these practices consists in collecting the sperm in her vagina after having made love and throwing it onto the fire while uttering a magic formula. If the husband witnesses this action or hears of it, he knows that he is doomed to die and may in fact do so, either from fright or by letting himself decline.

Sometimes husband and wife come to blows, but this fight usually turns out badly for the wife. Sometimes a wife may murder her husband by pushing him into a rushing river as the couple crosses a tree trunk above the torrent. Before colonization the Baruya were unable to swim, and the husband's body would be carried along in the swift current, ending up in enemy territory. A wife herself may seek refuge with an enemy tribe; but in that case she will come under the authority of other men and be deprived of the protection of her kinsmen. Furthermore, she risks being done to death by the Baruya in the next war.

Resistance may take the less direct form of infanticide. There are probably several reasons for killing a newborn child: fear of bringing up a first child, the desire to widen the gap between one's children, sometimes too the perfectly explicit refusal to bear the children of an unbearable husband.

Last, there is suicide, a common occurrence among the Baruya, both men and women, though more so among the latter. Suicide is a serious way to take revenge, for not only will the dead woman's spirit lurk about the village, trying to assault her husband and even her children, but on a less conceptual [*idéel*] plane it will immediately trigger an attack on the husband's lineage and village by those to whom his late wife had belonged, followed by the breakup of the alliance formed by the marriage. The question can be settled if someone is killed in the battle or if the husband's lineage pays compensation in the form of salt, bark cloaks, or cowries to the wife's father and mother.

Not all female suicides are necesarily or directly provoked by male violence. One of the most celebrated in Baruya history occurred in 1961, some months after the establishment of the first Australian surveillance post. A young woman from the village of Woniri had married a man from the village of Wiaveu. One day she was surprised in the act of making love with her husband's younger brother. She hanged herself out of shame. On hearing this, the men and women of her lineage and village (Woniri) decided to attack the inhabitants of Wiaveu. The Australian officer received warning of the decision. He set out with a small detachment of soldiers, disarmed the men from Woniri (while those of Wiaveu had had time to hide their weapons), and to punish them gathered together their bows, arrows, clubs, and shields, and burned the lot. He then set fire to the village of Woniri as an example.

Women use various forms of individual resistance or rebellion. Cases of group resistance appear to be rare. I have been told the story of how, a long time ago, at Warouaka, a group of young girls had lain in ambush, hiding at either end of a bridge, in the knowledge that a band of young initiates would shortly be crossing it. When the latter were halfway across the river, the girls suddenly rushed forward and provoked the youths sexually. The terrified boys turned on the girls, but one threw himself into the river and drowned. They say that the girls were savagely beaten and even that one was killed as a lesson to the rest. Since that time, the story is often retold during initiations, and sometimes before a wider audience. This anecdote gives one example of group resistance, of direct female aggression against those who reassert the superiority of the male by their avoidance of women.

Needless to say, when standing up to a man, either by refusing to cook or to make love, or, exceptionally, by committing murder deep in the forest, these women mean business. They have their reasons for resisting and for choosing these forms of protest. They resist male domination in thought as well as in deed, but their resistance does not necessarily mean that they have any quarrel with the actual principle of such domination. They resist, they rebel possibly, but so far as I know no female countermodel has ever been offered to the reigning social order. The ideas of the dominant sex appear to have remained the dominant ideas. That is the message that the old women shout at the young adolescent girls, banging their lessons on civic conduct into these juvenile heads with their digging sticks.

Male violence and repression

The men, meanwhile, close ranks whenever a woman happens to endanger the symbols of their superiority through the person of one of their number. Here, the physical and psychological repression that inevitably follows any kind of female resistance takes a rather special, exemplary, symbolic turn. For repression is generally confined to the kind of physical and verbal violence described above, and is performed by a man in his dealings with his wife. By the way, in other situations an older woman, sure of herself, can send a band of youths packing with obscene insults if they try to importune her daughter, pretending to ask for her hand in marriage. But things may turn out badly if the woman performs any of those gestures that are strictly forbidden women precisely because they directly undermine the superiority of

151

the men as a group. For example, even if an argument degenerates into fisti-
cuffs, the woman must never hit the man's face, especially his nose. We need
to recall here that the Baruya's nose is pierced at his first initiation, and that
pig's teeth or other ornaments designed to indicate his social status are
threaded into the opening in the septum. Should a woman so take leave of
her senses as to hit a man on the nose, she will be severely beaten, and no
one will take her side.

Indeed, if a woman should inadvertently, or worse deliberately, snap the
string holding up the little bark cloak that covers the man's buttocks, not only
will she be fearfully thrashed, but the men will then organize a ceremony in
order to reintegrate this victim of female aggression solemnly into their community. The man is dressed in new clothes, as the initiates are. The men then
kill one or more pigs belonging to the guilty woman and share the meat
among all the men in the village. They also send portions out to the *kwalanga*
in the neighboring villages. To realize the importance of this woman's crime,
we must remember that by showing his behind the man has been deeply
humiliated, having been reduced by a woman's act to the situation of a
youmbwaye, a first-stage initiate barely out of the women's world. For in
Baruya thought the little cloak is like a tadpole's tail; it evokes the myth of
men's origins as recounted earlier.

Among other, still more severe forms of repression, the remarkable thing
is that they all follow acts – committed by women – that directly threaten (or
appear to threaten) the very institution that produces and symbolizes the superiority of all men over all women, namely, the male initiations. In a famous
anecdote among the Baruya a woman, furious at having been pushed about
by the men in the dancing to celebrate the building of the ceremonial house,
before even the ceremonies themselves had begun, grabbed a torch and set
fire to the roof of the house. She was arrested on the spot and beaten; the
shamans informed her that they would put her to death for sorcery. She immediately went and hanged herself.

They also say that once a woman suspected of having questioned a young
initiate about the secrets of the male initiation rites was put to death, and the
boy as well. Her lineage was not permitted to exercise its right of vengeance.
Indeed, it was asked to pick from its midst a "brother," that is, a distant
parallel cousin of the guilty woman, and he was killed as well. All the men
from all the lineages then gathered shells and salt, and so on, to present them
to the guilty woman's lineage to compensate it for the murder. The laws of
lineage vengeance were thus waived for the sake of the general interest, in
the interests of the men, which were thus assumed to be identical with those
of society at large. If a woman, either accidentally or deliberately, came
across men playing the sacred flute, or making the bull-roarers hum, she was
instantly put to death and her lineage had the right neither to oppose this
action nor to demand vengeance.

Alongside these true (or imaginary) stories of female crime, to which the men have reacted as a body, are the various ritual practices which symbolize a kind of collective struggle by the men against the women. I have already described the former custom, which was common before the arrival of the white man but which has since grown less frequent, whereby the initiate from the last two stages would assault the women and the young initiates with sticks as the latter returned from their riverside ceremonies.

Women find themselves under men's protection and yet victims of their aggression. Before taking one last look at this dual, ambivalent feature of women's status, let us recall the four elements of the conflictual dynamics of relations between men and women among the Baruya – male domination, female consent, female resistance, male repression. In addition to the open repression that women and men exercise on each other is the self-repression that each sex exercises upon itself in order to cut itself off from and hold itself apart from the other sex and its sphere; to stay in its place, whether inferior or superior.

Insofar as violence between the sexes is mainly directed against women, male domination may be described as a relation of oppression. Does it necessarily entail exploitation? I have already replied to this question in the negative. But I should like to examine the question from a different point of view, with a brief description of the way men deal in practice with the various categories of women with whom they come into contact in the course of their lifetime, namely, mother, sisters, wives, daughters, and so on. In fact, these women fall into two categories relative to a man: those with whom he maintains deeply positive relations of mutual help and affection, in which quarrels and violence are proscribed (this category includes his sisters, maternal and paternal aunts, his parallel and cross female cousins, and his sisters' daughters). On the other hand, in his dealing with his wife or wives, his own daughters and his brothers' daughters (and potentially his brothers' wives, since he stands to inherit them should his brothers die), he wields authority and, at least where his wives are concerned, he exercises varying degrees of repression and even violence. As can be seen, the most extreme forms of male domination are directed toward those women whom a man has obtained in exchange for his sisters, hence inside the field of alliance, in other words on those women with whom he may legitimately have sexual relations.

Relations with the mother are more complicated. Until the age of nine a boy is dependent on her and on her affection. Then come the men to take him away, and she hands him over in a moving ceremony, gently pushing her son toward the young warriors who will carry him off to the world of men, beneath a hail of blows. All the women I have ever questioned after this ceremony have told me of their acquiescence and pride at watching their son going off to become a man, capable of protecting them and succoring them in their old age. It is only many years afterward that a man will be reunited

153

with his mother, by which time he has fathered several children himself, after he has brought her game twice in a period of a few months. The first gift of game frees him from the prohibition against speaking to her, which has restrained him ever since he became an initiate. The second permits him at last to eat in her presence, once more enjoying without danger the relations of commensality that exist between married couples and their children. By these two gifts, he bears witness to the suffering that his mother endured in order to bring him into the world and to raise him. Here we can observe the tremendous ambivalence in the man's relationship with his mother. She is the first women he encounters along the path of life, and this first woman represents protection, gentleness, and affection; yet it is without her and against her that the boy learns to live and become a man. Between a married man and his aging mother there exists an attitude of reserve and restrained affection, made up of long silences, whereas a mother and her married daughters are endlessly laughing, helping each other out, bickering, giving gifts to each other, attending to each other.

Significantly an initiate's two sponsors, who are supposed to protect him, educate him, and share his suffering, are taken from the maternal side. The older of the two, who is already married, represents the mother, whereas the younger, a matrilateral crossed cousin, represents his sister. He is a bachelor, and this status ensures that he will be in the men's house for several years to come, so that he is free to care for the little boy. In this way the nurturing, protective element of the female world is also represented within the world of men.

As for daughters, as we have already noted, they only leave their family to go and found another. Most of the time their father is affectionate though distant in his dealings with his daughters, especially once they become adolescents. It is their mother who cares for them constantly, giving them light domestic chores at a very early age. She scolds them, lets them play around her as she works in the gardens or makes her loincloths and string bags. Later, once her daughters are married, and especially with the birth of children, relations grow more intimate. Finally, when the mother is widowed and aged, she goes to live out the rest of her life with one of her daughters, where she helps with the children, helps raise the pigs, discreetly intervening in family life, though never openly contradicting her son-in-law.

Mother, sister: the two women to whom a man owes his birth and his ability to marry; two women toward whom he must refrain from all acts of violence (individual, physical or psychological); two women with whom he enjoyed "positive" relations in his childhood, but from whom he had to be separated in order to become what he is today. From the one, his mother, it is the others, his elders, his fathers, the men as a group who separated him. From the other, his sister, it is his father who separated him in order to find a wife for him (sometimes it is he himself that has exchanged her for a wife).

154

They are two "positive" women in the sense that they stand outside the world of sexual relations, because the incest taboo stands between him and them. These separations were necessary for him to be able to build his social and his subjective identity. The social and psychological break, with its attendant redirection of his thoughts and his feelings, occurs at a moment when, had he gone on living with women, he would have run an increasing risk of entering into greater and greater sexual intimacy with them. Yet Baruya men sometimes confess that, when all is said and done, they would rather have married their sisters, with whom they grew up and played, than some other girl.

Nor is this fascination with incest merely a desire or an idea, confined to the subjective, inner world of the individual. One quite frequently sees a Baruya marrying a fairly close patrilateral parallel cousin, a direct descendant of one of their respective grandfather's brothers, for instance. These marriages are publicly disapproved of and condemned as "dog" marriages, but they are excused at the same time, partly on the grounds that, after all, no other lineage had been prepared to give the young man a wife, that he would have remained unmarried, that the girl was consenting, and even that is was she who had wanted the marriage in the first place, and that, when one gets down to brass tacks, it is better to marry someone you know than someone you do not, and so on. In any case, there are certain objective reasons, "structural" necessities as it were, for the occurrence of these forbidden, incestuous marriages.

In a system of direct exchange of women, it sometimes happens that a male orphan has no sister to exchange, can find no lineage willing to give him a daughter, and thus remains outside the kinship system which is here incapable of balancing out matrimonial exchanges other than case by case, without ever interfering in the overall flow of such exchanges as it does in the system of "generalized" exchange. Those members of a generation who do not manage to fit into the system are left with two alternatives, either enforced celibacy, doomed to spend the rest of their lives in the men's house and hence never to become wholly men, or marriage with a "sister," which will release them from the men's house and make them men, but at the cost of some degree of stigma (which will not affect the children born of this union, however).

At the root of the fascination with incest though, beyond the pragmatic explanations associated with the actual mechanisms of the kinship system, which sometimes drives people to infringe its own rules, lies a further explanation, this time of an ideological nature: the belief that, at the origin of time, it was necessary, in order to create the present world order, to break the law to establish the law, to commit incest in order to ensure the descent of the first humans, who were then obliged to renounce incest forthwith. The philosophy of disorder as a necessity to establish order finds explicit expression

155

in the most secret of all the Baruya myths. It was related to me by Inamwe, the greatest of all the shamans, on 9 December 1974, at Port Moresby. I had taken him there to give him his first sight of the sea and to show him the films of the great male initiations, now edited, that Ian Dunlop and I had shot back in 1969. Here is a partially condensed version of this myth:

The first woman came out of the depths of the forest. She was called Kouroumbingac, and her name was a reminder of the forest, *Kourie*. She was accompanied by a dog, Djoue, for the men came after the dogs. The woman was hungry and said to the dog: "What are we going to eat?" The dog found a coconut, broke it open, and gave her some to eat. [In another version the dog finds a pandanus fruit and gives it to her to eat; now, the pandanus is the symbol of man himself. Men used sometimes to turn themselves into pandanuses.] The woman, after having eaten the fruit, became pregnant. The dog said to Kouroumbingac: "We're going to build a shelter here." He gathered all the materials, everything necessary, carrying it in his mouth, and he built the shelter. They both went inside, lay down, and went to sleep. The dog noticed that the woman was asleep. He penetrated her vagina and ate the head of the child in the mother's belly. Later, she went into labor, gave birth, and discovered that the child had no head. She threw it away; it was a girl.

The woman and the dog went off and reached a spot where there was room to perform ceremonies. Kouroumbingac found some trees bearing fruit. She ate some of the fruit and once again became pregnant. The dog, meanwhile, was in the bush. He did not wish to return. He was afraid she would scold him for having eaten the child's head. Still, he came back, but watched her from afar. After a while, she fell asleep. It was the spirit of the dog that had put her to sleep. The dog drew near to her, entered her vagina, and ate the child's arms and legs. Later, Kouroumbingac awoke and subsequently gave birth to a child that had neither arms nor legs. It was a boy.

Djoue the dog had once again gone off into the forest, but he left a trace behind him, a trail of blood, the blood of the infant that he had devoured. The woman spotted the stains and knew that the dog had eaten her children. She followed it to catch the dog and avenge herself. The dog, meanwhile, had hidden in a cave, in a hole in the rocks. There, his belly became so vast he was unable to move. At that point the woman arrived. She knew the dog was hidden in the hole, and she pondered what do to about it. She thought and thought, and her spirit caused trees to grow at that spot. She broke off some branches and used them to stop up the hole in the rocks.

Then she went back to the tree to gather some of the fruit she had already eaten. She filled her bag up to the top and looked for somewhere to sleep. She found a spot, ate, and then fell asleep. Once more she became pregnant. At that place there was a stretch of water, and reeds began to grow in the water. On awakening, the woman cut down the reeds and bound them to her arms and legs. She went into the water and went as far as an island that was standing in the middle of the water. She walked to the summit of the island, where there were trees growing, and she built a shelter, and when it was finished she sat down. But she thought that it would be better not to give birth in a high, dry place, and she went down to give birth at the water's edge. She gave birth and then examined the child. He was well formed, and it was a boy. She was happy to see that he was well formed.

Her house was not a house like the ones men live in nowadays. It was more like the lair of a wild boar. She started to heap more grass onto the roof. During this time, Djoue the dog saw that he was shut in on all sides. He thought and thought,

156

and in a single blow his spirit split the rock in two, smashing part of it into little bits. The spirit of the dog left the rock and flew away, crying, *"Krakra krakra kwara kwaraka."* It became an eagle (*bwanie*). It also became the mother of the eagle, who built her eagle's aerie very high up and placed her eggs, her young (*Kwarakwaraka*), in it. The skin and bones of the dog stayed shut up in the rocks and rotted, and they metamorphosed into animals, especially *bwaraka,* an [opossum-like] animal that lives close to water. Later the eagle returned and ate its own bones, in other words all the animals into which these had been transformed. The eagle does not eat as other birds do. It eats itself when it eats opossums.

During this time, the child grew. One day he started to cry out, and called his mother in tears: *"Kourambi, kourambi."* Even today, when Barwaya children cry they don't go *"wa, wa"* but, if you listen carefully, *"kourambi, kourambi."* When I, Inamwe, make flutes, two flutes (one uttering a high note, the other a low note), I play them and I give them to the men as they set out to catch opossums. When they reach a rocky spot, they play the flutes.

The men think that these flutes are there to chase away the spirits, the *yimaka* who live in the rocks in the mountain, and who also eat opossums. But in fact these flutes say, *"kourambi, kourambi,"* and that is the first man calling for his mother.

When the son of Kouroumbingac had grown up, he made love to his mother. A son was born, then a daughter. The mother was called Kouroumbingac, the son Kourambwe. Later, the brother and sister made love, and the ancestors of the Baruya and the ancestors of all men (of New Guinea) were born. This is why even today many Baruya still marry their sisters. I, Inamwe, during the male ceremony for the birth of a child, when I inwardly utter the magical formula of the eagle's name, *"krakra krakra kwarakwaraka,"* I take the spirits of the men, they fly off, and the men go back to their sisters. But in wartime, when I inwardly utter the formula *"djoue, duwa, duwa,"* then the wild dog rushes off, and he goes so fast he makes the enemy run out of breath. This is the formula that I utter when I smear the magical clays *namboutche* and *numwaka* onto the stone clubs. And with the aid of this magic, thanks to Djoue, the men become *aoulatta,* great warriors. The formulas take the enemy's breath away, and when we fire arrows at him he wearies himself trying to dodge them; soon he is breathless. We catch up with him and smash his skull with the stone club.

This is an admirable example of what the Baruya call "brief words," which express the basic things, the deepest underpinnings of the social and cosmic order, of secret and sacred lore.

Without a detailed examination of this myth, it ought to be fairly easy for the reader to spot several leading themes of Baruya thought. Woman appears on the scene before man. She drinks the milk of a coconut or pandanus fruit. The dog devours first the head, then the arms and the legs of both children, which she conceives without the direct intervention of man and, apparently, without that of Sun. Now, while penetrating the woman's belly, the dog does the exact opposite of what the Sun does. Instead of completing the head and limbs of the fetus, he devours them. He is a kind of anti-Sun, the negative of Sun. He then metamorphoses into an eagle, the Sun-bird, but also the bird of the shamans. And he also turns into a game bird, and chiefly a water game bird at that. He therefore joins heaven and water, men and Sun, and, as game, provides the material of all ritual gifts between men and women, and

157

between men and initiates. Last, he becomes a force that the shamans secretly put to work for the great warriors and hunters.

It was therefore as a result of a double incest (primordial incest between mother and son, secondary incest between brother and sister) that mankind exists today and that the present social and cosmic order was established. Therefore incest does not spell total disorder. It is a form of disorder that had to be transgressed in order to establish order. Once again we come back to the essential notion that it is necessary to transgress in order to create order. It was necessary for a man to transgress the menstrual blood taboo in order to go and snatch from beneath the women's soiled skirts the flutes that they had invented. Those who know that know that one needs violence and transgression in order to establish an inviolable order.

It is worth mentioning in passing that packs of wild dogs used to live on the slopes of Mount Yelia, a volcano that dominates Baruya territory. The world has changed for the tribe since the white men, armed with rifles, tried to catch these dogs in order to preserve at least a specimen. The packs fled to other territories, to other tribes, and abandoned the Baruya. Not entirely, all the same, for the only dog that a young Australian officer succeeded in catching managed to escape from the cage in which it had been shut up before it was to be shipped to the city by plane. Did it run away? Was it helped to escape? At any rate, at least one wild dog descended from Djoue remains to guard the mountains of the Baruya.

Thus, little by little the picture of relations between men and women among the Baruya takes shape. Women's nature is twofold, as are the powers of men. Violence lies at the heart of their relations, but not absolutely everywhere. It does not concern half the women with whom a man has dealings in his lifetime, namely, his mother, his sisters, his maternal and paternal aunts, his grandmothers and his granddaughters, and so on, and men would like to do what is forbidden them, that is, marry their sister, commit incest, and have no need of any other woman in order to reproduce life.

So the reader should beware of hastily concluding that relations between Baruya men and women are unrelentingly violent, that these people are indeed "savages." Let anyone tempted to think so banish the thought. As we have just shown, there is room, plenty of room, for tenderness, affection, and even passion among Baruya men and women. The exchange of women among men by no means precludes affection between husband and wife, between parents and children. If it really were the case that "arranged marriages," in which those concerned are not consulted, necessarily ruled out this kind of feeling, then the greater part of humanity must have also ignored such feelings for centuries and centuries, because the Chinese, the Arabs, and the Hindus also used to marry women whom they had for the most part never seen.

The fact is that a young Baruya girl might well fall head over heels in love

158

with some young fellow, and try to catch a glimpse of him or happen to be around as he passes by to get him to notice. And the young man in question, once he knows that a girl is interested in him, is often flattered, starts to take an interest in her, and gets to thinking that a woman who desires him that much would make a good wife. There are young girls who beg their older brothers not to promise them too soon and who confess that they are in love. Often the brother is not unfavorable to his sister's feelings and tries to discover whether the loved one might have a sister to exchange for himself or for one of his brothers. If so, everything works out fine. But sometimes things do not work out, and sometimes a young woman married against her will finds it hard to forget the man she loved and makes a pass at him. The outcome may be adultery, conflicts, rows, blows, and ultimately repression, which can be quite fearsome.

Young men too carry on in exactly the same way. There are all sorts of discreet ways to let a girl or woman know he fancies her. He can make up love songs for the beauty not yet betrothed, whose hand everyone seeks. The young man sings the names of the rivers that flow through the territory of the girl's lineage, and the message will be clearly understood. Adult men often protest against public pressure put on the young girl.

There are love songs, but love charms also, to attract the spirit of the person one desires. Possibly the greatest sign of love is for a wife to commit suicide after her husband's death. I know of at least two examples. A man committed suicide, and his wife, having looked for him everywhere, found him hanging from one of the trees in their field. She immediately hanged herself above her husband's corpse. The other case is that of the wife of the son of Warineu – one of those to whom I have dedicated this book. She did not wish to survive the death of her husband, struck, it was said, at an early age by an arrow fired by a *yimaka*. She hanged herself. Suicide is not merely a means of revenge against male domination. It is also an expression of love at its most desperate. And its mirror image, the *crime passionnel,* also occurs among the Baruya.

Although there is indeed competition, hostility, confrontation, and even violence between the two sexes among the Baruya, relations do not amount to a reign of terror or hell on earth. The institution of the principle of the general domination of all women by all men still leaves plenty of room for nonmechanical, highly complex, and even extremely contradictory relations among individuals.

With the Baruya, as with us, are all kinds of humor and playfulness designed to take the drama out of their confrontation and attenuate the fear of both sexes. The most significant examples of de-dramatization through play, to my mind, is a song that the boys and girls sing separately, but whose theme is precisely the symbol of male superiority, namely, sperm.

The song tells of a group of girls that had lingered in a garden and had

159

decided to spend the night in one of the huts that the Baruya build so as not to have to return to the village during forest clearance or while keeping watch over their crops. Suddenly, one of the young girls spied one of her cross cousins, a boy she liked and who liked her. He had come to see whether he could kindle a bamboo torch at their fire so as to light his way home. On entering the hut the young man saw the girls, some of whom were still quite little, and became aroused. He lit his torch, thanked the girls, and left, but he quickly doused his torch and came running back to ask to use the fire again. The girls let him kindle his torch again and he left, but he then repeated the maneuver. So the girls decided to watch what he was up to outside. They saw him hide and extinguish his torch before starting back to the hut. The young man's cousin then decided to play along with him. She quickly explained to the young girls how to drink a man's sperm.

The young man returned; they told him it was too late to return to the village and that he would do better to sleep in a corner of the hut. As night fell, his cousin started to caress him and drink his sperm. The other girls then took turns doing the same all through the night until daybreak. Having drunk him dry they then sent him off, jeering at him for his weakness. The women's song then breaks off.

The men's song takes over. It contains the following verses, which are never sung in front of women. The young man returned to the men's house and lay down beneath the building to hide. One of his cross cousins came and asked him what was wrong, and he finally told him what had happened. The cousin then told the other men. They called together all the men of all the *kwalanga* from all the villages, and they formed the long, very narrow (*puiganie*) corridor down which the young initiates who have just been separated from their mothers are made to run while being beaten. The cousin was sent to fetch the young man and this "women's man" was made to run through the *puiganie* beneath a hail of blows. He was brought back to the *kwalanga,* where succeeding orators lectured him at length on his improper behavior, after which each of the initiates in turn gave him their sperm to drink. This restored his strength and his "skin."

At that point, the young girls, proud of their exploit, reached the village. Imagine their surprise when they set eyes on the young man they had apparently "exhausted" standing there beside the path, decked out in all his symbols, his body glossy and his skin revived!

That is the song that the sexes sing as if in challenge to each other. It is hardly surprising that in the male version the collective honor of the men ultimately triumphs! But the girls had a good laugh while singing about what they were able to do with men and their virility.

These games, which hover on the brink of eroticism, pose no threat to the foundation of society. On the contrary, they demonstrate that each sex knows a good deal more about the secrets of the other than is officially acknowledged. But is not the main thing, surely, their mutual complicity in keeping silent about what they know in order to keep up appearances, safeguard the social order, and hand it down to the next generation? Surely too, is not this solidarity between the sexes a sign that both acknowledge the necessity of male domination?

Needless to say, it is the old men and women who know many things of which they are supposed to remain in ignorance (even so, it really does seem as if the old women know nothing about the nature of the bull-roarers). This shared knowledge does not alter the shape of their fate. But it does give women, particularly postmenopausal women, a freedom of speech and action that women of child-bearing age could never permit themselves. In Baruya society, women's authority grows once they have ceased to have those menstrual flows that represent such a threat to men, whereas their husbands' authority declines in the face of the rising generations of men and particularly of the great men. Of course, these old women have ceased to be of interest to men and kinship groups. By way of contradiction, it is one of these old women who preaches obedience and consent to the laws of male domination to young girls during the initiation ceremonies.

I might add a final example to illustrate the complexity of relations of power among Baruya men and women. As we have already seen, an *aoulatta* has the necessary authority to separate quarreling brothers and restore peace, or at least to impose a truce upon a group of kinsmen preparing to kill each other. Now women too, and particularly old women, could stay the right arm of an *aoulatta* about to break a truce concluded with an enemy tribe, as he prepared to smash the skull of a visiting member of this tribe. Often enough, a woman forewarned of what was being plotted would rush to the visitor to offer him betel nuts and lime, the traditional gesture of hospitality and friendship. This gesture would make him sacred, and no one could then kill him. Thus, women's power to give life could momentarily delay men's overriding power of death, the business of war, which was the permanent justification for men's domination over women.

8

Great men societies, big men societies

Two alternative logics of society

Now that we have analyzed in detail the various hierarchies that stem from the Baruya manner of organizing and interpreting their social relations, we may compare them with other models to be found in this part of the world, that is, Melanesia. Consequently, this chapter is written especially for anthropologists, and above all for specialists in New Guinea, but because its theme – the relations of kinship, wealth, and power – is general in scope it should prove of interest to other categories of reader.

Needless to say, we shall not be comparing systematically Baruya society with the fifty or so other Melanesian societies that anthropologists have studied since Malinowski (1922),[1] Seligman (1910),[2] even Codrington (1891).[3] A chapter would not suffice. We shall simplify our task by comparing the Baruya model with the form of social hierarchy that many still take to be the commonest in Melanesia, namely, the "big men societies." We shall base the comparison on Marshall Sahlins's article on the subject in 1963.[4] In it he broadens one's perspective by contrasting the logic of the merited and ephemeral power of the big man with that of the hereditary and almost absolute power of the chief of a Polynesian "kingdom." Many people's ideas of power in Melanesia before the arrival of the whites may be traced to this article.

[1] Bronislaw Malinowski, *Argonauts of the Western Pacific* (London: Routledge Kegan Paul, 1922).
[2] C. G. Seligman, *The Melanesians of British New Guinea* (Cambridge: Cambridge University Press, 1910).
[3] R. M. Codrington, *The Melanesians: Studies in Their Anthropology and Folklore* (Oxford: Oxford University Press [Clarendon Press], 1891).
[4] Marshall D. Sahlins, "Poor Man, Rich Man, Big Man, Chief: Political types in Melanesia and Polynesia," *Comparative Studies in Society and History* 5 (1963):285–303; republished in *Cultures of the Pacific*, ed. Thomas Harding and Ben J. Wallace (New York: Free Press, 1970).

The paradigm of the big man

The big man is a man who has acquired power through his own merit; this power is neither inherited nor inheritable. His merit lies in his proven superiority in various fields, for example, his skill and efforts as a gardener, his bravura in battle, his oratorical gifts, or his magical powers. According to Sahlins, none of these talents alone is sufficient to make a big man without one additional gift which apparently plays the decisive role in building the renown and power of this man, namely, his ability to amass wealth and redistribute it with astutely calculated generosity.

These talents, this wealth, and this skill in excelling in the competition of gifts and countergifts in ceremonial exchanges between his own and neighboring clans, between his tribe and neighboring tribes, little by little earn him the gratitude and loyalty of a certain number of individuals who become his obligees as well as the respect of a wider circle of people who know him by name and by reputation. There gradually forms around him a faction of close relatives, affines, and neighbors who willingly agree to help this man in his undertakings, either by performing services for him or supplying him with goods. He then relies on this faction in order to "magnify his name" well beyond the frontiers of his and neighboring tribes.

Now – one of the major points stressed by Sahlins – the wealth and power of a big man are built upon a series of contradictory practices that ultimately undermine the basis of his power. For he builds his power through application of the principle of reciprocity. A big man must give back what he has received if he wants to go on gathering into his hands an ever-greater quantity of wealth for redistribution. But in order to maintain and expand his power, the big man must gradually resort to opposing methods, delaying the moment of paying back to members of his faction what they have given him to help him make his name, receiving without giving, and possibly even levying a portion of the labor and produce of orphans, of young men without family, refugees, and so on, those who did or still do depend on him to gather enough pigs for a dowry in order to marry, for instance. Little by little, the growing centralization undermines his social base, which finally collapses beneath him, at which point his followers scatter and rally to one or another of his rivals who thus profit from his fall.

This contradiction arises not in the sphere of the production of means of immediate subsistence but in that of the production and circulation of means of exchange: pigs or their equivalent in shells, feathers, and so on, which are the material means of producing a certain category of relations and social status. It is this sphere which is the direct material basis of the big men's power.

For Sahlins, the type of power that represents a mixture of cooperation and domination and the type of person who embodies it do not emerge by chance but in certain tribal societies with a highly specific structure, which are numerous in Melanesia. These are societies without hereditary chiefs; they are acephalous, consisting of a certain number of local groups that are equal in political status, each responsible for administering its material resources and labor force. They are organized according to relations of kinship and segmentary residence, a structure that does not automatically entail the hereditary ascription of functions and positions of power to individuals who occupy by birth the points of segmentation of kinship relations (for example, the transmission of the father's social functions or wealth to his eldest or second son, or the transmission from an older to a younger brother, followed by a return to the oldest son of the older brother, and so forth). In other words, as John Barnes put it,[5] we are not here dealing with segmentary societies on the "African" model, referring of course to societies such as the Nuer studied by Edward Evans-Pritchard (1940),[6] or the Tiv studied by Bohannan (1954, 1957, 1968).[7]

For Sahlins, the big man and his power represent a specific institutional response to a particular type of society; they result from the logic underpinning its structures and are a response to the need for a supralocal political power in certain circumstances such as wartime, religious ceremonies, or exchanges with distant tribes. By his ambition and his initiatives, the big man thus serves as the means through which the wealth and efforts of several local groups are united for the furtherance of common ends. He serves as the unstable, provisional medium for supralocal political relations that have not yet reached the point where they would need to take the form of a permanent institution. Hence the striking contrast between the contradictory and ephemeral power of the Melanesian big man and the great kingdoms of Polynesia in which a permanent quasi-state supralocal power is exercised by the members of kinship groups that form a hereditary tribal aristocracy.

Sahlins suggests that the societies of Eastern Melanesia, the Solomon Islands, and the New Hebrides, where one finds "ranks" but no chieftainship, may perhaps represent transitional forms between these two types of power and social logic. But he does not carry his analysis any further and contents himself with ascribing to them the role of "logical" link, as it were, in an evolutionary pattern of social forms that runs from bands of hunters to societies governed by a state, via the acephalous horticultural tribes of Melanesia.

This synopsis seems to be the core of Marshall Sahlins's analysis of the

---

[5] John A. Barnes, "African Models in the New Guinea Highlands," *Man* 62 (1962):5–9.

[6] Edward E. Evans-Pritchard, *Nuer: A Description of the Modes of Livelihood and Political Institutions of a Nilotic People* (Oxford: Oxford University Press, 1940).

[7] Paul Bohannan, *Tiv Farm and Settlement* (London: H. M. Stationery Office, 1954); "Some Principles of Exchange and Investment among the Tiv," *American Anthropologist,* 57:60–70; with Laura Bohannan, *The Tiv Economy* (London: Longmans, 1968).

powers of the Melanesian big man. New Guinea specialists immediately expressed reservations and raised objections to this analysis, focusing on three points. First, in New Guinea, the land of the big men, there are many societies in which political power is hereditary as in Polynesia, even if their "chiefs" enjoy far more limited power. Meggitt cites the Wogeo, Motu, Orokolo, Manam groups, the Purari River people, and the Trobriand Islanders,[8] and of course we should add New Caledonia to his list. However, Sahlins never really claimed that all Melanesian societies corresponded to his "ideal type."

More important is the objection, once again excellently formulated by Meggitt, that emphasizes untangling what in the big man's power is assured him from the outset from what derives from his own merit. The problem is tricky because of the scarcity of ethnographic data available to us concerning the workings of these societies before the white man's arrival. Basing his analysis on the example of the Mae-Enga, Meggitt shows that the emergence of a big man, far from being a contingent event, only occurs within certain structural constraints that limit in advance the choice, freedom, and identity of the leaders. He describes in the workings of Mae-Enga society a great many situations that call for the coordination of large numbers of people, or that call for arbitration among individuals or groups in order to settle conflicts. Those who manage to contrive the necessary compromises are men who are "capable of putting people in a situation of indebtedness to them through the manipulation of traditional wealth." They "confer upon their group high reputation and a dominant position in the world of ceremonial exchanges," men whose network of social connections spreads well beyond their group and acquires great social and political importance in time of tension or conflict.

Meggitt shows that the function of all authority is in a sense part and parcel of the lineage structure, and that those men who are capable of embodying it can only come from certain points of segmentation within this structure. He also shows that the power of a leader is unlikely to diminish in time of conflict or sharp tension among neighboring groups, but that in time of peace there is room for shifts of allegiance and consequently for the big man's fall.

In other words, using the example of a society that, according to Sahlins, ought not to have produced big men owing to the emergence of its leaders at given points of segmentation in the lineage system, Meggitt ends up precisely describing those big men as defined by Sahlins. Faced with this divorce between idea and reality we may have little hesitation in concluding that Sahlins's thinking on the "structures" of big men societies does not tally with real life. For his view presupposes so great a social "fluidity," so great

---

[8] M. J. Meggitt, "The Pattern of Leadership among the Mae-Enga of New Guinea," *Anthropological Forum* 2 (1) (November 1967):20–35.

an absence of fixed points, that it is hardly surprising that one does not find this kind of society in New Guinea. The structures correspond rather to those of certain nomadic hunter-gatherer societies, but one does not generally find big men in these fluid societies.

However, Meggitt entirely agrees with Sahlins's statement that a big man is first and foremost a man skilled in accumulating and sharing traditional wealth. He explains that, among the Mae-Enga, a big man is rarely an expert in matters of ritual or a great warrior, and conversely an expert in ritual or a great warrior only rarely becomes a big man. A good warrior indeed seems to be viewed rather as a necessary evil, whose violence tends to become a nuisance in other circumstances.

Last, Meggitt says in a footnote that no notion of holiness attaches to the big man, as if accumulation and redistribution of wealth were insufficient to confer holiness on someone.[9] This comment is the second source of specialist criticism of Sahlins's views. Whereas a big man is certainly a Melanesian great man, not all Melanesian great men are big men. For in addition to the accumulation of wealth as Ann Chowning, superb scholar of ethnographic and historical sources, reminds Sahlins, Melanesia has two other avenues of power, namely, war on the one hand and ritual, magic, and sacred lore on the other. But she concedes that "there are only a few Melanesian societies of which it is reported [and confirmed] that a man can attain the highest prestige and the greatest influence, if not power, over others, without demonstrating his ability to accumulate and make the proper use of wealth. . . . But usually . . . competitions in economic achievement . . . are his main road to renown."[10]

Plainly the Baruya are one of those "few societies," but that is beside the point; we shall be coming back to this matter. The point is that, once we have acknowledged that warfare and sacred lore did represent two alternative roads to power and that there did exist Melanesian great men who were not big men, we still do not know how Melanesian men came to be great men. Without a concrete analysis of the social reasons and the mechanisms of production of these great-men-who-were-not-big-men, any account of the big men's power must necessarily be distorted and misapprehended. Sahlins indeed sensed this problem, adding a note of caution: "It is difficult to say just how important the military qualifications of leadership have been in Melanesia, since the ethnographic researches have typically been undertaken after pacification, sometimes long after. I may underestimate this factor."[11]

---

[9] Ibid., p. 35, n. 12.
[10] Ann Chowning, "Leadership in Melanesia," *Journal of Pacific History* 14 (1) (1979):72. See also Chowning, *An Introduction to the Peoples and Cultures of Melanesia* (Menlo Park, Calif.: Cummings Publishing Company, 1973), pp. 47–49.
[11] Sahlins, "Poor Man, Rich Man," p. 448, n. 13.

Three years earlier, in a remarkable article that Sahlins cited on the "political aspects of the system of ceremonial exchanges among the Kyaka (who belong to the Enga group and are neighbors of the Mae-Enga)," Ralph Bulmer wrote:

War and the Moka [ceremonial exchanges] were the two widest fields in which individuals achieved their position. . . . Men who are outstanding in the Moka are renowned over a wide area, as were successful war-leaders in pre-contact days, who also had to be members of powerful clans. It is hard now to reconstruct precisely how Moka leadership and war leadership were related . . .[12]

Therefore the picture of the Kyaka-Enga was rather different from the one of the Mae-Enga. Among the former, war played an important role in the production of their great men; yet, according to Bulmer, for them too, as for the Mae-Enga, "performance in the Moka is perhaps the most important single criterion and index of influence and prestige."[13] He goes on to point out, though without emphasis, that warfare was up to a point compatible with the preparation, coordination, and proceedings of the great ceremonial exchanges. War was detrimental to pig breeding, required drawing on one's livestock in order to compensate for the war dead and injured, interrupted for years exchanges between tribes that failed to compensate for losses inflicted on their neighbors, and so forth. In a word, war might promote great men, but they had to be able to make a successful peace before qualifying for the status of big man as well.

The aspect of ethnography and the theoretical problems with which I am concerned are encompassed in my analysis of the nature of forms of power and the various mechanisms of the production of great men among the Baruya. Having been lucky enough to have encountered the Baruya seven years after the end of their last tribal wars; having been admitted to their initiation ceremonies (which, even amputated of their war-related rites, still spoke volumes for their importance in the logic of their society); having had the opportunity of questioning directly great warriors who had only recently been disarmed by the white man; having observed the masters of the sacred objects and ritual lore in the performance of their functions – I am fairly well placed to grapple with the two major problems that bedevil analysis of the big man's power, namely, to untangle what is ascribed from what is achieved (as Ralph Linton puts it)[14] in the promotion of great men, and to identify the relations among the different functions that underpin their power, for example, male domination, war, shamanism, cassowary hunting.

One would certainly need many more such analyses before being able to

[12] Ralph Bulmer, "Political Aspects of the Moka Ceremonial Exchange System among the Kyaka People of the Western Highlands of New Guinea," *Oceania* 31 (1) (September 1960):12.
[13] Ibid., p. 5.
[14] Ralph Linton, *The Tree of Culture* (New York: Knopf, 1955).

draw conclusions. It is definitely not by comparing dozens of vague accounts that we can reach clear statistical and theoretical conclusions![15] The Baruya are probably an exception. Because I have been able to ask them questions that ought to have been put to the big men right at the beginning of the colonial period, perhaps their particularity may afford us a better glimpse of the (no less particular) social conditions that gave rise to the big men. What the Baruya reveal, by way of contrast, is that for big men to emerge it is necessary for the reproduction of relations of kinship to be intimately and directly bound up with the production of wealth. They reveal too that the direct exchange of women must have ceased (or almost ceased) in the production of relations of kinship and in the reproduction of the social groups that are based on these relations.

Let us take another look at the example of the Baruya, and try to compare their great men with the big men produced in other New Guinea societies (see Figure 13).

Strictly speaking, the two are only "half"-comparable, because only some of the Baruya great-man statuses are open to competition, and even then not to all individuals; the masters of the male initiation rituals (at least of those that take place openly) and the masters of the shamanistic initiations are ineligible to fight in the front line in battle and so to become great warriors.

Therefore those who own (through inheritance) the sacred objects (*kwaimatnie*) or possess secret lore (the myths of the master shamans) cannot be compared with the big men – not that there is no scale of greatness among them; greatness depends on their ability to perform their tasks. For instance, I knew two brothers who were masters of the shamanistic initiations. The elder, Inamwe, was universally acknowledged by the Baruya to be vastly superior to the younger one. The difference in prestige and authority was caused by much more than the simple difference between an older and a younger brother, important though that may be. The older brother was far more subtly and more profoundly versed in the myths.

Only the great warriors, the great shamans (excluding the masters of the shamanistic initiations), and the great cassowary hunters are strictly comparable with the big men in terms not of wealth but of individual merit, in terms of one individual's acknowledged superiority over all others engaged in the same undertaking. For none of these people builds his influence on the production and accumulation of wealth; nor does he accumulate wealth on the strength of his power. The only person who might be said to do so to

[15] One unfortunate example of ambitious comparisons based on inadequate material is afforded by Paul Sillitoe's article "Big Men and War in New Guinea," *Man* 13 (2) (June 1978):252–71. In another article, this time based on his own material, he supplies some interesting information about "horror of women" among the Wola (P. Sillitoe, "Man-eating Women: Fears of Sexual Pollution in the Papua-New Guinea Highlands," *Journal of Polynesian Society* 1 (1979):77–97).

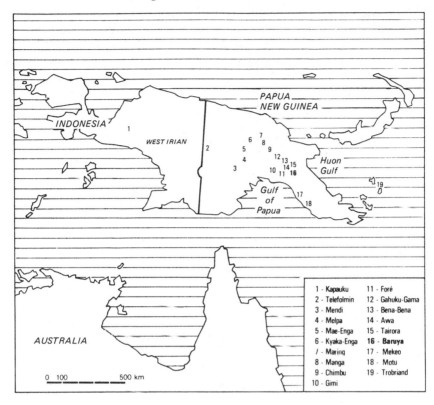

Figure 13. Territory of other New Guinea societies

some small extent is the shaman insofar as he receives gifts in return for his services.

The Baruya figure who most resembles the big man, because of his ability to produce and share material resources, is the *tannaka,* the great horticulturist; but his greatness increases in the shadow of war, and he rises above the crowd only because of the support he gives to the *aoulatta,* the great warriors, becoming their *tsimie.* What is more, although he is indeed one of the most effective producers of material wealth in his society, his products are not goods for ceremonial exchange but for subsistence, or pigs to be shared and consumed unaccompanied by any kind of ceremonial consumption. As for the prime means of exchange, salt, its manufacture does distinguish the *tsaimaye* from the common run of mortals but it is not enough to make him a great man. Nowhere in the logic of this society do we find the conditions required to produce a big man skilled in accumulating and manipulating wealth for exchange.

169

The production of great men

If we were to have a go at painting word-portraits, we should have to compare the only Baruya great man whose renown, like that of the big man, spreads far and wide beyond the frontiers of his own tribe, namely, the prestigious *aoulatta* or great warrior [pp. 174–5]. The names of the other Baruya great men are, on the contrary, carefully concealed from the outside world.

One has merely to compare the two types of New Guinea great man, whose common trait is that they both "represent" their group vis-à-vis outside tribes, to see the almost symmetrical contrast in the behavior, values, goals, and possibly even temperaments. There does indeed seem to be some deep-seated incompatibility, as Meggitt and Bulmer have suggested, between war and ceremonial exchanges. As they too are a form of competition for pre-eminence among local groups, ceremonial exchanges partially obviate the need for warfare and the warrior. Or, to paraphrase Carl von Clausewitz,[16] ceremonial exchanges are war carried on by other means. As the peaceful extension of war, they tend to weaken and undermine its role in intertribal relations.

Ultimately, the two contrasting heroes also contrast, within their own respective societies, with two types of men who occupy the bottom of the male social ladder, two negative characters as it were, who further magnify in comparison the greatness of the great man. Among the Baruya, the opposite of the great man is the *worianie,* who is good at nothing and good for nothing. Whereas in the big men societies, the big man's opposite is known in pidgin as a rubbishman, the outcast, the dregs of society, the man who lacks the means to marry, has no land, no kith or kin to support him; he is a man in need of assistance merely to stay alive, however wretchedly, who depends on others in order to exist (he may be an orphan, a younger brother, or a refugee). Now it is not at all the same thing to be good for nothing or good at nothing on the one hand, and to have nothing yet to be good for something on the other, to serve the big man who extends a helping hand to you. Yet both have in common the fact of being men on whom others can never really count or completely rely. In both cases, the great mass of ordinary men lie somewhere between these two extremes, neither all that good nor all that bad at anything in particular.

It is now necessary to look beyond these standard portraits and try to find out what, in social relations and structures, gives rise to the heroes. As we have already seen, Sahlins's hypothesis of totally fluid segmentary societies does not stand scrutiny. "It is not true that everywhere in Melanesia any man had an equal opportunity to achieve high status."[17] But if, as Sahlins sug-

---

[16] Von Clausewitz, *Vom Kriege* (Berlin: F. Dümmler, 1832); in English as *On War* (Harmondsworth, England: Penguin Classics, 1982), p. 119.
[17] Chowning, *Peoples and Cultures of Melanesia,* p. 45. See also Bronwen Douglas, "Rank, Power, Authority: A Reassessment of Traditional Leadership in South Pacific Societies," *Journal of Pacific History* 14 (1) (1979):2–27.

gests, the big man provides a framework for undertakings too great for the local political context, mobilizing the energies of large numbers of people or substantial resources in the general interest, the question is not merely what these societies lacked for permanent supralocal institutions to emerge but also what exists in these societies that allows the big man to personify and assume the burden of supralocal interests.

What exists is the production and the reproduction of life (relations of kinship) and of those social relations that lie beyond this sphere (intertribal relations, relations with the gods) and depend largely on the circulation and redistribution of material wealth and hence on their production. There is a direct, internal connection between material production and the reproduction of life and of social relations, a connection that does not exist among the Baruya or among societies of that type. For in the big men societies it is necessary to produce wealth in order to exchange it for women, to compensate for enemies or allies killed in war, or to make the sacrifices needed to stay on good terms with the spirits of the dead and the supernatural powers (cult of the dead, cults of male and female spirits, and so on). In other words there is no equivalence between life and life, as there is among the Baruya: that is, a woman for a woman, a warrior killed for a warrior killed. The fundamental principle underlying the workings of the big men societies is the exchange and/or sacrifice of wealth in order to reproduce life and society. This principle means not simply exchanging wealth for life. It would not be sufficient, I think, to develop fully the functions, the powers, and the personality of the big man; the exchange must be one without an equivalent in return.

Let us now take a look at what happens with the Baruya. Here, there is no need of a big man and his faction to organize the community ceremonies, to prepare for and conduct war, to negotiate peace, to foster trade and material exchanges with neighboring or distant tribes, to help young men find brides, grant land to refugees, adjudicate quarrels between villages or lineages, initiate hundreds of youths and girls. The material resources needed for all these activities of general interest are produced by each family and lineage working separately, and are redistributed either directly by them or indirectly under the control of the masters of the rituals, or again by the elders of the lineages, and so forth. Needless to say, among the Baruya too, all activities of general interest are ultimately controlled by a small number of leading personalities – mostly men. But these men do not exercise control because they contribute more than others to the material "financing" of the operation. The big initiations involve the mobilization of every family's resources; these are placed in the service of all, of the tribe, of the Baruya. Families may even be said to plan production of the requisite resources a long time in advance, for these ceremonies are occasions of much feasting and gifts of food to hundreds of visitors from neighboring tribes, and for weeks on end work in the fields slows down or even comes to a complete halt. The initiations are the occasion for the periodic reproduction of the Baruya tribe per se as a supralocal unit, as the substance and the permanent condition of the individual and group existence of its members. While reproducing this economic and political unity, this institution also reproduces the ethnic identity of all the tribes that partake of the same rites and culture.

The supralocal interests of the Baruya are satisfied by the tribal solidarity that exists among the lineages and villages. It is certainly a form of solidarity against other tribes, but it is based on two institutions, namely, the male initiations, and the mechanisms whereby the great men (the *aoulatta*, the *koulaka*) are produced to serve the tribe. Among the Baruya, the lineage is a strong unit, the clan is a weak one, and the tribe a strong one. In the "true" big men societies such as the Enga, the Melpa, the Kyaka, and the Chimbu, the lineage is strong, and so is the clan, but the tribe appears to be rather weak. I use the expression *true* big men societies deliberately, as the term *big man* and the portrait drawn by Sahlins have become such stereotypes, such a conditioned reflex that one even finds anthropologists applying the term *big man* to the great men of the society they are studying, and then wasting a great deal of time trying to explain that these big men are not like the ones found in the great societies of the Western Highlands who genuinely appear to be "true" big men and are described by Meggitt, Bulmer, d'Arcy Ryan,[18] or Strathern.[19] In what way are they not "true" big men?[20] Is it because they are first and foremost warriors and ritual masters, or because the redistribution of pigs in these societies is not extensive or is not competitive?

It is not merely the presence or absence of institutions such as male initiations or various mechanisms for the promotion of great men specializing in some social function or other, whether ascribed or achieved, that is the fundamental reason for the existence or lack of "true" big men. We may formulate this reason as questions: Do exchanges between groups and individuals depend on principles of equivalence and on mechanisms designed to restore rapidly the equilibrium between the exchangers (donors and recipients)? Or do they depend rather on the quest for nonequivalence in exchanges, on the principle of calculated disequilibrium or unequal exchange?

Let us take these questions and apply them to the Baruya. We have seen that the very principle on which the production of relations of kinship is based is that only a woman may be regarded as "equivalent" to another

[18] J. d'Arcy Ryan, "Marriage in Mendli," in *Pigs, Pearshells and Women, Marriage in the New Guinea Highlands,* ed. R. M. Glasse and M. J. Meggitt (Englewood Cliffs, N.J.: Prentice-Hall, 1969), pp. 159–75.
[19] Andrew Strathern, *Ongka. A Self-Account by a New Guinea Big Man* (London: Duckworth, 1979).
[20] To illustrate this approach is Cherry Lowman-Vayda's otherwise remarkable article: "Maring Big Men," *Anthropological Forum* 2 (2) (November 1968):199–243.

woman. The exchange of gifts of pig meat and services between the two families at the time of the decision to strike a marriage alliance is in no sense a dowry, bride price, or bride wealth; it is not an equivalent of the sexual services, children, and work that the young woman will be providing her husband. The gifts are a token and an expression of a decision to form an alliance; but this decision cannot be fully implemented in practice until the girl has reached puberty and the groom has left the men's house. We know too that the young man or the girl may on occasion break this alliance. The other family will take back the daughter offered in exchange or, if the girl's marriage has been consummated, it will immediately give one of this daughter's daughters in exchange for one of its sons. As for the pig meat and the services exchanged, these are now over and done with, and provided they have been carefully counterbalanced no one will be the loser. Consequently the Baruya take great care to give back what they have received, not in order to expunge their debts, but in order to counterbalance the debts of others toward them.

For in so-called primitive societies debts are never wiped out; they are balanced, or left unbalanced. The direct exchange of sisters between two men or two lineages in no way signifies that these two men and their lineages are no longer indebted to each other; on the contrary, it means that both are now dependent on each other for their reproduction, and that each is superior to the other as donor of a wife, but at the same time inferior as recipient.

The Baruya apply the same principle in war. Only an enemy's life can compensate for that of a Baruya, man or woman. Yet they apply the bridewealth principle when exchanging bars of salt, shells, or bark cloaks for a woman from a distant tribe with which they wish to trade. After a murder resulting in the breakup of a lineage and the exile of a portion of its members, who go to live with an allied lineage that gives them shelter and promises them land and protection, the hosts give to the victorious representatives of the splintered lineage a great quantity of wealth, salt bars, feathers, cowries, in order to "buy the name" of those they have incorporated and extinguish the residual rights of their former lineage over them. In both these contexts, life is exchanged for material goods, not for means of subsistence, but for means of exchange or for the means of symbolizing social status (feathers, cowries, and the like). We may say that in the big men societies individuals and lineages treat each other the way the Baruya treat outsiders with whom they wish to establish (nonceremonial) relations of trade and mutual help.

It strikes me that the principle of direct exchange of women has important consequences on the organization of material production in the Baruya economy. Because the production of relations of kinship does not depend directly on the accumulation of material wealth, there is little incentive to produce such wealth, pigs in particular. It is not that the Baruya have no need to produce the means of exchange in order to obtain what they do not produce themselves, but what they produce is salt, which they exchange nonceremonially, whereas salt is in itself a ceremonial object, one that is indispensable to the accomplishment of the rituals that mark the major events in the life cycle of the Baruya and their neighbors. Because the circulation and redistribution of pig meat (and a fortiori the circulation of live pigs, female especially) are not an essential issue in relations of domination between people and between local groups, Baruya women retain tight control over the circulation of pigs, live or slaughtered. It is not the place of women in the production of pigs that is highly diversified in New Guinea; it is their place in the circulation of the pigs, and that depends on the structure of relations of kinship and the other social conditions of production.

Incidentally, it is worth recalling that the Baruya state used to produce far fewer pigs than today, and that the growth in output is because of the advent of steel tools. Does this mean, as some anthropologists reason, somewhat mechanically, that if the Baruya did not develop the exchange of pigs it was because their output and their productive forces were limited, or does it mean on the contrary that their production was limited because it played no essential role in the production of social relations and was confined mainly to subsistence? I obviously incline to the second interpretation, while not denying the role of ecological and technological determinations. But I am convinced that the Baruya could have expanded their output of pigs before the advent of steel implements had they felt the need. Such an expansion would

---

The aoulatta:

He is indomitably courageous, capable of feats of physical prowess; master of exceptional spells that can make him invincible, possessing powers that enable him to "see" his enemies in his dreams and to know whom, when, and where to attack; he is a strategist.

He protects not just his lineage and village but the entire tribe.

He has few wives and children.

He spends more time watching the enemy or stalking him than clearing the forest and creating large gardens.

He has his followers who back his decisions, and his *djilika,* bodyguards, who maneuver with him on the battlefield.

His name and reputation are known among all the neighboring tribes.

He is the prime target when the enemy attacks, the chief rival of its own great warriors.

He stands out from the common run of men, from the simple warriors that make up the mass of the tribe, as numerous as "sweet potatoes."

He may intervene in issues connected with relations of kinship and act as a kind of adjudicator or referee.

His powers are not automatically handed down to his children, but he does leave them a great name to emulate.

If he uses his violence to further his own interests or oppresses the other Baruya and acts as a despot, he will be killed.

have entailed a change in the relations that have always existed in their agriculture between the extensive production of sweet potatoes and intensive farming on irrigated land. They would thus have been led to work harder using the same techniques, eventually working differently and employing different techniques.

It looks as though there is another complementary, though opposing, fact that might be dovetailed into this overall social logic, which ascribes a secondary role to the circulation of pigs while allowing women an important role in this circulation. This complementary fact is the great importance of game and hunting in relations between the sexes and in the reproduction of hierarchic relations between older and younger people, initiates and noninitiates, and so forth. To hunt there has to be game, of course, and the vast Baruya forests supply it in abundance (far more than does a savanna zone such as the Bena-Bena territory for example). However, here again, what is materially possible does not explain what is socially necessary.

For hunting is not all that important to the Baruya from the point of view of subsistence. On the other hand, it is essential to the reproduction of relations of male domination and of the mechanisms of the social production of men by men. The fact of giving game allows men to emphasize their superiority over women and youths. One is bound to observe that this article, which serves to mark one individual's dependence upon another, though owing nothing to the work of women, owes nothing to that of men either, as it

---

The big man:

He is shrewd, cautious, calculating, a good speaker, convincing.
He pursues a strategy of gifts and countergifts.
He is a great producer, but above all a great accumulator and redistributor of wealth.
He is polygamous, with many wives and children.
He receives help from those whom he has helped, particularly young men in search of a wife but wanting the pigs and other forms of wealth needed for a dowry.
He represents first and foremost his lineage, his village, and clan, as well as his entire tribe in certain circumstances.
His name and reputation are known far and wide.
He stands apart from ordinary men, and particularly from those young warriors with "bloodshot" eyes whose impetuous violence can be a nuisance in peacetime.
He intervenes in affairs relating to kinship between lineages and in political relations between clans, arbitrating disputes.
He bequeaths to his children wealth, a name, and partners in other tribes whom they may use in turn to aggrandize themselves within the network of ceremonial exchanges.
If he turns this reciprocity into exaction, he will gradually become a despot. Sooner or later his faction will abandon him, and he will fall. Or he may even be murdered.

is produced by nature. So the only thing that counts in differentiating men among themselves is their skill in hunting and their individual magic powers (what we call luck in our culture, but luck is not a Baruya concept). The Baruya are keenly aware of this distinction since they remark that "the pig is to women what the *kapul,* game, is to men; the pig is the women's *kapul.*"

According to the logic of this society, which ultimately rests on the principles of kinship (namely, the equivalence of women) and of men's dominance of women, pigs (which are the joint products of the labor of women and men, but in the production of which women play the leading role) are essentially kept within the sphere of subsistence. On the other hand, game, which is the product of an exclusively male activity, nearly always lies outside this sphere and serves as an object of ceremonial exchange.

At the same time, however, because women retain extensive control over the production and distribution of pigs, men perform a series of ritual gestures to mark the slaughter, dismembering, cutting up, and cooking of the animal.

Irrespective of the practices relating to the pig, game is ritually more important and is an additional social limitation on the development of farm production, which is the principal material condition of stockbreeding. For all these connected reasons it would have been difficult for a dynamic process of expansion of output and accumulation to have taken root in Baruya society; it is significant that the occasions of setting in motion such a process occurred in the production of salt, in order to exchange the latter for the white man's implements. Now salt, although used in the rituals, is an article that circulates essentially like a commodity, and it does so under the men's control. Salt and game are the principal means of trade and social exchange among the Baruya, and both their "production" and their circulation are exclusively controlled by men.

Just a few words more on the big men societies before concluding this chapter. In this discussion I have referred only to the Mendi, the Melpa, the Mae-Enga, the Kyaka, and other societies in the high valleys of the New Guinea interior. All these societies are interlinked within a vast network of competitive exchanges that periodically take place on ceremonial sites, in the midst of rejoicing and dancing, in what are known in New Guinea as pig festivals. These networks have distinct names, *tee* among the Enga, *moka* among the Melpa, *maku* among the Kyaka, and are interconnected.[21] Periodically, when the pig festival comes around to their tribe, hundreds of men mobilize their personal material resources and those of their kin, neighbors, and affines, and they set out in pursuit of renown, influence, and political

[21] See D. K. Feil, "Women and Men in the Enga Tee," *American Ethnologist* 5 (1978):263–79; and "Enga Women in the Tee Exchange," *Mankind* 11 (1978):220–30; Andrew Strathern, *The Rope of the Moka* (Cambridge: Cambridge University Press, 1971).

power, doing battle by means of gifts and countergifts of pigs, dead or alive, feathers, shells. The aim is to show oneself ever capable of giving back more than one has received, systematically seeking to cap one's rivals in the flow of gifts and countergifts.

But in these societies the exchange of material wealth is not confined to the sphere of ceremonial exchanges, to peaceful competition among big men, before the admiring eyes of hundreds of spectators, who contemplate the long rows of pigs tied to stakes while listening to the harangues of the big men as they proclaim their gifts and the names of their recipients. The reproduction of life and the production of relations of kinship are entirely dependent on the exchange of women for wealth and, in another sphere, all intertribal political relations imply "economic" exchanges, the circulation and redistribution of wealth. The very nature of social relations, the logic underpinning the workings of these societies, calls forth and stimulates the production and circulation of material wealth for the sake of their reproduction; they supply a wide range of circumstances and pretexts in which the differences among individuals and clans in the production and redistribution of wealth acquires social significance.

It is hardly surprising that the big man should be foremost among the great men in these societies, leaving far behind him the warrior or the expert in matters of ritual. He is ever present and often necessary (helping one of his kinsmen to assemble bride wealth in order to marry, or negotiating peace with a neighboring tribe and seeking a means to compensate its respective losses in men and goods), and redistributes more wealth than anyone else.

Let us now turn from the role and glory of the big man and look at the system of social relations that produces him, examining how the existence and development of the sphere of ceremonial exchanges affects the workings of relations of kinship and the institutions of male domination, particularly the male and female initiations. It is enlightening to observe that there are no true male initiations in these societies, although adult men do perform male cults in honor of female spirits, fertility goddesses, and so on. We shall be coming back to this matter. In other societies, such as the Chimbu, people speak of the rapid decline of male initiations or of their mere residual survival since the white man's arrival which put an end to warfare and gave fresh impetus to the ceremonial exchanges.[22]

Another aspect important to the functioning of these societies is that the principle of the direct exchange of women is in no case put into practice, although they are perfectly familiar with it. Among the Mendi, for ex-

[22] Paula Brown, "Marriage in Chimbu," in *Pigs, Pearshells and Women*, ed. Glasse and Meggitt, p. 95. See also P. Brown, "The Chimbu Political System," *Anthropological Forum* 2 (1967):36–52 and her portrait of a big man in "Kondom," *Journal of the Papua and New Guinea Society* 1 (2) (1967):61–71.

ample,[23] it is even explicitly condemned because it abolishes the movements of wealth created by marriage and makes it much harder to enter into relations of ceremonial exchange with their affines.[24]

Sometimes, as with the Melpa or the Chimbu, although there is no true acknowledgment of women debts between two clans, one does find a kind of vocabulary or language of "exchanges of women." But A. and M. Strathern suggest that it is the language of the *moka* exchanges, for in them an "exact reciprocity implies equality and peace. . . . By contrast, imbalance in reciprocity implies superiority and a measure of hostility."[25] One ends thus in the reverse situation of that found with the Baruya. Among the Melpa, the recipients of women are superior to the donors, because they give bride wealth and riches, part of which goes into ceremonial exchanges and consequently into the competition between clans and between tribes.

In these societies, therefore, the ceremonial exchanges and the requisite production and circulation of wealth exert permanent pressure on all social relations (and primarily on the first among them, namely, relations of kinship). Specialists in these societies have supplied specific examples of the way in which constant pressure affects relations of kinship.

A. Strathern shows that, among the Melpa, a girl's parents will endeavor to extract greater bride wealth from the suitor's parents. Where there is no direct exchange of women the equivalence between wealth and women may be measured according to several criteria of equal value. Among the Melpa the bride wealth is comprised as follows: shells, which are paid in order to "cut off the head of the girl," that is, separate her from her lineage; "pigs for the girl's vagina," that is, to authorize the husband to have sexual relations with her; and, finally, the fattest hog, which must in no case be omitted, for the girl's mother – "the mother's head pig." The girl's parents try to increase the first two items of this bride wealth, not out of any concern to obtain the exact economic (or any other) "value" of their daughter, but under pressure of the "general competitive context of *moka* exchange arrangements."[26] Such is the influence of these exchanges on relations of kinship that A. Strathern

---

[23] See Ryan, "Marriage in Mendi."

[24] The Baruya now recognize this point in their own way. In 1979, following the murder of Panandjuyac, the tribe held a series of big meetings. Some of the older men claimed that if people were going to start murdering their daughters left, right, and center, after they had taken such trouble bringing them up, they would have to start demanding bigger dowries. The discussions were stormy, and I was struck to hear young men accusing their elders of wanting to discard the traditional principle of the equivalence of women. One of them exclaimed, "If we do as you say, then only rich young men will be able to marry!"

[25] Andrew and Marilyn Strathern, "Marriage in Melpa," in *Pigs, Pearshells and Women*, ed. Glasse and Meggitt, pp. 157–8. See also M. Strathern, *Women in Between: Female Roles in a Male World* (London: Seminar Press, 1972), chap. 5.

[26] Andrew Strathern, "The Central and the Contingent: Bridewealth among the Melpa and the Wiru," in *The Meaning of Marriage Payments*, ed. J. Comaroff (New York: Academic Press, 1980), pp. 57–8.

states that "a marriage is fully established when the affines make *moka* with the breeding pigs a young couple have been endowed with."[27]

With the Tombema-Enga, Feil has shown that many of those who by their gifts enable a young man to gather up his bride wealth do so not in the name of any strict obligations of kinship, but because they hope, through his marriage, to expand their circle of *tee*-exchange partners. Among the Kyaka, Bulmer has demonstrated similar processes. Although matrimonial alliances open the door to a fresh series of exchanges, it is *maku* exchanges in return that ensure the stability of the marriage and, through it, that of the alliance. Generally speaking, the establishment of relations of exchange has a profound effect on the relative importance of the various categories of the kin to a given individual. The more distantly related one is, the more the relation of Maku exchange becomes the predominant factor in relations between kin, and it tends to devalue "genealogically calculated agnatic kinship outside the expanded family or lineage."[28]

Furthermore, these relations of exchange are not limited, as are relations of kinship. Although it is rare for an individual to feel genuinely concerned by the relations that his affines maintain with their affines and they with theirs, he is quickly concerned by the economic and political situation of his partners within the network of competitive exchange to which all belong. Whereas, among the Kyaka, the word *maku* is still strictly confined to competitive exchanges, among the Tombema-Enga social relations are now subordinated to the *tee* competitive exchanges as a general rule. All relations of debt of whatever kind between individuals and groups are "settled" or compensated for in the course of the *tee* ceremonies. These relations thus ultimately appear to be so many aspects of the *tee*. They take its form, and submit to its logic and its dynamic, in the sense that the ceremonial exchanges function as a kind of clearinghouse for all the debts incurred in the business of social relations. They serve as the occasion for the payment of bride wealth, of blood price for a murder, to compensate losses borne by one's affines or enemies in war, and so on. The actual substance of all these different debts, the material wealth of all the different lineages, is displayed and circulates in open view. The big men stand in the midst of this general, multifarious movement, which mainly follows the course of the *tee*. They are able to give more than others or to give in the place of others. They occupy the key positions in a system that little by little tends to take over the management of all debts and all material obligations of individuals and groups and ultimately, through the need to produce and maintain the flow of material wealth, to take over the management of social life in general.

There can be no doubt that the social importance of these exchanges and

[27] Ibid., p. 65.
[28] Bulmer, "Political Aspects of the Moka Ceremonial Exchange System . . . ," p. 10.

179

the role of the big men have grown with colonization. Now that war is prohibited, economic exchange alone remains as an outlet for competition. Furthermore, colonization has released a flood of once-scarce traditional wealth into the interior of New Guinea, for example, shells and feathers. It has introduced implements and techniques that have increased the productivity of agricultural labor and, consequently, facilitated the increase in the number of pigs bred for the exchanges. For the young people, wealth is daily becoming an ever more vital condition of marriage and access to adult status, whereas among the Baruya that condition is still the initiation ceremonies. Before going into this last point, namely, the absence of initiation in the big men societies, it is worth stressing how different the status of women in these societies is from that of Baruya women.

This difference cuts two ways. On the one hand, inasmuch as wealth in terms of pigs plays an essential role in society, and inasmuch as the exchange of pigs depends primarily on the labor of women, the female labor force in big men societies is a far more important social factor than among the Baruya. Men's exploitation of this labor force becomes broader and, paradoxically, it is the women who, by the work that they put into raising pigs, enable men to appropriate the labor and the person (sexual and other services) of other women.

On the other hand, the woman plays a different economic role in the sense that it is through her that the wealth of her bride wealth flows into the hands of her lineage and broadens the relations of ceremonial exchange. She is a necessary conduit for the circulation of wealth, and the stability of her marriage, its durability, and its success have a direct bearing on the economic circumstances of the lineage. Under these conditions, the woman would appear to enjoy a greater measure of "autonomy" than the Baruya woman, although she also appears to be more exploited. However, if she is the wife of a big man she is not alone in being exploited, for the landless young men or those whose parents are unable to pay their bride wealth work alongside her for their benefactor.

In big men societies, which were periodically rent by war, the question of land became particularly important when the population was more numerous and production more intensive. Now, the intensification of competitive exchanges directly led to an expansion of output and of labor productivity, and with it the risk of land disputes. War and ceremonial exchange were therefore both mutually supportive and mutually exclusive, because war interrupted the process of exchange, wrought havoc with pig breeding, demanded pigs to compensate for the war dead, and thus made them unavailable for exchange, and so on. In his latest book on the Mae-Enga, Meggitt even goes so far as to state that "The basic preoccupation of the Mae is with the possession and defense of clan land. Participation in the Tee, as in other prestations, is but a means to this end."[29] This defense may be an exception connected with the scarcity of land among the populous Enga tribes, but this exception is already sufficient to overturn the situation afresh, and tends to subordinate the exchanges of ceremonial goods themselves to a strategy of land redistribution among the tribes and clans.

It now remains for us to analyze the second salient feature of the big men societies of the New Guinea interior, namely, the absence of male and female initiations and the presence of male cults of the spirits of fertility, wealth, and success in exchanges. Two particularly interesting examples are offered by the cults of a female spirit and of a male spirit among the Melpa and the Gawigl, which are known to us through the work of Vicedom and Tischner (1943–8),[30] Strauss and Tischner (1962),[31] and more lately A. Strathern (1970, 1979).[32]

The following is a brief sketch of the founding myth of the cult of the female spirit as presented by Strathern [paraphrased here], based on his own and Vicedom's material:

There once lived in the forest two unmarried brothers, who saw parrots come regularly to eat fruit from a tree. The younger told his brother to shoot one down. The older brother did so, but the bird was injured and flew off. The man took a morsel of meat with him and followed it, eventually finding a beautiful girl whose arm was bandaged. He offered her the meat. She took it, thanked him, and went into a house. [In fact she was the parrot he had injured.] He then saw her run out of her house and go to rub her sex against the trunk of a banana tree. When she returned, he took a fragment of shell and stuck it into the trunk. When she rubbed herself again, she cut herself and "made a vagina." Later, her sisters came and all of them, except the youngest, entered the house, became "hot," and, after a while, went to rub themselves against the banana tree and cut their sexes. The youngest of the sisters remained outside the house, then left the spot. The man made skirts for the girls, gave them meat, and brought them to his home, where he gave three of them in marriage to his brother and took four for himself.

One day, he quarreled with the woman he had injured when she was a parrot, and she went off to weep in her garden. A storm broke and the youngest sister appeared to her; she gave her a bundle of dance decorations and some cordyline branches to give to her husband, and told her to tell her husband to open the bundle behind his men's house [in this society, the men sleep in separate houses from the women]. The husband took the bundle, did as she had told him, and, when night fell, he heard spirits dancing around his house. Next morning, he found stones painted different

[29] M. J. Meggitt, *Blood Is Their Argument* (Palo Alto, Calif.: Mayfield Publishing Company, 1977), p. 9.

[30] G. F. Vicedom and H. Tischner, *Die Mbowamb* (Hamburg: Friederichesen–De Gruyter, 1943–8), 3 vols.

[31] H. Strauss and H. Tischner, *Die Mi-Kultur der Hagenberg-Stämme* (Hamburg: De Gruyter, 1962).

[32] Andrew Strathern, "The Female and Male Spirit Cults in Mount Hagen," *Man* 5 (4) (December 1970):572–85; "Men's House, Women's House: The Efficacy of Opposition, Reversal and Pairing in the Melpa *Amb Kor* Cult," *Journal of Polynesian Society* 88 (1) (1979):37–51.

181

colors, and he knew that the woman-spirit had come to him in the form of these stones. He started a cult to her, to her who had not become a human woman like her sisters, and since that time, the men say that when they sacrifice pigs to this spirit, they do not share the pork with their wives.

This myth is also to be found among the Huli who live near the Mendi, among the Wiru, and so on.

It is worth comparing this myth with that of the Baruya in which the woman plants a bat bone into a banana tree trunk, the man impales his sex on it, and, maddened with pain, grasps a bamboo knife and slits the woman's sex.

The cult of the Virgin Woman, goddess of fertility, seems to spread from the south to the north, from the Ialibu, neighbors of the Mendi, to the Melpa, and still farther to the Kyaka and the Maring.[33] The Melpa fetch experts in these rituals from the south, and the cult is organized by one or two big men who pay them, regarding this payment as a kind of bride wealth paid to the woman-spirit, whom the experts bring as wife to all men. The rituals are repeated after an interval of some months and last several weeks. They culminate in the construction of a men's and a women's house into which enter the adult males wishing to be initiated. Some are dressed in male, others in female, symbols. They go to sleep beneath the same roof, eat beneath the same roof, but in separate areas. There is no exchange of food between the two halves. They then bury the uterus of a sow in an oven dug out of the ground in order to satisfy the earth and ensure the fertility of the pigs and an abundant harvest. Pigs are sacrificed to the ancestors, and the sons of the big men are shown the sacred stones used in the sacrifice. The men consume sacred food prepared by the experts in order to protect them against the women's menstrual blood. Everything ends in dancing performed by the officiants of the cult, dressed as men and women, and by a great sharing of pig meat, without compensation, to the hundreds of people who come from neighboring clans and other tribes to celebrate the end of the cult in an atmosphere of general rejoicing.

As for the cult of the male spirit, it is based on a myth that tells of how a childless couple one day found a baby, a boy, in a river. During the night, the child, who was a spirit, tore off the head of the sleeping woman and ran away with it. The next day the husband set out with his brother in pursuit of the spirit. They bottled it up in a grotto where it had taken refuge, seized it, and the husband took back his wife's head. The spirit promised to teach him the magic formulas needed to make women beautiful and fertile, harvests abundant, and wealth plentiful. With the head and the magic formulas the hus-

---

[33] R. M. Glasse, "The Huli of the Southern Highlands," in *Gods, Ghosts and Men in Melanesia*, ed. Lawrence and M. J. Meggitt (Oxford: Oxford University Press, 1965); R. Bulmer, "The Kyaka of the Western Highlands," ibid.

band brought his wife back to life, and the spirit became a stone that is now the object of a cult celebrated by the men, from which women are excluded.

Among the rituals of this cult is the erection of a gigantic stake, the *porembil,* whose significance is phallic. The masters of the ritual bury "cold" plants to make the earth fertile, and distribute pigs' livers to the sons of the men celebrating the cult. The men eat in silence, and they must all finish eating together, for to do otherwise would be a sign of death. The experts then throw magic bundles across the fire to ensure the success of the *moka* exchanges. The cult ends with gifts of pig meat to the crowd, and the big man who "financed" the celebration of the cult then dances excitedly in front of everyone, shouting out, "I have had the pigs cooked, I am dancing, I am celebrating the cult to the finish."

Let us now compare this cult with the Baruya male initiations. Strathern finds three themes or fundamental objectives in these ritual practices. They are identical with those of the male initiations of the Baruya or of the different Eastern Highlands tribes such as the Awa, the Bena-Bena, the Gahuku-Gama, and so on. Their first objective is to overcome the duality of the world of women, as givers of life and death, to receive the power of a female spirit, or more precisely to seize hold of it in order to control it. This spirit is a virgin and hence does not present the dangers of menstrual blood and the pollutions of the sexual reproduction of life. The second objective is to confirm men's superiority over women in the process of procreating children, and above all in the ability to produce sons; to assert the superiority of the male over the female in the cosmic forces that make fertile the earth, domestic animals, and so forth. Last, its purpose is to establish and deepen the solidarity among men, but only among those who celebrate the cult, that is, the men belonging to one or two clans, apparently never those of the tribe as a whole.

These three objectives are common to the initiations of the Baruya, the Awa, Fore,[34] Gimi, and to the secret cults of the Melpa, Gawigl, and others, with an understanding of these objectives and of the founding myths, which also contain comparable though frequently inverted patterns, let us now compare the social aspects of these ritual practices.

Among the Baruya, the initiations are for male children and adolescents. The cult is for adults who are fathers of several children. The initiations are obligatory for all the youths in the tribe. The cults are organized by volun-

---

[34] Philip Newman, "Religious Belief and Ritual in a New Guinea Society," in "New Guinea: The Central Highlands," ed. J. B. Watson, *American Anthropologist* 66, special issue (1964):257–72; P. Newman and D. Boyd, "The Making of Men: Ritual and Meaning in Awa Male Initiations," in *Rituals of Manhood: Male Initiation in Papua New Guinea,* ed. Gilbert Herdt (Berkeley: University of California Press, 1982); L. L. Langness, "Ritual, Power and Male Dominance," *Ethos* 2 (3) (1974):184–232; R. M. Glasse, "Marriage in South Fore," in *Pigs, Pearshells and Women,* ed. Glasse and Meggitt, pp. 16–37.

teers belonging to one or two clans. They are partly financed by a big man. The costs of the Baruya initiations are borne above all by the initiates' families and by the tribe. The masters of the Baruya rituals are native Baruya. Their function is hereditary and carries no material remuneration. The masters of the cults are outsiders; their function is ascribed, although it can be "purchased." They are paid in shells, feathers, and so on, which are also used as dowries and gifts in ceremonial exchanges. The Baruya initiations are directed against enemies and women. The cults are aimed at women and indirectly at enemies. The paramount aim of the initiations is to enable the men to secure their control over life and strength. The aim of the cults is the control over life as a source of wealth to enable a man to hold his position in the intertribal network of *moka* exchanges. The initiations entail physical trials and take place in an atmosphere of collective obedience to the masters of the initiate rituals, and in the midst of a crowd of relatives and onlookers. The cults entail no great physical tests, other than the obligation to keep silent and to dance; they take place in an atmosphere of collective obedience (including the big men) to the masters of the rituals. Last, the initiations are celebrated with gifts of game presented by adult men to the young initiates, and with the handing out of food to the onlookers, without any competition, in an atmosphere of giving, but without any countergiving; the cults, on the other hand, are celebrated by means of sacrifices to the ancestors and the sharing of pig meat without incurring any debts or obligations. The cults are supposed to multiply the quantity of wealth destined to circulate in the competitive exchanges, yet rest upon a principle that contradicts the logic of these exchanges, namely, the free gift, or gift without countergift. Furthermore, the big man does not occupy the front rank in this context, yielding to the master of the rituals (the *kwaimatnie*-man, among the Baruya), while continuing to amass still greater prestige and influence through his greater contribution to the material expense of organizing the cult.

Might we then hypothesize that the development of competitive exchange and of exchange-oriented production may have led first to the disappearance of relations of kinship based on the direct exchange of sisters, where these existed, and subsequently to the disappearance of the collective male and female initiations? By gradually replacing the role of war in intergroup competition, these exchanges may have done away with the link that formerly existed between war and the male initiations. Could it be that the people's growing economic interdependence has diminished the need for that immense apparatus of ideological control, the initiation? For, after all, in order to instill the attitudes and principles of male domination into young Mendi, Enga, Melpa, and Kyaka boys, it is now enough merely to separate them physically from their mothers and take them to live in their men's house without subjecting them to initiation rites!

More profoundly though, if we do assume that systems of kinship based on the direct exchange of women may formerly, in New Guinea or else-where, have been more important than today, that the principle of the equivalence of women used to exercise greater influence, or represented a more widespread standard than today in the organization of marriage alliances, then why, and in what circumstances, did the principle of the equivalence of gift and countergift lose its power? Under what circumstances have its terms (a life for a life, a woman for a woman, a death for a death, a pig for a pig) become converted into varied forms of wealth and, in the last analysis, into varied forms and quantities of human labor (male and/or female, collective and/or individual)? The hypothesis according to which these systems may once have been more important or more widespread than today rests on our knowledge, drawn from archaeological and ethnobotanical findings, that the arrival of the sweet potato, brought from America by Portuguese and Spanish sailors four hundred years ago, probably wrought far-reaching changes in the New Guinea economy. The sweet potato was added to the traditional tuber of Asia and Oceania, the taro, and, thanks to its adaptability to high altitude climates, permitted the occupation of high valleys and previously uninhab-ited zones. Furthermore, sweet potato yields per acre are superior to those of the taro.

The question, if meaningful, concerns far more than the Baruya, the Melpa, New Guinea, or even Oceania. It is in fact the question that Claude Lévi-Strauss asks at the end of *Elementary Structures of Kinship* (1949),[35] in which he discusses systems in which the choice of spouse is not directly determined by the structure of the system but depends on criteria external to kinship, such as wealth or the status of the future spouses (one might marry the daughter of a chief or of a rich cattle-owner, and so on). He calls these systems of kinship complex-structured systems. One encounters these complex-systems in New Guinea too, based not on the principle of "generalized" exchange, which imparts to the exchange of women for bride wealth a general thrust and direction, but on the principle of "general" exchange, without any particular preference or direction, that is, women for exchangeable wealth.

In the last analysis, the big men are a particular variety of great men, arising wherever competitive exchanges have diminished the relative impor-tance of war and warriors; wherever boys and girls learn to take their place in society without recourse to large- or small-scale initiate machinery; wher-ever exchangeable material wealth can be exchanged for anything, and above all for women. But, as between the Baruya and the Enga or Melpa, I see many intermediate societies, many transitional forms that suggest that, de-spite the diversity of languages and within this cultural diversity, systems and laws of transformation of the social structures encountered in New Guinea

---

[35] Reprinted (Boston: Beacon Press, 1969).

may exist. (Incidentally, those of my colleagues who have specialized in the hunter-gatherer societies of the Amazon, the Achuar, or Jivaros of Ecuador, for example, find much in common between the Baruya great men and their Amazon warriors).

Take the Maring, who live in the valleys of the Bismarck Range of mountains, on the fringes of the Melpa and Karam groups. They have been closely studied by Roy Rappaport,[36] A. Vayda, and Cherry Lowman-Vayda.[37] Lowman-Vayda, in a fine, extended article, shows that in the Maring society the big men are first of all great warriors and great men endowed with supernatural powers that enable them to communicate with the ancestors. A clan usually has only one of these ancestor-spirit-men. It is he who organizes the sacrifices to the ancestors and thus partly controls the social use of pigs. Because he is the only person capable of communicating with the ancestors, he represents the interests of all the members of his clan. But his function is not automatically handed down to a successor. Several members of his clan gather before the remainder of the men in the clan and start to smoke green tobacco and chew leaves. The first to choke on the smoke is designated thereby as the successor to the "man-of-the-ancestors' spirits." Alongside him, each clan has a "man-who-possesses-the-magic-of-war." He is the guardian of a pair of sacred stones and of the rituals that enhance the warriors' strength and enable them to bewitch enemy warriors. These stones are kept in a special house, and the fight-medicine-man is hedged about by a great many taboos. He is assisted by a number of men possessing war magic, and by shamans who are not empowered to give orders to the other members of the clan. The fight-medicine-man does not fight in the front rank. As with the Baruya, the Maring do have great men that are great by virtue of their functions and their individual ability to perform those functions. The relationship between what is ascribed and/or achieved with the Maring is simpler than with the Baruya because functions are inherited within the clan and redistributed among a certain number of candidates belonging to that clan by means of a selection process. There are exchanges of pigs, but in the form of meat, not of animals on the hoof. In other words, although people speak of big men in this context, we are in fact dealing with great men: the invincible warrior, the ancestor-man, the man in possession of fight magic, not with the big man of the Enga or the Kyaka, the manipulator of men and wealth. Another point to note is that the Maring have two coexisting systems of kinship, one based on the direct exchange of women, the other based on the exchange of bride wealth for a woman. Furthermore, they used to be able to offer a live woman in compensation for an enemy warrior killed.

[36] R. A. Rappaport, *Pigs for the Ancestors* (New Haven, Conn.: Yale University Press, 1968); "Maring Marriage," in *Pigs, Pearshells, and Women*, ed. Glasse and Meggitt, pp. 117–37.
[37] C. Lowman-Vayda, "Maring Big Men."

Great men societies, big men societies

Among the Manga in the same region, studied by Cook,[38] we find the Maring's two kinship systems, but the former is not the occasion of an exchange of wealth, whereas the latter is accompanied by bride wealth which is paid after the birth of two children and on the occasion of a pig festival. Here again, the great men are the great warrior and other figures, but one finds no "true" big men. The same duality is to be found among the Telefolmin, studied by Ruth Craig, where the big men are very different from those of the Highlands.[39]

In the vast group of societies in the eastern provinces of the Highlands, on the fringes of which the Baruya and the Enga live, one often finds initiation systems close to those of the Baruya – among the Awa, the Tairora particularly, but also among the Bena-Bena, the Gahuku-Gama, and so forth. In almost all cases, however, they practice not the direct exchange of women but the exchange of bride wealth, and sometimes, as with the Bena-Bena, live pigs, not pig meat, which puts heavier strains on each family's livestock. Yet, there again, the foremost of the great men on the public scene is the great warrior, and alongside him the masters of the rituals, of whom very little is said in the specialist literature. But there is scarcely any sign of "true" big men.[40]

Does not this presentation contradict what I have been saying? Here we have societies with collective male initiations which, even if they only last a few months and imply no radical separation of boys from girls, are similar to the Baruya society. But these societies like the big men societies also practice marriage by bride wealth and competitive exchanges of pigs; yet they do not seem to have any true big men capable of dominating the others by their generosity.

In fact there is no contradiction to my hypothesis, for I am saying that one finds big men societies not where there is no (or no longer any) direct exchange of women, but where *exchanges of whatever type,* of women, pigs, enemies slain in battle, *have ceased to be based on the principle of the equivalence of whatever is being exchanged.*

Kenneth Read, the great pioneering student of the societies in the eastern provinces of the New Guinea Highlands, already took this view more than twenty years ago, in a stimulating article on "leadership and consensus" among the Gahuku-Gama.[41] He pointed out that, for the Gahuku-Gama, the fundamental principle is the equivalence of individuals, or at least among

---

[38] E. A. Cook, "Marriage among the Manga," in *Pigs, Pearshells, and Women,* ed. Glasse and Meggitt, pp. 96–116.

[39] Ruth Craig, "Marriage among the Telefolmin," in ibid., pp. 176–97.

[40] L. L. Langness, "Marriage in Bena-Bena," in ibid., pp. 38–55; "Sexual Antagonism in the New Guinea Highlands: A Bena-Bena Example," *Oceania* 37 (1) (1967):161–79.

[41] K. E. Read, "Leadership and Consensus in a New Guinea Society," *American Anthropologist* 61 (3) (1959):425–36; "Nama Cult of the Central Highlands," *Oceania* 23 (1952):1–25.

men on the one hand and women on the other (for the males dominate, and the sexes are nonequivalent). He further stressed that this society seeks to promote the "strongest" men, the prime arena for the expression of strength being war, the next most important being the production and redistribution of wealth in the "pig festivals." But no big man emerges in these exchange ceremonies. Why? Because "the major cycle of festivals is governed by rules which are expressly designed to permit [the reproduction of] parity. The group holding the festival, for example, should not kill and distribute pigs which exceed their guests' ability to repay."[42] There is the answer. To be sure, relations of kinship are based on the exchange of goods for women, and this system heavily influences an individual's chances of becoming a great man, for "certain adult prerogatives . . . are withheld from him until he has repaid the debts accumulated on his behalf . . . at his initiation and his marriage."[43] But the system of exchanges and the key social logic are based on the principle of the equivalence of exchanges and of the promotion of fundamentally equivalent adult men, even if it does leave room for the "strongest" to outclass the others to the benefit of all, whether in war or in production.

In other words, when all is said and done, beneath the chaff of words, and despite the unwarranted use of the term *big man* to designate any great man with power in Melanesia, the big man as described by Marshall Sahlins is probably the exception in this part of the world.

Ultimately, one wonders what it is that has led to the hereditary, definitive association, in certain societies, of the division of functions and status with distinct social groups (as among the Baruya), and why this hereditary division has come to serve as a point of departure or pretext under which certain groups "deserve" to appropriate a portion of other people's labor and resources embodied in their functions in the name of the general interest. This question brings us to the possible dissolution of forms of common ownership of resources, and to the birth of castes and classes, but it would take us way beyond the scope of this book.

---

[42] Read, "Leadership and Consensus," p. 430.
[43] Ibid., p. 428.

1. The village of Wiaveu, where the author lived. Situated on a terrace above the river, it is surrounded by large gardens of sweet potatoes and protected from pigs, both wild and domestic, by high fencing. The houses are concealed in thickets of bamboo and areca trees. *(Photograph by J.-L. Lory.)*

2. A woman digging up earth with a digging stick in order to plant taro seedlings. The soil has been completely plowed by pigs. In the background is a banana tree, and behind it are the mountainous slopes covered with primary and secondary forest. The woman carries her newborn baby in a net bag held around her head by a headband. *(Photograph by P. Lemonnier.)*

3. Clearing the forest. Inamwe, the great shaman, uses a stone pickax to chop down a tree that he had previously decorated with magic leaves. He works from a scaffolding, which allows him to attack the trunk well above the stump. Note that his body posture is very different from that of our woodcutters. *(Photograph by M. Godelier.)*

4. Group of women returning from the gardens. They are dressed in capes of bark. The woman *on the right*, who has a heavy load on her back, carries her baby in a net bag on her stomach. *(Photograph by J.-P. Lory.)*

5. Prayer to the Sun, part of a ceremony performed by
the men in honor of one of them who has just had a child.
The men whistle and send their breath up toward the Sun,
while they simultaneously snap their fingers. Note the two
eagle feathers, mark of the shamans, as well as the *ypmoulie,* the bandeau headbands of red, the color of the
Sun. *(Photograph by M. Godelier.)*

6. A little boy learning to use a bow and arrow. Note that
he wears feminine clothing because he is not yet an initiate. *(Photograph by M. Godelier.)*

7. Construction of the *tsimia* (large ceremonial house). The women carry bundles of straw to thatch the roof and throw them toward the men, who avoid looking at the women. *(Photograph by I. Dunlop.)*

8. Part of the first-stage initiation ceremony. In the night, mothers accompany their little sons as far as the doorway of the men's house. *(Photograph by P. Lemonnier.)*

9. Passage from the feminine world to the masculine world. A man carries on his back a young initiate who has just left his mother, and brings him running toward the world of men through a double row of warriors who lash them with branches. *(Photograph by J.-L. Lory.)*

10. The nose piercing of young boys, who are firmly yet gently held by their "sponsors." The master of the rituals pierces the septum with a bone needle. *(Photograph by J.-L. Lory.)*

11. Beak of the hornbill, symbol of the penis. *(Photograph by M. Godelier.)*

12. The insignia of the *tchou-wanie:* the beak of the hornbill, symbol of the penis; a ring of rattan completed by two sharpened pig's tusks, symbol of the vagina. *(Photograph by M. Godelier.)*

13. Arrival of the master of the first-stage rituals and his cousins. The first and the last men carry a bark cloak filled with the magic food. The second holds a baton decorated with cowries upon which are attached the pieces of wood for the nose piercing. The last one solemnly holds up the *kwaimatnie. (Photograph by P. Lemonnier.)*

14. Ymbainac, who has just had her first period, is shut away in a hut constructed at the bottom of the village in a space reserved for women, prohibited to men. *(Photograph by M. Godelier.)*

15. Initiation of a young pubescent girl. They rub her breasts and belly with nettles. Her "sponsor" holds her and gives her a small piece of wood to bite on so that she will not cry out in pain. *(Photograph by J.-L. Lory.)*

16. During the initiation ceremony of the first stage, warriors threaten to shoot their arrows into the thighs of the young initiates. One of them holds a leaf in his mouth onto which he has bled. The narrow shield, decorated with the painting of warriors, is the shield of the *aoulatta* or great warriors, and only protects part of the body. *(Photograph by P. Lemonnier.)*

17. Standing before Ypmeie, grand master of the third-stage ceremonies, two masters of first-stage ceremonies brandish a club painted in war colors to evoke the legendary exploits of ancestors. *(Photograph by M. Godelier.)*

18. Davaine, the greatest cassowary hunter in the valley of Wonenara. He wears through his nose a wild pig's tusk and two quills from cassowary feathers. At the crest of his helmet is a white parrot feather, the mark of initiates of the fourth stage, and of married men. *(Photograph by I. Dunlop.)*

19. *Koulakita,* ceremony for the initiation of shamans. *On the right,* Tchouonoondaye, master of rituals of the first stage, advances hunched, carrying on his back the feathers of the future shamans. *On the left,* the shaman master of the ceremony seizes hold of a feather and leaps about in the fire, looking in the darkness for a future shaman upon whose head to attach the feather. *(Photograph by J.-L. Lory.)*

20. At daybreak, in the silence of the valley, and hidden from all view, the shamans leave for the forest; eagle feathers on the tops of their crowns and whips in their hands are for driving away evil spirits. *(Photograph by J.-L. Lory.)*

21. Trading salt with another tribe. On the left a Youndouye feels the weight of the a bar of salt that he has just been given by a Baruya *tsaimaye* (salt maker). The two tribes, who do not speak the same language, are associated by a pact of friendship and trade. *(Photograph by M. Godelier.)*

22. A *tsaimaye* pours pure water into gourds filled with the ashes of salt cane. As it passes through, the water will pick up the saline elements, which will then be extracted by evaporation. *(Photograph by M. Godelier.)*

23. Discovery of the Baruya in 1951 by a column of soldiers and porters, led by Jim Sinclair. *(Photograph by J. Sinclair.)*

24. Elections for the National Assembly in 1968. An Australian officer supervises voting by members of the Youndouye; they have never seen or heard the candidates. *(Photograph by M. Godelier.)*

PART THREE

Recent transformations of Baruya society

9

The colonial order and independence

As the reader is already aware, Baruya society as it existed before 1960, before the arrival of white authority, no longer exists. In 1967 I encountered two missionaries working with the Watchake, another Anga group separated from the Baruya by the highest peaks of the Kratke Range and by vast, almost impassable forests. They pointed to one of the peaks and pronounced the words that never fail to quicken the pulse of an anthropologist: "Why don't you go over there and see the Baruya. They were discovered only recently and they still dress as before. They can't have changed too much."

Indeed, my first contact with the Baruya was a shock. Hundreds of men, decked out in feathers, armed with bows, arrows, and shields, were devoting a great deal of their time to archery practice. And here it was an hour or two from the government outpost where the officer in charge of the region lived with a few soldiers and policemen. Near the outpost the shields disappeared, bows and arrows were held discreetly in the hand or hidden in the tall grass. But, on the whole, the society seemed to be holding up, almost intact. However, as I was to discover later, whole sections of the edifice had already disappeared, and had started along the slow road into oblivion, in the memory of adults. Such customs as displaying the dead on platforms, wrapped in cloaks of tree bark, or assembling and transporting the bones of the deceased a year or so after death for a second funeral ceremony had been forbidden by the Australian authorities for reasons of public hygiene and were never to be resumed. The main male initiation rites had been thoroughly reorganized to conceal their essence from the white men, missionaries and government officials who visited the valleys from time to time or lived there. More deeply, a whole series of rituals relating to war had been amputated, whereas others had been reinterpreted to fit in with the altered circumstances. It took the trust of the Baruya and several years' mental effort to reconstruct their vanished customs and to track down, where possible, the original meaning of what remained.

191

Recent transformations of Baruya society

The Baruya were no longer what they had been even seven years earlier, namely, a sovereign tribe ruling over a territory that its ancestors had conquered and enlarged over the centuries at the expense of indigenous groups. Until the end of the nineteenth century the Baruya had lived in the Marawaka Valley, where their ancestors had taken refuge. At the beginning of the twentieth century they began to push into the neighboring Wonenara Valley, where they gradually came to occupy half the territory. The land was fertile, the forests rich in game, and the valley's few inhabitants retreated before the Baruya. When Jim Sinclair arrived in the valley in 1951, the Baruya, as I have said, suggested that he help them settle their score with their enemies the Yuwarrounatche, who were still holding out in their two fortified villages. The Baruya had at first considered killing the white man and his soldiers, but they thought better of it after he offered to demonstrate the powers of his weapons. He asked them to line up a row of thick shields and selected several sturdy Baruya warriors to shoot arrows at these targets. He inspected the impacts and praised those warriors who had succeeded in piercing a shield right through. Then he lined up his soldiers and ordered them to aim at the middle of the shields, which splintered apart under the impact of the rifle bullets. He then asked the Baruya warriors to examine the size of the holes in the wooden shields, and it seems that the warriors were convinced of the superiority of the white man's weapons and their magic. The next day, when Jim Sinclair ordered his soldiers to present arms before the Australian flag raised before his tent, a Baruya, Bwarimac, who was later to be named village chief, fell into a trance at the site of the gleaming bayonets. He had been possessed by the "spirit of the white man," as he was to explain to me later. Jim Sinclair, who recorded the incident in his logbook, never learned of the attempts to capture his powers or to kill him. In any case, the first white man spent less than a week with the Baruya; he was only passing through.

But it would be wrong to suppose that Sinclair's coming marked the beginning of the white man's influence on the Baruya. As we have seen, the white man and the colonial domination that they brought with them were preceded by their tools, which had already come into the hands of the Baruya. The introduction of these tools had very different consequences for the men and for the women of the tribe.

To obtain steel tools, the Baruya set about producing more salt, which led them to enlarge the area planted with salt cane and to solicit more intensively the services of the salt makers. With the help of steel tools the men were able to clear greater areas of forest and to produce more tubers for the same amount of labor as before. There was more to eat and the number of pigs increased. For the women, on the other hand, forbidden by the traditional division of labor to use hatchets and machetes and lacking any new productive force to replace their traditional tools, the increase in agricultural pro-

192

duction and pig raising meant a greater expenditure of labor. The traditional distance separating the roles and the productivity of the men and women in the division of labor grew wider.

Moreover, the superiority of steel tools[1] greatly reduced the importance of cooperation in the various phases of the labor process, such as clearing the virgin forest, cutting tree trunks into stakes and planks, and the like. Individual forms of male labor gained in relative importance, thus diminishing the functions of mutual economic and material assistance as well as the relations among kin and neighbors which had formerly played a role in production. For production could now be organized to a greater extent within the relatively narrow framework of the family, monogamous or polygamous. The material complementarity of husband and wife (or wives) thus came to be a closer, more everyday affair. Jim Sinclair noticed that almost all the men were carrying steel tools, although stone adzes were still to be seen here and there.

Therefore even before the arrival of the white man, when the Baruya replaced their stone tools with tools of steel, they had already started to become economically and materially dependent. The steel tools were more productive, but it was not the Baruya who made them, and for a long time they had no idea that these tools were made by "white men." Nor did they know that the increasing influence of the white man and his wealth in New Guinea was partly responsible for a series of historical events that shook Baruya society between 1930 and 1940.

For indeed in that period the territory of the Baruya in the Marawaka Valley was brutally invaded by two enemy tribes from Menyamya, the Tapatche and the Yopenie, who launched simultaneous attacks on every Baruya village in the Marawaka Valley. The terrified inhabitants sought refuge with neighboring tribes or with Baruya families occupying part of the Wonenara Valley, who had created a sort of bridgehead there and had been slowly increasing in size since the beginning of the century.

The local tribes banded together to form a united front (including part of the Andje tribe, hereditary enemies of the Baruya) against the invaders who, although they belonged to the Anga culture, "spoke another language," as the Baruya say today. After a year of continual hit-and-run attacks, the invaders returned to their own territory. It is probable that the invasion of the Tapatche and the Yopenie was provoked by the expansionist pressure exerted by tribes that had experienced a phase of economic and demographic growth after entering into contact with the Europeans. Conclusive evidence is lack-

[1] Maurice Godelier, in collaboration with José Garanger, "Outils de pierre, outils d'acier chez les Baruya de Nouvelle-Guinée," *L'Homme* 13 (3) (1973):187–220; Beatrice Blackwood, *The Technology of a Modern Stone Age People in New Guinea*, Pitt Rivers Museum, University of Oxford, 1950. Richard Salisbury, *From Stone to Steel. Economic Consequences of Technological Change in New Guinea* (Melbourne: Melbourne University Press, 1962). William Townsend, "Stone and Steel Tools in a New Guinea Society," *Ethnology* 8 (2) (1969):169–205.

ing, but it seems as though the invasion, although part of a centuries-old movement of expansion by the Anga groups of the Menyamya region, was the consequence of the growth of trade and contact with the Europeans.

The consequences for the Baruya were significant, for after the departure of their enemies and the reconquest of their territory many of those that had sought temporary refuge with the Baruya pioneers in the Wonenara Valley decided to remain.

This new distribution of the Baruya population somewhat relieved the pressure on scarce land in the traditional Baruya territory in the Marawaka Valley. But the price was increased pressure on the groups of the Wonenara Valley and especially on the Yuwarrounatche, who had already yielded part of their territory to the Baruya pioneers. It was to "finish off" the Yuwar-rounatche, as they put it, that the Baruya sought to enlist the aid of Jim Sinclair and his troops after the latter arrived on their territory one morning in 1951, led there by Watchake guides who were well acquainted with the "Batia," makers of salt, whom the Australian wished to discover.

During all the years of indirect, oblique influence of the white world on the Baruya, they remained a sovereign tribe, freely reorganizing their way of life in response to the events and changes that overcame them. But the changes took on an altogether different aspect with the pacification of the Eastern Highlands in 1960 and the forced submission of the Baruya to the policies of the Australian colonial administration. The region was declared a "limited access zone," which meant that whites and other outsiders were not allowed to reside or move about more than a few miles from the outpost. This arrangement lasted until 1965. In the meantime missionaries of various Protestant denominations had set themselves up in the authorized zone. In 1967 I, an anthropologist, arrived; on my first trip I spent nearly three years in Wiaveu, the Baruya village farthest from the government outpost and the other whites. At the time there were no roads and the only link with the outside world was by light plane or helicopter. In 1979 volunteers from the Baruya and neighboring tribes completed a path passable only in the dry season, extremely dangerous, crossing the mountains at nearly 3,000 meters, and flanked by dizzying drops. The same year the Baruya – as did their traditional enemies the Yuwarrounatche – bought their first vehicle, a small Toyota truck, in order to transport their coffee and sell it at a better price in the city, from which they brought back goods purchased at lower prices, including a particularly desired commodity, beer. For New Guinea had gained its independence in 1975, and the free sale of beer, once limited to whites and Chinese, was authorized for all.

Let us return to the Baruya under colonial rule. The period was brief, as it lasted only from 1960 to 1975. It was long enough however to produce irreversible changes in Baruya society, and these transformations gathered momentum after independence. We shall briefly survey these changes, even

194

though, having observed them for several years, I have abundant material on the subject. But it would take almost another book to present and analyze this material in detail.

To colonize is first of all to pacify, and to pacify is to use force to prevent the recourse to force in settling conflicts within a tribe or among tribes. Henceforth, conflicts and other disputes were to be brought to the attention of government representatives, the commanding officer of the outpost, and he was to judge them according to the law, a law built around the principles and objectives of a different society: Australia, member of the Commonwealth, whose legal system was largely inspired by that of Her Majesty the Queen of England.

The repression that accompanies all pacification was confined, for the Baruya, to the burning of one of their villages, which had taken up arms to avenge the suicide of one of their women married in another village. The guilty parties were arrested and thrown in prison. But the Baruya, like the other tribes of the region, could not fail to take the meaning of the repression visited upon their friends and neighbors the Youndouye, in the course of which three members of the latter tribe died by gunfire, including a woman shot down in a garden by a sergeant. The Youndouye had killed one of their enemies who, appointed "village chief" by the white officer, had gone to the outpost to learn what his new functions were to be. Just a few months before the Youndouye had been at war with the man's tribe, and they had six dead to avenge. They killed the man and threw his corpse to the dogs and the pigs. The officer felt compelled to "make an example of them" and undertook a punitive expedition which resulted in three dead and a long train of prisoners. One of the prisoners, a great shaman, thought that he could change himself into a bird and fly away. He threw himself off a high rock and fractured his pelvis; he is still alive today, broken in two and twisted, and he moves about on a pair of crutches.

It is easy to guess the consequences of the new social order. The Baruya had henceforth lost their political sovereignty, one of whose attributes is the right to use force to settle problems within the tribe or outside it. With warfare forbidden, the Baruya men automatically lost one of the foundations of male domination, the monopoly of armed violence. In a sense "pacification," the intervention of a white authority that settled their disputes in their name but instead of them (based on laws and customs external to the tribal context), made all Baruya, regardless of sex, minors in their own eyes. The men were the ones who lost the most because they now found themselves "like women," deprived of the right to use violence. In this respect the distance between the sexes has been reduced, but by force.

Without war, the old Baruya still say, life has lost much of its pleasure. Above all, the social mechanisms, the ideas and symbols that served to make good (in some cases great) warriors of boys were now without purpose,

195

anachronistic, useless. The heroes now are the veterans. In the evenings in the men's house, they recount their exploits to young initiates who know that there will never again be a splendid pitched battle or a well coordinated ambush. The Baruya lost no time eliminating from their initiation ceremonies the rituals intended to prepare youths for war, to prepare them to kill and handle the blood of enemies, to protect themselves from the pollution of this blood and the vengeance of the victims' spirits. Little by little the initiatory machine has disintegrated and whole sections of it have collapsed, leaving here and there in the rituals traces that point to the missing pieces, whose former existence the young no longer even suspect. Sometimes, as I more than once had the occasion to witness, an old man forgets himself and begins a ritual now useless. He is quickly stopped in his tracks by the men who were between twenty and twenty-five years old in 1960 and who are today the *apmwenangalo,* the accomplished men of their society. They tell him, a little curtly, to pipe down.

But if war with neighboring tribes is forbidden, hostility persists, fed by the tales of former warriors and by a few lingering disputes that the white peace has made it impossible to settle. In particular, the tribes that had had to retreat before the Baruya and thus lost part of their territory would like very much to recover it. Their sole recourse is to persuade the colonial administration that their claims are legitimate and that it should return to them the lands that were once theirs. Hence the incidents along tribal borders and the interminable legal wrangling before the officer who calls together the old men of each tribe, collects their testimony, and seeks to establish and mark the borders of their tribes. The administration's policy has been in general to maintain the status quo by "freezing" borders as they were when the whites arrived. For these reasons there is still considerable discontent among those who believe that, without the coming of the white men, more favorable circumstances sometime in the future would have enabled them to recover part of their land by force and intertribal diplomacy. But there now remains only one way to make peace: by the exchange of women and the exchange of goods. In this new political context, the matrimonial alliances between tribes, which had sometimes marked the end of war, have acquired greater importance and become more frequent. Consequently, those women who agree to leave their tribe to live with another, enemies only yesterday, play a greater role than before.

Colonial relations have modified the status of women in another respect. Now physical violence by husbands on their spouses is punishable by law, and wives thus have an incentive to resist their husbands more often and more openly. Above all, in a society where the direct exchange of sisters made divorce impossible, divorce is now recognized as a right. But this right, it goes without saying, benefits the women chiefly. For the first time and with the support of extratribal law and authority, they can break an alliance forced on them by fathers or brothers. Few women dare to do so, and one was killed with an ax by her husband when she left him to live publicly with her lover (who already had two wives). The husband, a young man who had worked for the whites, turned himself in to a government outpost, and threw the bloody implement on the officer's desk, telling him to go and look for his wife in the garden where he had killed her, reminding him that he was not a "little child" and knew how to settle his affairs by himself, as custom required. The man was sentenced to three years in prison, during which time he learned to drive a Land Rover. He returned with redoubled prestige for having both followed the customs of his tribe and taken a further step into the white man's world. But the Baruya are aware that their entire system of marriage based on the direct exchange of sisters is threatened by the direct autonomy, more hypothetical than real, of women. Women now have some "say" in the choice of their future husband. As the barriers that separate the sexes tumble one by one, boys and girls know each other better than in the past and have more occasion to meet one another before marriage. The male initiates' fear of women has diminished. Except for the *mouka* and the *yiveumbwaye,* who are still strictly shut up in the male area, initiates often have occasion today to meet their sisters and their fiancées, and even to catch sight of their mothers. The Baruya have recently softened the custom that used to forbid a married man to speak to his mother or eat in her presence before he was at least thirty years old and had several not-so-small children. Now men married for five or six years with small children can take part in rituals during which they are liable to encounter their mothers.

Moreover, with the departure of many men, married and unmarried, to work on the plantations along the coast, sometimes for many years, the women have become accustomed to the absence of direct supervision by their husbands. To be sure, a woman is closely watched by the men of her husband's lineage, because she lives with them. But, more often than in the past, she relies on the material aid of her own family and her brothers, who give her plots of land to cultivate; and she is more likely to take care of her nephews and nieces and so forth. Adulterous liaisons are becoming more common with the men who remain in the village – who will one day have to answer to the absent husbands or fiancés. Prostitution, once completely unknown in this society, has been introduced by policemen and soldiers from other regions stationed at the government outpost for long months, often without their wives. Some of these men offer money or other gifts to Baruya women to make love with them. Still others make similar advances to boys. For many older Baruya these changes are a sign of the disorder and licentiousness that have taken hold of the family and society since the arrival of the white men. Everyone believes that the first line of defense against these disorders lies in the preservation of the male and female initiation ceremonies. These ceremonies, deprived of the rituals once aimed at outside enemies, are more than ever becoming the symbol and the instrument of male domination, seen as the inviolable principle of the social order. But violence has not disappeared from relations between men and women. On the contrary, each day sees its new share of occasions and examples of feminine resistance or indifference to the traditional practices and symbols of male domination. It is thus not by chance that the victims of the five murders committed among the Baruya since the arrival of the whites have all been women.

The second consequence of colonization, after the suppression of the warrior function, was the arrival of missionaries representing three Protestant denominations, two of which immediately plunged into intense competition for the conquest of the souls of the Baruya. In 1960, a few weeks after the construction of the government outpost, a family of linguists arrived from the Summer Institute of Linguistics to learn the Baruya language and translate the Bible into that language. The undertaking proved to be long and difficult. A translation of the Book of Genesis was not completed and published until 1975. Such a project demands a great deal of scholarly spadework, concerning both the language (description of the phonology and grammar of the Baruya language) and the interpretation of various elements of Baruya thought and principles of social organization. This scholarship has crystallized into the production of a dictionary – still far from completion – of the Baruya language. The missionaries' "work" changed somewhat after independence. In addition to translating the Bible, the Summer Institute of Linguistics produced a number of short booklets in Baruya intended to provide, for those who knew how to read, basic information about geography, meteorology, how to use money, how to buy and sell, and the like. The attempt of these missionaries to implant "modern" institutions and ideas (not all of which concerned religion for that matter) in the language and culture of the tribe is strikingly different from the activities of the other missions, which educate and instruct the population of New Guinea in pidgin English.

The second mission that came to work with the Baruya was the New Tribes Mission, an American Protestant group so named because its chief aim is to convert "newly discovered tribes." Like the first group, these missionaries seek to establish their influence over indigenous cultures by conducting their activities, where possible, in the local language.

The third mission, however, has adopted a completely different strategy, and its social influence is much more profound. This mission is sponsored by the well-organized Lutheran Church, which has chosen a New Guinean bishop as its head and receives generous support from the German and Australian Lutheran churches. The influence of the Lutherans has been considerable because they were not content to preach the work of Christ and to set an example of Christian living, but immediately set up an educational system. Starting in 1964 they opened schools where pupils learned, at first in pidgin, to read the Bible as well as to write and count. This undertaking was encouraged by the Australian colonial administration, which had neither the intention nor the means to create a public school at Wonenara and could only laud the Lutherans' efforts.

And the Baruya responded. Many parents sent their boys to the missionary school, and for the first time an institution other than the men's house and the system of initiations began to take on the function of socializing the young. Now this institution ran counter to and contradicted Baruya society and ideas in three ways. For a start, the children sitting next to each other in the classroom came from all the tribes of the Wonenara region, whether enemies or friends of the Baruya. Second, several little girls from the Baruya and other tribes soon appeared at the school. The men's privileged access to knowledge was from this moment on under modest threat. Finally, and most significantly, because the principal goal of schooling was to evangelize the population, instruction was accompanied by an aggressive and exceedingly contemptuous attitude to local "pagan" customs and to these people, who had remained "in the dark, in ignorance of the Truth, of the true light which is the word of Christ, who died on the Cross two thousand years ago in a place called Israel, to redeem the sins of all men, the sins of black men and the sins of white men" (typical Sunday sermon by one of the pastors). The Lutheran Mission launched direct and frontal attacks on the Baruya belief system, on the myths and above all the initiations and shamanism. The Lutheran missionaries forbade their pupils to participate in the initiations, to wear the Baruya costume, or to have their noses pierced. Above all, they presented shamanism and magic as the work of the devil, while at the same time seeking to find out as much as possible about what went on during the initiation ceremonies for boys, girls, and shamans (to which they were not invited).

Much more than the Australian colonial administration, which had refrained from attacking Baruya customs so long as they posed no "threat to public order," the Lutheran missionaries taught the Baruya that their culture and customs could be despised, indeed were despised. The Baruya reacted in diverse ways. Some pupils decided that they would "follow the way of the missionaries" and would have "nothing more to do with the loincloths of their fathers." Most of the adults, however, set about concealing or rearranging their ancestral customs. But some, while maintaining the traditions, decided to put their trust in the world of the future, not for their own sakes, but in order to give a head start to their sons and their lineages. Such was the case of the greatest Baruya shaman, who sent his two sons to the Lutheran school and for a long time had them educated outside the initiate system.

In addition to assuming responsibility for the education of part of their youth, the Lutherans have resorted to two forms of intervention in Baruya society which the other missions do not use. First, they have little by little introduced their "evangelists" into each tribe; these live with the population and from time to time (sometimes every day, depending on their zeal) issue calls to prayer or religious services. In the beginning these evangelists came from the tribes of the north coast of New Guinea, where the Lutheran Church has put down strong roots. They arrived with their families, set themselves up in a village, received a patch of land to cultivate and preached in pidgin. Their children went to the Lutheran school alongside those of the policemen and the soldiers at the government outpost.

But gradually these evangelists from other regions have been replaced by Baruya, Wantekia, or members of other local tribes who have themselves been to the Lutheran school and are able to evangelize, pray, and sing in their own language. This process has continued since the independence of New Guinea in 1975. Today there is an evangelist with his family in every village in every tribe of the Marawaka district. These evangelists are somewhat better paid than formerly, but they receive no more than fifty kinas per year (the kina is worth just over seven [1981] French Francs). They are permitted only one wife. According to the Lutherans, like all other Christian missions, one cannot be baptised without renouncing polygamy. The "proper" way of marrying, the Christian norm in the organization of kinship, begins with monogamy. As a result, an essential element in the functioning of Baruya kinship relations has been devalued, and an important instrument of male domination has at the same time been undermined.

The other aspect of the Lutherans' missionary practice that has strongly affected Baruya society is their role in the economy of the tribes in the vicinity of the new government post at Marawaka, where the mission moved after the transfer of the post from Wonenara. In 1968 the mission had opened a trading store in Wonenara, then the site of the government post. The store sold articles in great demand among the local populations, notably machetes, hatchets, Japanese canned fish and meat, rice, cloth, work overalls, shirts, blouses, dresses, and the like.

Well organized, backed by a commercial company owned by the congregation, which imports its goods directly from Japan and Australia and possesses its own boats, using the regular light plane service (also owned by the congregation and piloted by white missionaries), managed according to Western accounting principles whose effectiveness is due to their purely commercial character, the mercantile activities of the Lutheran missionaries in Wonenara and later Marawaka flourished. To give an idea of the profitability, the initial outlay in 1968 was 200 Australian dollars, which was used to purchase a few cases of canned fish, some bags of rice and bars of soap, all of which were sold at a profit. The money was immediately reinvested to buy a larger quantity of goods which were also sold at a profit, and so it went. At the end of the year, after deducting the cost of transporting the goods by air and the salaries of the store manager and his assistants, 14,000 Australian dollars worth of goods had been sold or were in stock. This figure indicates a substantial rate of profit. It also suggests what might be the rate of profit enjoyed by the major capitalist trading firms of the Pacific operating in New Guinea, Burns Phillip and Steamships, as well as by the great copra, coffee, and rubber plantations which until 1975 were almost all owned by Australians or Europeans.

Therefore, barely a few years after the submission of these tribes, the Lutherans have introduced one of the essential ingredients of a market economy, namely, retail trade; and not just any market economy, but its modern, Western, capitalist form. To be sure, the missionaries have not directly modified the conditions of production, but by offering a great variety of desirable goods they have helped to foster or strengthen needs created among the Baruya and their neighbors by the products of capitalist industry. Most important of all, they have created needs money alone can satisfy. To obtain money the Baruya have had to enter into new relations of production. For this, they had but two alternatives. Either they could submit to the pressure of the Australian colonial administration by "signing" (?!) a two-year contract to work in the coffee, copra, and rubber plantations on the coast or on distant islands; or, again in response to pressure from the colonial administration, they could clear new land in the forest for planting coffee and other cash crops.

In short, the Baruya had the choice of becoming rural proletarians, or petty commodity producers, or some combination of the two. Part of the money earned on the plantations or from the sale of a few bags of coffee quickly found its way to the store newly opened by the missionaries. Since then the flow of money into and out of the hands of the Baruya has never ceased to grow. Amplified by the spread of wage labor and small-scale commodity production, the flow has split into several circuits in recent years because the Baruya have decided to open their own "house of commerce," imitated as well by several neighboring and rival tribes. The power of the Lutheran mission, stemming from its ability to educate a part of the young, to establish a network of evangelists covering all the tribes of the region, and to offer a regular supply of coveted European goods, has spurred sharp criticism from the competing missions, in particular the American New Tribes Mission. The latter says that the Lutheran mission is a church built on money and power that has forgotten the lesson of Christ, which is to lead a life of poverty and charity. In the eyes of the American missionaries the Lutheran mission, like that other archenemy, the Catholic Church, is an institution devoted to no more than the pursuit of worldly ends, a social force perverted by the Devil.

Except for the battle of the churches for the conquest and eternal salvation of the souls of the Baruya, the various missionaries are alike in that they have all mounted a frontal assault on three elements of Baruya culture and society: polygamy, shamanism, and myth. The missionaries without exception are eager to know who among the Baruya men and women are the shamans. All spontaneously see in shamanism a form of sorcery, in a word the work of the Devil. The shaman is to the missionaries what the great warrior was to the Australian administration at the beginning of the colonial era. The shaman is the potential adversary who must be identified and, for some missionaries, eliminated. As the reader can imagine, the representatives of those two leading institutions, the state and the church, lost no occasion to pick the anthropologist's brains on this question, but in vain!

One final and rather important element among the many differences regarding the work of the missions among the Baruya and their neighbors needs to be underlined. From the start the Lutherans declared their outright hostility to the very existence of the great male initiation rites. Since they did not live among the local populations, the Lutherans knew almost nothing of the female initiation rites. Before independence they forbade the children who came to their schools to participate in these initiations, just as they forbade the pupils they had sent to be educated in English in the schools of other regions to return home at the time of the initiations. Since independence such forms of direct intervention have become less common. But the Lutherans are still openly hostile to the continued existence of the male initiation rites, and they sometimes even threaten to reveal to the women what they have learned about these rites.

The other missions, which live in much closer contact with the population, show no hostility toward these institutions. The missionaries have witnessed and are thus familiar with most of the rituals that take place in the open – those for men, not for women. They correctly see in these rituals an important piece of ethical machinery which spectacularly imprints in the consciousness of young Baruya a set of moral norms not dissimilar to the Ten Commandments: thou shalt not kill (at least not a law-abiding Baruya); thou shalt not commit adultery; thou shalt not steal (from your neighbor's garden), and the like. For such laws are indeed proclaimed by the masters of the rituals and mark the various stages of a boy's initiations. But there is a striking difference between these moral precepts and their Judeo-Christian equivalents, for the sanctions that they carry with them have nothing to do with the gospel or the legal principles of the state, colonial or postcolonial. The sanctions are dictated by traditional tribal law. The victim of an offense may take the law into his own hands, and the most common form of justice among the Baruya has been the death of the guilty party or parties.

A fundamental contradiction has arisen in the heart of Baruya society. It affects society as a whole, but it particularly undermines the machinery of male domination, namely, the male initiation rites. For the traditional principles of good behavior among the Baruya presupposed the political and juridical sovereignty of the tribe, and the equality of each lineage and each individual before the tribal law. This equality gave to each Baruya the right to settle his own disputes with reference to the law of the tribe. But it is now forbidden (although not impossible) for the Baruya to employ the sanctions provided by custom. The victim of a transgression must now turn to the representatives of the state, for it is a principle of every form of state, be it colonial or independent, repressive or liberal, that no man may take justice into his own hands.

For the Baruya, however, the transition from colonialism to independence was accompanied by a change in the way in which the state intervenes in their society.

During the colonial era the Australian administration appointed in each village a *luluai* or a *tultul,* whose responsibility it was to see that the members of his community did not break the law or, if they did, that they were brought immediately before the colonial authorities. This individual also had the task of assembling the population of his village for the colonial census taker or for the medical teams that came to diagnose diseases or combat epidemics. Each year he had to persuade a certain number of men, adults or even adolescents, to go to work on the coastal plantations. As we have seen, the administration at first sought to appoint big men and especially great warriors to these functions. Since independence a system of councils elected by the population has replaced the *luluai* and the *tultul,* and these councils are an element of local power. We should note in passing that this kind of reform had been introduced even before independence in regions of New Guinea that had been more profoundly subject to white influence and for a longer time than had the Baruya in 1975 or even in 1981.

Of course the councillors (*consol* in pidgin), like the *luluai* before them, serve both as representatives of their local communities before the administration and as representatives of the administration before their local communities. But unlike the *luluai,* they are elected from among several candidates by all men and women over eighteen years of age. Thus for the first time a woman can, by voting, accomplish a political act strictly equal in value to that of a man. Indeed a woman could even stand as a candidate, although to this day no woman has done so. Most of the candidates are young men between thirty and forty-five years old. The youngest were thus ten years old or so in 1960; they have lived in the men's house and were initiated in accordance with tradition. The oldest were twenty or twenty-five in 1960 and already married. They had even done battle against their enemies. But all are too young to have been *aoulatta,* although it is said that some were well on their way. Today the *consols* count among their number shamans, *kwaimatnie*-men, and even the descendant of an enemy lineage which had come over to the Baruya two generations earlier and was still not fully integrated five or six years ago. This man has become the representative of his village, a Baruya village recently rebuilt facing an enemy village in order to keep an eye on its expansion. It was from this latter village that the representative's ancestor had originated.

203

Recent transformations of Baruya society

When Australia granted independence to Papua New Guinea in 1975, the Baruya, like their neighbors, correctly grasped that most of the white men would be leaving, and they were afraid of finding themselves defenseless, face to face with their old enemies after only fifteen years' truce. So the Baruya began to build new villages along their frontiers to watch over and defend against the enemy villages. The warrior function has thus not disappeared from Baruya social life, but it has been reduced to the level of virtuality, a latent function no longer supported by the institutions and practices that were once linked to war.

As a rule the *consols* know pidgin, which they have learned either at school or on the plantations, through contact with foremen and workers from very different linguistic and cultural backgrounds. More and more *consols* are young men with several years' schooling, who are minor state employees, such as male nurses, employees of the Department of Rivers, Lakes, and Forests, and the like. These men are quite unlike the big men who in other regions of New Guinea have continued to dominate their societies after independence and have in some cases been elected to the National Assembly.

Another essential aspect of the changes now occurring in Baruya society is that the Baruya now elect representatives of their region to the National Assembly. The candidates run on the ticket of one or another of the national parties, on a platform consisting of a few slogans, calling for roads, schools, funding for increased coffee production, and so on. The candidates come from different tribes, and several tribes band together to vote for a particular candidate. The first representative to be returned for the Marawaka region was an Andje, from the tribe most hostile to the Baruya. He was a brilliant young man who had been to the Lutheran school and had served as a medical assistant in the health service. The Baruya had voted for him overwhelmingly. A year or two before his election, they had given him a woman and he had given them one in return. He was active in the National Assembly and was greatly mourned when he died in 1978 in an airplane crash on one of the peaks that dominate the Gulf of Papua. In 1979 an election was called to replace him, but this time the Baruya were divided among themselves and they put up two candidates. The seat slipped the grasp of the tribes of the Anga linguistic and cultural group. The winner was a young forestry engineer from a tribe in the Kainantu region; he immediately joined the prime minister's private office.

To put the Baruya society of today in proper perspective, we have still to consider two essential links in the chain of transformations (simultaneous or successive, convergent or opposed) that the society has undergone in the last twenty years. First, a number of young Baruya have become government officials or have assumed positions of responsibility in the Protestant Church or the trading companies. Second, the coffee-growing trade has given rise to men of sufficient wealth to become small-scale entrepreneurs, who are increasingly behaving as if they were big men.

Let us cast our minds back a bit. After a few years the Baruya lost much of their enthusiasm for the "Bible school." They felt that the boys could learn to speak pidgin without going to school, and that learning to read and write pidgin only led to lowly jobs as evangelists in the missions or as trading store clerks. Therefore the Baruya asked that their children be educated in English. When I say their children I mean only some of their children, including a few girls, for the Baruya had acquired the habit of sending only one son in two to school, sending the others to the men's house to undergo training for initiation (although, as I have said, the homosexual practices and a whole range of rituals associated with war had by now been eliminated). In response to the desires of the Baruya and their neighbors, the Lutherans have set up a school that provides education in English. But the Lutherans are no longer alone because the government has opened a nondenominational state school in Marawaka which admits children from all the tribes in the vicinity of the government post. Out of 150 pupils in 1979, 20 were girls. Some of these children will one day go on to a teacher-training college or university. How many? It is impossible to say, especially now that school enrollments have considerably increased throughout the country, and the number of students already exceeds the number of jobs available in the civil service, the missions, the trading companies, and elsewhere.

Indeed, there is already a small group of young Baruya men who represent a new kind of great man. They were seven or eight years old when the white men arrived in the region, and they were thus too young to have been initiated. They went to the Lutheran school with other boys who were older and had therefore been initiated. They were therefore more susceptible to European cultural influences. Remarked upon for their intellectual abilities, they were sent by the mission to schools scattered around New Guinea where the teaching was carried on in English. Six or seven of them have had successful careers. One is a lecturer in mathematics at the University of Technology in Lae, another is a forestry engineer, another a police official near Madang, another a government official, and still another a pastor. These men, still under thirty, are gradually becoming folk heroes because they understand English, earn more than what one can earn from growing coffee or from work on the plantations, and use the money they earn to help their kin and affines. They are slowly taking the place of the *aoulatta*. Their attitudes toward the traditional customs have significantly changed since their youth. Then, without a thought to the consequences, they copied the white man's contempt for their initiations, their myths, and other elements of their culture. All these young men, except the pastor, have returned to undergo the initiation rites, at least the main ceremonies. But even more than the men of their age who stayed with the tribe they are profoundly ignorant of the most secret of rituals, those that are no longer practiced and will soon no longer be mentioned at all. Almost all of them today favor the preservation of the male and female initiations. They look upon these initiations as their roots, their identity. As one of them said in English on the occasion of their last *mouka* initiations in 1979, the initiations are like "what the Europeans, the white men, call culture."[2]

They too see the initiations as the source of the Baruya's "strength." But it is no longer only magical and warlike strength that aids in the struggle against enemies and evil spirits; it is rather the moral and physical strength that a young man needs in order to resist the temptations of the city, hunger, the urge to steal, prostitution, gambling, unemployment, and the sorcery of distant tribes. It is the strength not to spend all one's earnings on beer or gin, not to quarrel with the workers from all over New Guinea, who club together according to tribe and region on the great copra and rubber plantations. In a word, as some of the missionaries already point out, the male initiations have lost their sacred character and have acquired an ethical character; they have become lessons in civic morality, taking their examples and raw material from traditional culture, but after having uprooted it and directed it toward different goals. For the male initiations once again work in two directions: toward the interior, where they are still directed against women, designed to create and reproduce male domination; and toward the exterior, where the enemies are no longer the neighboring tribes but the dangers that spring from the development of a cash economy, from emigration, from the dismemberment of the value system, from the changing role of men and women in their society, from the severing of certain functions such as war, and from the uprooting or truncation of such functions as shamanism and control of the rituals. As this process moves both ways, it preserves, while at the same time amputating, the principles which used to underpin the thought and workings of a society in order to withstand the march of history; the society is pitting itself against itself in order to adapt to something that was originally imposed from the outside but is gradually becoming a part, a cog, an internal functional goal of that same society.

Today the spirits still manifest themselves to the young initiates, to the *mouka* who formerly would have grown up to be *aoulatta;* but now the spirits communicate by sending the cassowary feathers that used to designate the future great hunters of the "wild woman" of the forest. The warrior function is disappearing, but its substance and its signs are being transferred to other functions – traditional ones such as cassowary hunting, or new ones such as

[2] The Baruya word for the white men is *waiaka,* which in fact means the "reds," those whose skin is sunburned.

206

the hunt for university degrees and positions of authority in state and private institutions.

Shamanism retains its vigor. In 1979 a grand initiation ceremony was held for a new class of shamans, men and women, the first of its kind in six or seven years. Here again the mutations and the remodeling go deep. Cut off from its direct links to warfare, Baruya shamanism has kept its therapeutic function almost intact. Healing consists as always in driving out the evil spirits that threaten the existence of the Baruya and dispatching them in the direction of their enemies.

Little by little a division of labor of sorts has grown up between the shamans and the doctors or nurses sent by the administration to treat the population and help in the fight against major epidemics. Traditional Baruya culture had already paved the way for this division of labor, because the shamans only treated internal illnesses. Accidents, external afflictions, or malnutrition could therefore be dealt with by Western medicine. The only area of overlap is that of internal sicknesses, which might have been causing general weakness and loss of tone, vomiting, or even excretion of blood. They were formerly treated by a series of shamanistic cures intended to cast out the evil spell, and the doctors treat them with antibiotics. European and New Guinean doctors today cooperate more and more with the shamans, and sometimes encourage them to visit their patients and look after them.

Caring for the sick also means interpreting in terms of Baruya culture the miseries that are the lot of humans. The missionaries are hostile to this interpreting, but the Baruya set great store by it.

However, a far more serious obstacle to shamanism than the opposition of the missionaries lies in the forces that drive so many young Baruya to leave their villages for two years and sometimes more in search of work on the coast and in the cities. But a shaman can only be initiated if he commits himself to remain with the tribe to protect it against death. This is not a problem for women, since they have little occasion to travel outside Baruya territory, but things are different for the men of the rising generations. There is already a sort of "shaman recruitment" crisis, which the Baruya (at least, those over thirty-five) recognize and lament.

An event that occurred in 1978 clearly illustrates the action of these contradictory forces. As I have said, the greatest of the Baruya shamans, the master of the *koulakita* or shaman initiation rituals, had sent two of his sons to the Lutheran school. One of them became a pastor and has consistently refused to have anything to do with the initiations, be they for men or for shamans. The other is a forestry engineer and, although he by no means rejects Baruya culture and shamanism, his occupation nevertheless prevents him from living among the Baruya. In 1978 the great shaman died without having passed on all of his secrets to his brother, who was to have inherited the responsibility of the *koulakita*. During the burial ceremony, while the corpse painted in blue clay was being carried into the mountains, in a sitting posture, on the shoulders of first one volunteer and then another, a group of young warriors suddenly appeared and swept down upon the cortege. In the course of this attack a young man collapsed in a trance. The spirit of the departed great shaman Inamwe had entered the body of the young man, who was none other than the son of the shaman's brother. And so the powers of the greatest of the Baruya shamans had been saved, not by his brother, who had not inherited his secrets, but by his nephew, who had been possessed by them.

In October 1980 at the time of the *koulakita* I, like everyone else, expected that this young man in his turn would become a shaman. But in spite of the insistence of his father, the new master of the rituals, and of the men of his lineage and many more besides, he refused even to appear at the place of the initiations. He stayed at home, for he knew that if he took part in a single ritual he would be "discovered" by one of the shamans officiating with his father and that an eagle's feather would be placed on his head as a sign of his election by the spirits and by Venus, the supernatural source of the healing power of the shamans. The affair was thus a failure; the nephew's "possession" by the spirit of his uncle had not succeeded in restoring to the tribe the protection that it had enjoyed under the exceptional powers of the departed great man. Perhaps the nephew will not refuse to become a shaman on the occasion of the next initiations. His current way of life would be no obstacle. He is a young man, twenty-seven or twenty-eight years old, who has worked little on the plantations, speaks pidgin poorly, and leads the life of a horticulturist. Perhaps his attitude can be attributed in part to his cousin the pastor. Sometime before these events, the mission sent him to work and preach among the Baruya. He pays frequent visits to his family and to his village, and his influence on them is considerable.

The role of the last category of the traditional great men, the masters of the male initiations, the *kwaimatnie*-owners, is not about to disappear, far from it, and hence they retain significant prestige and authority. More than ever they are the guardians of social, cultural, and tribal identity. They have inherited a role whose significance is enriched by all of the elements analyzed so far, namely, their links with the tribal ancestors, the Sun and the Moon, the secrets of male domination and those of the promotion of great men. Today they receive the additional support of the new great men, the young who have taken up successful careers in the new community, the nation state of Papua New Guinea.

In a world where the force of tradition is undermined by social change, where individuals are less and less inhibited by the old rules, it is no surprise that certain lineages now openly challenge the supremacy of the Kwarrandariar, the lineage of the Baruya clan that holds the exclusive right to initiate adolescents or the *tchouwanie*. Therein lies the meaning of the hesitant attempt made in 1980 by a Boulimmambakia to initiate the new *tchouwanie* alongside, or instead of, the Kwarrandariar. His ambition was of short duration and ended in shame, beneath the withering sarcasm of the new master of rituals who is himself a young man whose authority is not yet firmly established. (Indeed he is said to be under the thumb of one of his three wives. As a result he is much more vulnerable than his predecessor, his celebrated brother, Ypmeie, who already possessed a *kwaimatnie* before the arrival of the white men and had helped to produce the last of the traditional great men.)

Competition for the control of the ritual functions is growing even within the lineages. Among the Wombouye, masters along with the Tchatche of the rituals marking the separation of boys from the world of women, a segment of the lineage that previously did not control these rituals now claims the right to do so. In 1979 the men of this segment displayed a *kwaimatnie* that they had allegedly obtained sometime before from a master of rituals in the Menyamya region, the territory of the Baruya's ancestors. Several generations earlier the ancestors of this segment of the lineage may have shared with the other segments the right to initiate the *mouka*. But after a murder they were obliged to split off from their lineage and take refuge among their allies. Today, however, there is no longer any basis to the balance of power that permitted the exclusion of this lineage. There are no more wars, no more vendettas. Reconciliations that in the past would have been difficult are now possible and even desired. Moreover, the Baruya rule has it that even if the authenticity of the *kwaimatnie* purchased in Menyamya for some salt is doubtful, even if the right of these men to participate in a ritual function is of uncertain legitimacy, the matter must nevertheless be handled within the lineage; the other clans have no right to intervene. Thus, although the male initiations have been preserved since the arrival of the white man, along with the functions and the powers of the *kwaimatnie*-men, the structure has been weakened from within by the outbreak of crises of "legitimacy."

Because of the preservation of the male and female initiations and the Baruya rituals surrounding birth, marriage, and death, the production of salt remains indispensable. But salt, as we have seen, was more than an object of ritual exchange; it was also the principal means of commercial exchange between the Baruya and their neighbors. However, with the exception perhaps of bark cloaks, feathers of birds of paradise, or pigs' teeth (needed for making the baldrics that the *tchouwanie* and the *kalave* wear across their chests), everything materially necessary to Baruya life and not produced by themselves can be purchased for money in one of the stores in the Marawaka post. Salt has thus lost its role as the principal means of exchange, retaining only its function of social exchange, the magical means of acting on the life and the strength of humans in their moments of trial (initiations and child-birth, for example).

The production of salt has therefore greatly diminished. The irrigated fields of salt cane are gradually becoming taro gardens. Young Baruya show no great desire to be initiated to the technical and magical secrets of produc-ing salt. Although there are still many salt specialists today, their replacement appears to be in doubt. Inexpensive commercial salt used for cooking has naturally become an object of daily consumption. But as such it does not compete with the traditional salt of the Baruya, which serves as an object of ritual consumption or as a means of exchange, a form of intertribal money that draws part of its intertribal value from its use as a ritual food by neigh-boring tribes, even those of different languages and cultures.

These changes have greatly reduced the status of the *tsaimaye*, the tradi-tional salt maker. Furthermore the salt trade has ceased to be dangerous. In the past an expedition to the neighboring tribes to buy bark cloaks or stone tools in exchange for salt carried with it a serious risk of being killed and even eaten. Nowadays one can come and go as one likes, protected in prin-ciple by the power of the state.

Finally, we cannot conclude this analysis of the recent transformations of Baruya society without touching on the new role of money and wealth. Every Baruya today must have money. Women obtain money by selling a few sacks of sweet potatoes and vegetables to government officials, missionaries, or the state, which must feed columns of porters or the workers hired to build roads or to prepare landing strips. Pigs are increasingly raised for sale in the local market, and some of the money thus earned goes to the women. But for the most part what money they have comes from the men. Money is a new form of material dependence for women in addition to that already entailed by the old division of labor still in effect in agricultural production.

Men on the other hand have at least three ways of obtaining money. A man may choose to respond to one of the appeals of the administration which is in constant need of short-term unskilled labor for a week, a month, or even more. Or else a man can go to work on the coastal plantations, for a period of always at least two years. At the time of my first trip to New Guinea, in 1967, the earnings of the plantation workers were very low. They lived shut up in compounds grouped according to language and region. They were fed on rice and fish, and they were given tobacco and a little spending money, which they spent in the plantation store. The planter thus made a double profit: on the workers' wages and on the sale of goods. At the end of two years each worker was returned to his region by airplane, after having been paid the sum of his net earnings, which had been put aside for him so as to prevent his spending it all before returning home. In 1967 a worker's net earnings over two years amounted to thirty Australian pounds, about sixty or

210

sixty-five U.S. dollars at the time. With this money in hand a Baruya would immediately head for the stores in the cities, Steamships or Burns Phillips, and would buy a blanket, crockery, axes, and so forth. As a rule he arrived home with half the money earned, but within a few weeks none of it remained. For on returning to his village he could scarcely avoid distributing all or part of his purchases and his savings in the form of gifts to his brothers, brothers-in-law, wives, cross cousins, maternal cousins, and the rest.

In view of these facts, it is difficult to deny that the plantations were a scene of capitalist exploitation of man by man. This is not to say that the Baruya themselves felt exploited, much less that they recognized the mechanisms by which they were being exploited. They complained about the discipline and the poor food, but they described with pleasure the boat and airplane trips, the drunken beer sessions, the local women or the prostitutes with whom they had had a good time, and so on. Since independence things have changed, and the government has taken steps to improve pay for rural workers, who earned twenty-five kinas on average – around 167 [1981] French Francs – per two-week period in 1979. But compared with salaries four or five times higher in the cities, especially if compared with the substantially increased prices of goods imported form Australia or Japan, rural salaries remain quite low.

Regardless of the rate at which his labor power is exploited, and regardless of whether or not he is conscious of it, a Baruya who leaves his village to work in the city or on the coast and returns with gifts and money acquires a certain prestige, although less now than in the first years of pacification, when leaving one's village was an adventure. More often than not the adventure was voluntary. Young men wanted to see the world, and the colonial administration only exerted pressure on individuals to "sign" work contracts if the number of volunteers was insufficient to meet employers' demand for labor.

To see the world, to learn pidgin, to return home bearing gifts, these things were and remain beyond the reach of women. A new divide arose between the sexes, continuing and in part renewing the foundations of male domination: a continuation because, yet again, male superiority is built on a virtual monopoly of contacts with the outside world and on the knowledge and know-how that can only be acquired from such contacts.

Even without becoming rich, a man who emigrates and is exploited outside his own society involuntarily creates new social and material conditions for the domination of women by men within his own society. But a man who works on a plantation does not become rich. To do so he stands a much better chance planting or selling coffee.

After the collapse of Brazilian coffee production in the early 1970s it became advantageous for countries like New Guinea to produce coffee for the world market, even in small quantities. The variety of coffee grown, robusta,

211

brings the direct producers up to one kina or more per kilo. Growing coffee does not require a great deal of work, and some of it, such as the harvest, shelling the mature fruits and washing the beans, can be done by children eight to ten years old. Baruya society traditionally left young boys free to play until the time of their initiation, whereas girls were already taking part in some productive tasks in the company of their mothers. Now that the production of coffee has taken its place alongside subsistence production, more use is made of the labor power of girls than before.

With the prospect of earning easy money, money principally intended to buy necessities or luxuries, not to be accumulated, every Baruya has taken to growing coffee, using plants distributed by the Department of Agriculture. But some have planted on a much larger scale than others. Their ardor in clearing fields for coffee, in pressing women and children into service for harvesting, and then carrying the coffee grains in sacks on their heads or backs to the government post, there to be purchased by an employee of the Department of Agriculture or a private company, all this productive effort strikingly resembles the ardor of the old *tannaka,* those tireless land clearers and gardeners who devoted themselves to meeting the needs of war and warriors and so of the tribe in general. But this time their ardor no longer serves the interests of all. It is aimed primarily at bringing wealth to one man and his family, even if they cannot keep this wealth for themselves, since the social logic of kinship relations obliges people to share with those around them the better part of what they have earned. The principle of the equivalence of women and of the equivalence of lineages in the direct exchange of women, creating as it does a constant incentive to participate in noncompetitive exchanges of goods and services, thereby helps to lessen the social impact of the growing economic inequality among individuals, families, and lineages.

This principle operates still more profoundly outside the redistribution of money. For only some soils are fit for growing coffee, and the Baruya know perfectly well which land is best suited. In other economic systems the individual or collective owners of this land would be able to capitalize on their privileged situation. This is not so among the Baruya, because their system of land ownership still allows each Baruya to ask of those who have received women from his lineage the right to use one of their parcels of land for a time on condition of reciprocity. Moreover, in everyday agricultural practice the clearing and preparation of large gardens still require the cooperation of a certain number of men, often brothers-in-law, cross cousins, and so forth. In short, this system of land ownership, which the Baruya have automatically applied to the coffee gardens, makes it difficult at present for particular lineages to attain a position of economic domination on the strength of their ownership of the best coffee gardens. However coffee growing poses a delicate problem, because the grower must retain the right of access to the land on which coffee is planted for many years. Those who plant the coffee trees may be inclined to believe, after a number of years or perhaps even a generation, that the land on which their coffee grows belongs to them. The Baruya recognize this danger and have discussed it in their assemblies, but do not regard it as a serious threat.

Two aspects of the new economic and social developments are of particular interest. On the one hand, the position of women with respect to the factors of production has not changed. The right to use land to plant coffee is still accorded by men and, if the production of coffee or other cash crops continues to develop among the Baruya, sexual inequality will only be reproduced and enlarged on other grounds. On the other hand, there is something new in the agreements reached between two men or between two lineages to cooperate in planting coffee on land that belongs solely to one of them, because this kind of agreement implies a long-term commitment. It is no longer a matter of one or two years, the time required to grow some sweet potatoes or taro in a garden that the borrower will then leave fallow while thanking the owner. The agreement is for ten years and more, although the area of suitable land is limited, since in the mountainous territory of the Baruya good coffee-growing land is rare, and poor land demands laborious improvement. The obligations created by the generosity of those who share their coffee gardens may therefore prove to be long-lasting, and they may give to the lenders considerably greater social influence than was enjoyed by those who in the past allowed their land to be used by others, since more or less everyone did so. But here again, the prestige and the influence will belong to men and not to women, and to certain lineages rather than to others.

Finally, alongside agricultural wage labor and small-scale production for the market, a Baruya has two other ways to earn a living. First, there is government service. Civil service pay is high if compared with that of an agricultural worker or a small coffee grower. Therefore a few Baruya, having attained the rank of head of a government post, policeman, or university lecturer, have become rich men though still young (between twenty-five and thirty years old). In 1979 the head of a government post earned one hundred kinas per fortnight (around 800 [1981] French Francs), four times as much as a farm laborer, and if he lived in the bush his living costs were minimal. These officials thus have savings, and some of them are able to buy prestigious consumer goods. The university lecturer bought a used car and, as soon as the track across the mountains reached Wonenara, he made a triumphant visit to his native village of Wiaveu. The inhabitants were extremely proud of him. Since the end of the track is twenty minutes by foot from his village (which is perched on the top of a steep hill), they decided to extend it to the very foot of the slope and to build a shelter to serve as a garage when the great man comes to visit them.

Young civil servants moreover are passionately interested in the political and economic development of their country. They listen to the radio in pidgin and in English; they follow the debates in the National Assembly, read the newspapers, support various political parties in power or in opposition, in particular the nationalist Pangu party, and all want their tribe to benefit from development. As we have seen, they encourage parents to send their children to school and at the same time favor the continued existence of initiations. Each one of them provides financial support for the education of some of these children. As far as the tribe's economy goes they are all in favor of increasing the production of cash crops. One of them, who had learned something about accounting and management, helped his clan to create a company known in Baruya as Kwaimandjiya ("We shall try") and in English as the Baruya Trade Store.

The company is a joint-stock one, financed out of the savings of the Baruya and several neighboring tribes; it also benefited from a government start-up loan. At the time, the minister of finance in Michael Somare's government (elected after independence, but which fell in 1980) was Barry Halloway, an Australian who had fought for the independence of Papua New Guinea and who had become a citizen of the country after 1975. Halloway had been member for the Eastern Highlands before becoming minister of finance, and it was to him that a young Baruya came to obtain the initial loan. In 1979 the minister granted the man the sum of 8,000 kinas (approximately 55,000 [1981] French Francs), which he deposited in a bank. With this money and that of the stockholders he had two stores built, one in Wonenara and the other in Marawaka; he hired employees from his lineage and from among his other relatives, bought an initial stock of goods, and then a small Toyota truck. With the truck he could buy supplies directly and at a better price in Kainantu, a small town ten hours' travel (in the dry season) from Wonenara, along a track that, as things stand now, is dangerous in any season for passengers and trying for vehicles. Young men had to be found to learn to drive and maintain the truck. Their stay in the city and their training were financed in part with money given to me by a number of French foundations for the purpose of conducting my research and aiding the Baruya.

We are now witnessing the emergence of a new kind of man who looks as if he is taking his place among the great men of the new Baruya society: the commercial entrepreneur. The man of whom we have spoken has invested a significant sum of money drawn from savings on his salary. Since he is a government official the question arises for the administration as to what to do about an official who is also a private entrepreneur. But the company he created is a limited liability company, and he is only an adviser. He approached several Baruya government officials who like himself can accumulate savings on their salaries, requesting them to become the major stockholders in the company. Some of them at first refused out of prudence, but also because they harbor the desire to do the same thing for their lineages.

214

The colonial order and independence

This time we can clearly discern the emergence among the Baruya of the big man, who calls upon the cooperation of his lineage, his affines, and supporters, while at the same time serving the interests of both his lineage and of his tribe, and even those of the neighboring tribes. But the last have also entered into the competition. The Yuwarrounatche, the neighbors and enemies of the Baruya in Wonenara, recently bought a Toyota truck to go into the same business. One of their members – he too is employed by the state as a chauffeur and mechanic at the government post – serves as their adviser.

To understand the social role of this new kind of man, we must consider once again the nature of retail trade in New Guinea. As the example of the Lutherans shows, such trade is an easy way to earn a lot of money quickly, much more than can be obtained from the small-scale cultivation of cash crops or even the salary of a government official, and without the effort required to cultivate the land or to emerge victorious from academic competition at school and the university. Everywhere in New Guinea, Europeans, Chinese, and New Guineans are opening stores along roads, near plantations, in the cities. Many of them – especially among the New Guineans – quickly go bankrupt. There are too many stores and the initial investment often insufficient, the appetite for profit too strong, and the management bad. The owners can never lower their prices and in the end their customers desert them or only come if they have no alternative.

Not till after 1970 did a handful of Baruya return from the cities or the plantations with a bit saved, and start to build what are called in pidgin *kenti* (small shops), each one independent in its village. A *kenti* is a little bamboo shack with a board for a counter, two or three other boards for shelves, and a door equipped with a padlock. The owners bought a few cartons of cigarettes, two or three bags of rice, some cases of canned goods (Japanese mackerel, Australian corned beef), and sat waiting for customers. These businesses were not overly successful. They faced competition from the mission store, which was better stocked and undercut their prices. Then this mercantile activity was subject to constant pressure from a different social logic: relatives, neighbors, and friends bought on credit, and they frequently expected the goods that they came to buy to be offered to them as gifts.

A few of the *kenti* still survive today, run by young men twenty or twenty-five years old returning from the plantations and beginning, like their elders before them, to dream of getting rich quick. But like everyone they have to buy their supplies from the mission stores or the store run by their Baruya "brother." They could also go into the city to buy their goods themselves, but the trip by air and the shipping costs would be expensive, or else they could pay the chauffeur of the truck owned by the Baruya Trade Store to transport them and their goods.

We see how contradictory are the effects of retail trade, even in the rather efficient form of the better-managed "trading companies," on the social and

215

economic development of the Baruya and their neighbors. On the one hand, this trade performs a service, because it makes available to the population tools, means of subsistence, and luxury items that are a source of utility or pleasure. The trade meets the needs of the population and even creates new ones by constantly enlarging the range of products offered (Japanese watches, plastic raincoats, children's clothes, and the like). By spreading the influence of the monetary economy, retail trade stimulates small-scale cash crop cultivation and departures for the plantations, the two principal sources of money for the vast majority of Baruya men. But on the other hand, by showing that much money can be earned without engaging in tasks of production, retail trade is turning part of the Baruya youth away from material labor. Furthermore, and this is the essential point in the current development not only of the Baruya but of New Guinea and similar countries, retail trade brings wealth to a few individuals but does not genuinely create wealth. It is easy to observe that among the Baruya money earned in various fashions quickly finds its way to the mission stores or to the Baruya Trade Store, where it becomes concentrated in a few hands. Wealth circulates and becomes concentrated (money is thus redistributed), but it is not created. Its sources are elsewhere, in the growth and diversification of cash crop cultivation and in labor performed on the plantations or in the service of the state.

Here is the crux of the problem. The few Baruya who created a joint-stock company promised that those who owned shares would regularly share in the profits and receive dividends. There was thus an explicit promise that everyone would make money together. The group that runs the company never ceases to proclaim that it serves the interests of all, and especially those who have put up their savings. But already by the end of 1980 cracks had begun to appear in this appealing façade. The Tchatche clan was accused of helping itself to money that belonged to all to pay for airplane trips to the city. People wondered where one of the clansmen had been able to find the money needed to pay compensation of 1,280 kinas to an enemy whose head he had cut open in a fight that broke out over a woman after a drinking session. In short, a two-sided movement is developing. Some, who still hope to benefit from it, continue to support the company and the man who symbolizes it. Others are losing patience and beginning to complain, and a few are thinking of starting another company. In the past, when the *aoulatta* or great warrior became a despot he was harshly judged. In the future, the wealthy entrepreneur will lose the support of his stockholders if it is shown that he is helping himself instead of helping them.

In this way some of the conditions that foster the emergence of big men are slowly starting to arise; these new "big men" are entrepreneurs who help others while helping themselves, who one day go too far and are forced to relinquish their power. But the nouveaux riches among the Baruya are only retail traders, not "true" big men. Nowhere does their social structure provide an incentive for them to convert their money into pigs, feathers, or shells, or to adopt a calculated strategy of ceremonial gifts and countergifts that would bring them direct returns in glory and authority. The Baruya nouveau riche buys luxury goods and is interested in consumption and pleasure. Another sign of "distinction": two Baruya recently "bought" Chimbu wives, one of them paying 685 kinas. To be sure, the payment of bride wealth for a wife is nothing new for the Baruya, but what is new is in these two cases was that the dowry was in money rather than in bars of salt and bark cloaks and that the women came from far away. The two Baruya met their wives in the city or near a plantation. In language and in culture these women are completely unrelated to the Anga tribes with which the Baruya have established matrimonial ties in the past, by exchanging their traditional forms of wealth for women. The goal of these exchanges was above all to establish or consolidate trading relations with the woman's tribe. But things are not the same with the young Baruya who have chosen Chimbu women. Of course it may well be that the brothers and cousins of these women harbor an ulterior motive in letting their sisters go off to live among the Baruya. The latter inhabit a marginal region still covered with forest, and the men may have had it in mind to pay regular visits to their brothers-in-law in order to buy bird of paradise feathers, a species that has disappeared from the Chimbu territory but that plays a leading role in their ceremonial exchanges. The principal motive of the Chimbu men nevertheless lies elsewhere. Being a populous tribe they lack sufficient land; as it is their custom to marry with a bride wealth, they need a great deal more money than the Baruya to reproduce their social structures, and they resort to all sorts of methods to obtain it. The reader may well imagine the life these women lead, foreigners by language, culture, custom, and ideology, irrevocably separated from their community except for brief visits from their relatives (and these visits are costly, since the trip must be made by airplane or truck).

But a movement in the opposite direction has also begun. Two Baruya men, still in their thirties and belonging to the generation of males that entered the men's house in 1960, have completely cut themselves off from their tribe and have married into the communities where by chance their jobs had led them. They now live with their brothers-in-law in coastal villages whose culture is completely different from their own. In addition to his wife one of them received a patch of land and some coconut trees, and he now produces copra to pay his wife's bride wealth. He had a letter sent to his family explaining that he was giving up all rights to the Baruya woman who was promised to him. The other Baruya, who had become a policeman, married a woman on the north coast where he was stationed. He too paid a dowry.

Like other Baruya these men chose to marry outsiders, but instead of bringing their wives back, they settled away from home. Both kinds of marriage contribute, in opposite yet complementary ways, to the birth of new

217

social customs, ones that both build on tribal traditions and efface them. Such a metamorphosis in traditional local communities is only possible because the white man has created a higher power, the state, which provides an incentive for men, wealth, and ideas to circulate throughout the country on a scale completely different from that of the past and for reasons that have nothing to do with tradition. This metamorphosis, which has made of each local unit a contradictory mixture of several different levels of reality and power, tribal powers and state powers, is what the formation of a nation is all about: a nation politically independent in that its citizens elect their own leaders from among themselves but, like all the young nations of Oceania, dependent upon the capitalist world and the great powers that dominate it in Europe or in Asia.

Such are, all too briefly, the contradictory transformations and metamorphoses wrought in Baruya society by the belated imposition (in 1960) of a colonial order, one of the last of a bygone era. No sooner was it established than this order gave way to the authority of an independent nation state, without the Baruya ever having much say in the matter. By 1981, in a society which only thirty years earlier had been using stone implements to act upon nature, the figures of power had been profoundly unsettled. Some of these figures have disappeared, others have virtually collapsed, whereas those that remain must make their peace with the new facts of life and the powers that be.

The warrior function has almost disappeared, the old *aoulatta* are dead or are peacefully waiting to die, surrounded by great prestige and respect. But everyone knows that there is not much place in the future for exploits such as theirs. Prestige now goes to the young men who like the *aoulatta* before them have conquered in the outside world; but these men become state officials or employees – some have already reached high rank – in the missions or private companies. In the near future one of these men will be running for election to the National Assembly, as the representative of all the tribes of the Marawaka district.

With the disappearance of warfare much of the role of the great gardener or *tannaka* has also disappeared, for he was the pillar and the source of material support for the warriors' effort. Of course his other sources of prestige remain. On the occasion of the initiations or the innumerable public meetings held to settle a dispute, discuss building a school or buying a truck, he is always the first to send bags of sweet potatoes and taro harvested and cooked by his wives, and to come bringing armfuls of sugarcane. He now has the option of investing his strength and talents in the production of coffee with the sole aim of enriching himself if he so wishes.

As for the *koulaka* or shamans, they are at present only moderately threatened by modern developments. Of course, like the *aoulatta* they have lost their role in war. But since every act of healing among the Baruya concludes with an act of aggression against their neighbors and former enemies, the shamans alone are carrying on the age-old battles of their tribe. With the *kwaimatnie*-men they remain the principal guardians of ancestral thought and custom. They are no doubt threatened by the activity of the missionaries, but until now the latter have only succeeded in converting two Baruya. On the other hand, because the shamans only treat internal diseases and "afflictions," there is no real conflict between them and the doctors. Most of the doctors are ready to collaborate with the shamans, something that is perfectly possible in view of the changing ideas and attitudes of the medical profession in Europe and in New Guinea. But if one day a young Baruya returns as a pastor to preach the gospel to his own tribe, mounting a frontal attack on the functions of the shamans and the traditional interpretations on the sources of evil, sickness, and death, things could quickly change. The young Baruya, who today refuse to become shamans only because they want to keep their freedom of movement and the option of leaving their tribe, may very well refuse to do so for other reasons tomorrow, for ideological reasons turning on religious "conviction."

As for the *kayareumala,* the cassowary hunters, their status is not yet threatened, although it may be in the future by use of firearms if the number of gun and hunting permits increases. At present increasing permits is not the policy of the administration. But the young Baruya who accompany officers of the administration on forest patrols often lasting several weeks, who see them shoot cassowaries, which everyone then eats without ceremony, will they not one day soon be tempted to forget that for a Baruya the cassowary is the "wild woman" of the forest, which only a handful of inspired hunters have the power to trap?

But things have not yet gone this far. For as we have seen, aside from its value as a feat of hunting skill, the cassowary hunt is a symbol of male domination and will retain its prestige as long as that domination lasts. Moreover some of the values formerly associated with the warrior function have been shifted to the activity of the hunt. Young males who once could have become great warriors today receive messages from the "spirits" telling them that they will probably become great hunters of the cassowary. And the "spirits" choose these future hunters from among the boys who do not go to school, who live as in the past in the men's house.

For since 1979 the Baruya have decided to send to school only those boys who show the aptitude and the desire to study. Indeed, many children run away from school and prefer to be initiated in order to live in the "men's house" and to hunt in the forest with boys of their age. Of course they will learn to speak pidgin but, since they will not learn to read and write, they will become gardeners; from time to time they will leave the tribe to work two years or more on the coast, or they will become coffee planters. In the course of time they will be joined by Baruya of their age who were sent to

219

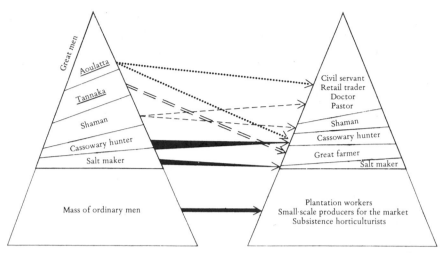

Figure 14. Changes in the Baruya hierarchies since the colonial era

school but who only succeeded in remaining there a few years. It is among the young Baruya bound for a more traditional life that the spirits choose the future shamans and cassowary hunters. As for the salt makers, also tied to the preservation of the male initiation rites, they have the important function of producing an item of ritual consumption that is still vital to the reproduction of traditional Baruya social relations, but they have lost the function of producing the tribe's principal means of commercial exchange, for money in the form of coins and bills has replaced salt.

Of all the figures in the social hierarchy of the Baruya, there remain to be considered the *kwaimatnie*-men, the masters of the male initiation rituals. Although for a time shaken by the disappearance of war and the deliberate policy of certain missions that sought to prevent the initiations of the children who attended their schools, the function of the *kwaimatnie*-men is still of the utmost importance for every Baruya. This function is a symbol of continuity, tradition, and identity. Since the Baruya perceived that their initiations gave the young the moral and psychological strength to resist the perils of life in the cities and on the plantations, the initiations have once again been directed along two lines, against two sources of disorder: one internal and traditional, namely, women; the other external and profoundly new, the difficulties of life outside the tribe that every young Baruya faces. Today as yesterday, a young Baruya man must be "strong" in the face of the challenges of life, and the Baruya woman must recognize his superiority and remain faithful and hard working during the years of his absence (see Figure 14).

Even to this day, then, we find delineated at the heart of Baruya society, albeit under slightly altered features, the domination of men over women. In principle, women are now protected against male violence by a new force, that of law and the state. But the law has not prevented five of them from being done to death by men since 1960. Women have been given the same political rights as men, and they are entitled to vote to elect consols or members of the National Assembly. Although a tribeswoman will have little difficulty forming an opinion of a Baruya running for election to represent her village, it is still out of the question for her – simply through lack of information and experience of the outside world – to arrive at a well-informed opinion of a Baruya seeking election to the National Assembly, still less of him as a representative of the party to which he belongs.

The distance between men and women has narrowed over the last fifteen years. A whole series of attitudes and signs of submission on the part of the latter toward the former have vanished, those that concern body attitudes, ways of moving about, and the things said between the sexes and the way in which they are said. The Baruya have eased the taboos that formerly kept a man apart from his wife, mother, and daughters. It is no longer uncommon (it was unthinkable when I arrived, in 1967) to see a young father holding his child in his arms and looking after the infant for a while before handing it back to its mother. The world of women, the world of the reproduction of life and baby care, has ceased to pose quite such a threat to men and their masculinity.

Personal relations have changed a good deal. The traditional attitudes and ideology of male domination have already taken some hard knocks. In three essential ways, however, nothing has yet seriously changed in the relations between the sexes. To this day, women are still excluded from land ownership; tribal law survives; and, concerning the land, which is the prime condition of material existence, women are in no sense, not even formally, the equals of men.

Although no one is entitled to resort to armed violence, men still continue to commit such violence on women. Among the Baruya, people kill with the hatchet or arrows. The men still go around their daily business with an ax slung over the shoulder and a bow in the hand to clear the forest and shoot a few birds along the way – perfectly normal and necessary in a society that depends on forest farming for its subsistence. What is remarkable, twenty years after colonization, is that women are still forbidden to touch or wield axes or adzes. The men may give them little machetes as gifts, which are efficient for cutting down dead wood in the forest, but none has yet given his wife or sister an ax.

The last field in which relations between the sexes remain highly unequal is that of money, and everything connected with the getting of it. But here the Baruya are still far from living in an industrial, cash economy, in which all means of subsistence must be bought. The women produce their own food, their skirts, their string bags, and where these aspects of their material

221

life are concerned they are independent of the men. They are not, however, in the strategic operations such as forest clearance, erecting fences around the gardens, and other activities crucial to the production cycle; they did on the other hand enjoy, and they still do, a certain measure of autonomy within the production process.

Concerning access to money, the situation of the women has undergone a slight change in the last twenty years. Initially, they were allowed to earn a little by selling sweet potatoes and other vegetables to the administration of the missions in order to feed the workers at the government post, the mission employees, the sick undergoing treatment at the dispensary, prisoners, and so on. But the demand (for a few hundred kilograms of potatoes a day) was too low to cover the cash requirements of hundreds of women. So for many years the women depended for cash on the men (husband, brothers, or father gone to work on the plantations). This situation still exists, but two things have changed. The Baruya have gradually begun to sell their pigs inside the tribe. Needless to say, when they kill a pig, it is generally to share the meat among their kin and affines; they have to do this, as the direct exchange of women still exists and therefore implies reciprocal gifts of pig meat among the families that have decided to form an alliance. But they are sending increasing quantities of meat to the market. A sixty-kilogram pig can bring in around fifty kinas (400 [1981] French Francs). As the women have traditional rights over their pigs, the men share the proceeds of the sale with them.

The same goes for coffee, which the women harvest, shell, dry, and often carry as far as the government post. Here again, the men share the proceeds with the women. These are new departures, which are altering economic relations between the sexes, but are still far from making women financially independent of men. One thing though, and this is important under Baruya tradition, a woman can do as she likes with what money she has. This tradition still survives, and today she will most likely buy rice and fish to eat with her women friends, sisters, or mother; or she may buy clothes, adornments, mirrors, and so forth.

This survey of what has changed in relations between the sexes would be incomplete if we failed to stress one fact that is at least as important as the abolition of war and the introduction of legal protection for women, namely, the girls and some young women are now gaining access to education through schooling.

In 1974 a formerly shy young woman, who had lived with her husband at the government post field hospital and had quickly learned pidgin, told me that she had gone of her own accord to the "Bible school" to learn to read and write and that she had noticed that she learned more quickly than the boys. "Ah, if only I'd been a man!" she concluded. I do not think that she was merely – or even mainly – giving vent to penis envy, and the anecdote shows how far change transcends the question of sexuality.

222

Nowadays the girls not only go to the Bible school, but some also go to the English-speaking school. Some take their studies further, and as has happened in all the tribes that have been in contact with the contemporary economy and the state for some years, they go on to become nurses, teachers, university students, and the like, following in the footsteps of their brothers, who have now become civil servants. Certain Baruya applaud this evolution, and I can cite one significant example. In 1980, when it became necessary to find a wife for a young mathematics lecturer, who wanted to marry within the tribe, the families concerned by the marriage chose for him a bride able to read and write, who understood pidgin and the rudiments of English and would thus be able to go and live with him on the campus.

If the Baruya have been struck to discover the intellectual abilities of their womenfolk, they were no less astonished by the following incident. At school the children play all sorts of sports. One day a girl showed that she could run faster than most of the boys her age. Men and boys expressed mingled admiration and regret, for here women were encroaching upon what had till then been an exclusive male preserve, namely, trials of physical prowess, whether in training for war or for the sheer thrill of competition.

Understandably, these changes come as a blow to the traditional symbols and norms of male superiority, which still continue deep down to organize Baruya society and which still serve men as a point of reference, as a conceptual frame on which to fashion their personalities and self-images. The outcome of contradictions can sometimes be tragic. In July 1979, for instance, a young Baruya killed his wife with an ax and then turned himself in to the commander of the government post, a New Guinean from the Gulf of Papua region. The brothers and uncles of the victim wanted to execute the culprit, who was taken to the town for judgment and sentence. He refused to utter a word before the court.

I have talked over his behavior with the Baruya in an effort to understand its meaning. Several explanations have been given, and even if none is the correct one, they are indicative of a state of mind and of a state of society. It was explained to me that the young man had returned to the village some months earlier, that he had been expelled from school because he was a poor pupil and regularly failed his exams. On his return he had been bitterly rebuked for his failure by the members of his lineage and all those who had helped finance his schooling. Some had asked him to pay them back, as they had been counting on him to help them in turn later on. So he decided to go to work on the plantations in order to earn some money. But his young wife then reproached him for leaving her so soon after their marriage. As she was sharp tongued, she must have said something wounding to him, so the young man went back to live in the "men's house." Rumor has it that certain men took advantage of the situation to urge his wife to leave him. But that was impossible, as her husband's lineage had already given a wife to hers, which made her the *ginamare,* the wife given back in exchange. So, to cut a long story short, we do not know what really happened. What I did learn was that the murderer had already contemplated committing the crime a few days earlier. He had told the others in the "men's house" that he would be going to Marawaka for some days. In actual fact he never made the journey and is reported to have been seen watching his wife from afar as she went into the forest; but she was accompanied by her younger brother, and his presence had stayed the murderer's hand. The opportunity arose a few days later when his wife's mother asked her daughter and son-in-law to go and fetch wood in the forest. He went off alone with her into the forest, armed with an ax, and killed her.

Whatever the objective value of interpretations of the crime, they clearly reveal some of the sources of conflict in Baruya society today, such as the hopes placed in young people sent to school, the pressures on them, how women react when their husbands express their intention to leave them for two (or more) years to work in the plantations, the way other men exploit the situation to press their own suit in the absence of a fiancé or husband, the fear and resentment felt by men who have been publicly humiliated by the mockery and resistance of certain young women, who are far less inclined to submission than their elders. For this murder bears tragic witness to the women's newly acquired social power. The situation is unstable and shifting, but it painfully unleashes both the contradictions of the old Baruya social organization and those emerging with the new.

I thus come to the end of my journey. From among the many possible courses, I have chosen to explore Baruya thought and society by starting with an analysis of relations between men and women, and by trying to understand the logic that lies behind all the different hierarchies and forms of power that have their roots in the mechanisms of male domination, by which I mean the production of great men who have risen above their fellows by virtue either of their functions or of their merit.

We have tried to show how this edifice gradually crumbled and changed even before the colonial shock, though still more so afterward. As a producer of great men, not big men, Baruya society throws a different light on the big men societies and on their deep structures. But comparison with New Guinea, Africa, or the Amazon raises general theoretical questions that we shall briefly discuss in the concluding pages of this book.

224

Conclusion

10

The ventriloquist's dummy

First, a brief reminder of what we set out to do in this book. Several years in the field have yielded an abundance of systematically observed empirical facts and brought me into ever-closer contact with the attitudes and patterns of thought of the Baruya. I am now convinced that the dominant factor in their behavior and social organization was, not the relation between men and women, which means nothing in itself, but the multifaceted and partially contradictory configuration of relations between men and women in every area of their lives. My purpose in this book has been merely to reconstruct as clearly as possible the mechanisms and the internal logic of the social practices and ideas around which this configuration of relations revolves. I began by looking at Baruya society before the colonial shock (which is of only recent origin), and then went on to observe the transformations and mutations that have occurred since this shock up to the present day, six years after Papua New Guinea's accession to independence.

In order to continue my theoretical analysis of Baruya society, I would have to turn to a very different approach which would supply the material for another book. This approach would set out from a crucial principle of science which is that the particular always belongs to a class of like facts. No particular society can be fully accounted for in terms of itself, for the simple reason that each society has a past which spills over into its present and prevents our understanding it purely in terms of its present conditions of existence. At the same time, history demands explanation, and cannot itself explain everything. These thoughts are immediately applicable to the Baruya, and we shall confine ourselves to a single example, namely, the kinship system that is characteristic of their social organization. As we have seen, the production of relations of kinship among the Baruya depends primarily on the principle of direct exchange of women, and the Baruya language uses different words to refer to parallel cousins and to cross cousins.

Now there are dozens of societies in the world today that practice direct exchange of women and whose languages also distinguish between these two varieties of cousin. Some are hunting societies, others agricultural societies. Some live in Australia, others in America or in Oceania. Precisely because of this particularity, the Baruya immediately belong to a class of social facts that need to be analyzed. The way in which they belong to this class indicates what this theory ought not to be seeking. For the very diversity of societies that possess this type of kinship system already shows that its existence cannot be accounted for by hunting or agriculture, still less by this or that particular form of hunting or agriculture. In order to pursue our theoretical analysis of Baruya society we shall have to turn our backs on it temporarily, or at least approach it on a different plane, systematically comparing it with all the other societies with which it is comparable, whether by resemblance or by contrast. This approach is only justifiable if we first assume the existence of laws that govern the structural transformations of the various forms of social organization that have either succeeded each other or coexisted in the course of history. We shall not be pursuing this approach – at least not here – but we shall nevertheless be extending the theoretical perspectives opened up by this analysis of Baruya society and try to use them as a basis on which to formulate some problems of a more general order.

Let us return to the formula of male domination among the Baruya for a fresh look at its component parts. We are now familiar with them. Women are really, actually separated from control over the means of production, destruction, and exchange. The men therefore control in practice (and sometimes enjoy a monopoly over) the material means of existence, as well as over the social means of governing and even thinking. They are in charge of and control the strategic phases in the practical process of producing the material conditions of existence, for example, forest clearance, protecting crops from wild animals; in the reproduction of life they also claim to play the leading role by conceiving the child in the mother's belly, by nurturing with their sperm both fetus and mother, with the aid of the Sun, the divine father of all human beings.

On closer examination, we find that the various components of male domination belong to two types of social reality, whose effects when combined are compounded. On the one hand, women are prohibited from land ownership; they are separated from the production of the means of destruction and exchange. This directly visible social reality is daily experienced in practice and exists both in thought and outside of it. Second, the assertion that men play the principal role in the making of a child is a reality that exists first of all in thought, a conceptual [*idéel*] reality, just as socially real as all the other components of male domination, but whose mode of social existence is particular in the sense that it consists foremost in a series of symbolic gestures, rites, and practices in which the Baruya engage in order to demonstrate men's dominance in the process of reproduction of life.

228

Let us dwell for a moment on what is generally meant by a symbolic practice. It is a means of transmitting ideas from the world of thought to the material world or nature, while at the same time turning them into social relations, into social matter. Symbolic utterances and gestures transform ideas into a directly perceptible social and material reality. But it would be wrong to think that the Baruya see their symbols and rites as mere play-acting, as a representation of fundamental realities that act upon them in a generally invisible manner for them. The symbols are not mere signs; they are also means of acting directly upon these deep-seated though invisible realities. Their symbolic practices are a good deal more than play-acting, since by acting out these invisible realities they press them into the service of their social order. This belief in the concrete efficacy of symbolic practices means, for them, that to show something symbolically is to demonstrate it, because it is to act and produce results that are daily verifiable and verified in the multitude of visible signs of men's superiority over women. Now this belief was shared by both sexes, and these shared representations constituted the main silent and invisible strength of male dominance. Today, the clash between Baruya culture and other cultures and religions that are seeking to replace their ancient customs is liable to shatter this belief and shared outlook in some people's minds. Christianity, or other aspects of Western culture, are therefore going to have to furnish alternative evidence of male superiority.

Let us return to the way in which the Baruya conceive the origin and essence of male dominance. To explain the origins of this dominance they claim that men had once laid hold of the powers that formerly belonged to women and added them to their own, after having rid them of whatever may have been harmful to them. To the outside observer, it seems as if these powers of which women are said to have been dispossessed had no existence outside the symbolic utterances and practices that asserted their existence, unlike land or weapons, from which women are daily and visibly separated and which exist outside thought. We are not saying that these two types of separation stand in opposition to each other in the way the real and the imaginary worlds do, because the imaginary world is part of the real world and is socially just as real as the other elements of social life.

Why do the Baruya come to attribute to women, in thought, powers that thought immediately sets about confiscating and adding to those of men? It seems to me that the point of all these efforts is to diminish the social importance of the incontrovertible evidence that it is in the woman's belly that children are conceived and from her belly that they are born, and that it is then to her milk that they owe their survival. It is as if men, already concretely dominating the process of production of the material conditions of existence, had endeavored by means of thought to magnify their role in the reproduction of life and hence to deprecate the primordial role that women patently play in this process. It is as if men wanted to abolish or diminish

229

their dependence on women in the process of the reproduction of life and to rob women of the powers that they wield by virtue of the particular role that they play in this process. But by asserting the legitimacy of the imaginary violence done to women in order to magnify men, because of the beneficial results to all, the myths simultaneously legitimize the violence done to women in all areas of life, and primarily in the social mechanism in the reproduction of life, in the workings of relations of kinship, which are based on the principle of the exchange of women between groups by the men who represent them.

We return to two general theoretical problems. What do human groups gain from exchanging women? Why are men more representative of these groups than women, and why is it they who assume responsibility for defending the interests of the group? Here, we can no longer rely on the explanations given by the Baruya themselves, and we must seek objective, non-intentional explanations for these social facts.

Why is the control of the process of the reproduction of life such an important issue in classless societies? Could it be that, in these societies, living individuals are more important to the reproduction of society than are the material means of production? This assumption would explain why relations of kinship function as relations of production in such societies. But why do groups need to exchange the means of reproducing life among themselves? Why can they not find the means of their reproduction within themselves? Is there something within their conditions of existence that ceaselessly drives them to separate in order to exist, yet to overcome this separation in order to go on existing? Are there then objective reasons, over and beyond the process of the reproduction of life, that explain why it is the social organization of this process, the production of relations of kinship, that both establishes this separation and enables it to be overcome by means of exchange?

Even if there are unintentional reasons to account for this separation and exchange among the groups that form a society, we still need to find out why it is the men and not the women who represent these groups, and why it is the women and not the men who are given to others. Are there areas of social life outside kinship that propel men into the forefront and thus make them more representative of society than women?

When one asks the Baruya why are men as they are, and why do they behave as they do, why do they have a monopoly of war and hunting, why do they occupy the leading position in the process of production, forest clearance, and so on, they offer two kinds of reasons. Men are stronger and they are more mobile than women. But it would be a mistake to take the division of labor as we find it among the Baruya for a reality that explains society as a point of departure, when it is in fact a point of arrival. For although one cannot deny that it takes a great deal of combined physical force to clear the virgin forest using stone implements, it does not explain why women do not make their own digging sticks, even though they could. It does not explain why it is the men who make them and then give them to the women, thereby reasserting women's dependence on men in the process of the production of their material conditions of existence. The division of labor is not the point of departure of the social relations by which production is organized. It is itself a point of arrival, the outcome of both a certain state of the material and intellectual productive forces that a society employs to act upon its environment in order to extract from it the means of existence, and of the relative position of the two sexes vis-à-vis resources, in other words, of their respective relations to the conditions of production.

Thus it is very difficult to distinguish the unintentional elements from the intentional ones in the content of social relations, and hence to perceive their relations, to construct a theory of the causes and mechanisms that give rise to them. It seems to me that the place of women in the process of the reproduction of life may, up to a certain point, exclude them from those activities that require great mobility, such as war or big game hunting, as well as from exchanges with the outside world, owing to the potential danger of armed violence. It is also possible that the differences in physical strength may help to explain why material activities demanding a great expenditure of energy in a short space of time are reserved for men.

There is no single cause, nor even an ultimate cause, of the diverse forms of male dominance encountered in history. I see rather a series of causes, which are not intentional at bottom, and which arrange themselves into a sort of hierarchy because certain ones play a more important role in the mechanism by which their efforts are combined into an outcome that is never the same from one society to another, or from one era to another. The assumption of unintentional reasons for the existence of male dominance would be sufficient to refute any conspiracy theory, but it should in no way be taken to mean that men, finding themselves in a socially advantageous position for unintentional reasons (which though meaningful obey no teleological imperative) have not worked intentionally and collectively to reproduce and widen this advantage. The Baruya men have undoubtedly done so in the case of making digging sticks for women. But it is also the case during the initiations when the men reveal to the young initiates that it is they who make the bull-roarers and twirl them about their heads, producing the bellowings that strike such terror into the women and little boys from afar during the men's ceremonies. The women and children are led to understand that these are the voices of spirits come to mingle with their brothers and fathers. In male power, violence combines with ruse, fraud, and secrecy, all of which are used consciously to preserve and widen the distance that separates and protects men from women, as well as ensuring their superiority. But we must not forget that Baruya women have their own secrets, protecting them from men and constantly reminding them that women have powers too.

Consequently the relation between the conceptual and the nonconceptual [*idéel* and *non-idéel*] in the real world cannot be construed as the relation between a reflection and the reality reflected. Thought does not reflect; it gives meaning to situations born of causes and forces whose origins do not lie solely in the conscious or the unconscious. Thought invents and produces this meaning by constructing systems of interpretation which engender symbolic practices, which are themselves so many manners of organizing and legitimizing, which also produce male domination over women and thereby become social relations. It would be simple if thought could confine itself merely to reflecting or representing society, but the whole difficulty of scientifically analyzing the conceptual [*idéel*] factor in the real world stems from the fact that thought not only represents society but itself contributes to the production of society.

We need to adopt this outlook in analyzing a society's ideas about the body and what it has to say not only about the bodies of men and women but, with the aid of their bodies, what it has to say about sexuality and its sexual discourse. For in all cultures, the differences that sexuality entails for each sex (different organs and different bodily substances) become the terms and vocabulary of the discourse that sexuality is constantly expected to produce on the social and cosmic order, together with the evidence that it is supposed to adduce in support of this discourse. In societies where men do dominate women and permanently subject women to particular forms of ideological, social, and material violence, sexuality is constantly called in to prove to the men who commit it, and to the women who are subject to it, that this domination is perfectly "legitimate." We all know that, when it comes to oppression, the domination of one section of society by another (sex, caste, class, or race) is fully justified and legitimate only if the victims themselves become the guilty parties, those primarily responsible for their own fate.

What could be more evident in seeking grounds for social differentiation than finding the basis in the body, or in "nature" as we like to say; and where male domination is concerned, in the difference between the body of man and that of woman? In themselves, needless to say, the bodily substances do not speak and are meaningless. Yet in all societies they do in fact speak – and not mere gibberish either. Indeed, they scream and, from one point of view, sexuality is an indiscreet screaming chamber for relations of oppression and exploitation. As we have seen, for the Baruya, it is the menstrual blood, as opposed to sperm, that is the chief supplier of irrefutable "proof" that women are merely victims of themselves. But, of all languages, body language has the advantage of extinguishing discourse, interrupting the flow of words, and stifling verbalization in a subjectively experienced consent that is

232

equally an acknowledgment of the rightness of things as they are. For indeed a Baruya woman has merely to see the blood start to flow between her thighs for her to hold her tongue and mutely consent to whatever economic, political, and psychological oppression she may be subjected. Consequently one of the functions of thought, which is not merely to explain but also to convince, is in fact totally accomplished in the language of the body and in its fantasies. When language about the body becomes the language of the body there is nothing more to be said about society and the universe. All that remains is to experience a social and cosmic order to which the body has already submitted, beyond conscious and deliberate discourse. It is in the body rather than in consciously argued thought that "intimate conviction" finds fulfillment and completes the demonstration that thought requires.

Consequently, when one presses Baruya men with direct questions such as: "But why can't women inherit land? Why don't they make their own digging sticks?" one is met by silence; then comes the answer: "Because they're women"; and if one insists a little, they start to talk about menstrual blood, pollution, and so on. So sexuality seems to behave rather like a ventriloquist's dummy, one of those dolls that suddenly starts talking about anything and everything; held at arm's length by a man who seems to be saying nothing, merely asking questions and waiting for the answers, whereas in actual fact he is both asking the questions and giving the answers.

In fact, what is clear is that in any society, over and beyond personal relationships between individuals of either sex (beyond the concrete relations that bring them face to face with each other as father, mother, son, daughter, brother, sister, relative, friend, stranger, enemy, exploiter, exploited), sexuality is subordinate to the conditions of reproduction of social relations. The conditions of reproduction of social relations are not subject to sexuality, which is therefore obliged to fall back on its own resources to produce a discourse that does not originate with it in essence and which transcends it, since it legitimizes the social order to which it is obliged to submit. The subordination that we are talking about here is not merely that of one sex to the other; it is the subordination of one sphere of social life to the conditions imposed by the workings of other social relations. We are talking about the place of this sphere in the reproduction of the deep structure of society, not merely of its position on the surface of society, within the visible hierarchy of collective institutions and individual behavior patterns. "Over and beyond any personal relationship" does not mean "prior to any personal relationship," for we are speaking here not of any chronological order of priority, but of a structural priority, in other words, of the place that a social activity occupies by virtue of its functions in the process of production and reproduction of societies.

What is needed here is a whole "history" of sexuality, and a comparative theory of the languages of the body, and anthropologists today are among the first, if not the first, to tackle this subject.[1] We need to know how sexuality is affected by its subordination to this or that social relation and, first of all, needless to say, to the reproduction of this or that relation of kinship. To show that the language of the body, the meaning of bodily substances, is probably subject to transformational laws, through the transformations of kinship systems, we shall compare the Baruya theory of the body with another theory, again from New Guinea, namely, the Trobriand Islands, familiar from the celebrated work of Malinowski and, half a century later, that of an American anthropologist, Annette Weiner.[2]

The society of the Trobriand Islands is a hierarchic matrilineal society. At its apex a hereditary aristocracy controls the land and the so-called *kula* exchanges of ceremonial goods with the outside world. The Trobriand theory of the process of the reproduction of life is roughly as follows: A child is conceived in its mother's belly when two elements combine to form the internal substance of the fetus; in the blood of the mother is incarnated the spirit belonging to the mother's clan, an ancestor, *baloma,* which penetrates her in the form of a child-spirit, *waiwaia.* The child-spirit is therefore the provisional, historically transient reincarnation of an immortal spirit, of a *baloma,* which lives with the other *baloma* of all the matrilineal clans in a small island off the Trobriand Islands.

Therefore the woman conceives the child alone, and the child belongs to her, and to her brothers who are formed from a mixture of this same blood and of various child-spirits from the same clan. Here, sperm is not thought of as the principal substance of the child, its internal substance, but as a substance that helps to nourish the fetus and to shape it; hence the practice of repeated coitus during pregnancy, to fortify the child and help it to grow in the mother's belly. As with the Baruya, the child is made up of bodily substances and a spiritual principle, but here the spiritual principle is not the Sun, the superfather of men, but an everlasting being that exists outside of time and within the course of time, from generation to generation. Because the woman serves as the place in which these spirits (male or female?) are reincarnated, she occupies the central place in the process of the reproduction of life. It is a very different theory from that of the Baruya women, and their social position is much superior, but one should be wary of concluding that this society is therefore a matriarchal one, for in matrilineal societies, women produce children for their brothers, who do not make love with them,

---

[1] From a very different standpoint, Michel Foucault has embarked on a history of sexuality in the Western world: *Histoire de la sexualité,* vol. 1, *La volonté de savoir* (Paris: Gallimard, 1976).

[2] Annette Weiner, *Women of Value, Men of Renown* (Austin: University of Texas Press, 1976), esp. chap. 2, pp. 25–60; "Trobriand Descent: Female / Male Domains," *Ethos* 5 (1) (1977): 54–70; "The Reproductive Model in Trobriand Society," *Mankind* 11 (1978): 175–86.

whereas with the Baruya, men sire children with the women that have taken the place of their sisters. We could go on to compare in even greater detail theories of the body with those of other societies in Oceania or Africa, whether matrilineal or cognate, with or without classes; but our analysis already hints at the real reasons why blood and sperm, though meaningless in themselves, invariably convey society's messages, and why we do not need to look elsewhere for the reasons that underlie their meaning.

Nor is this meaning to be found in some substance taken in isolation, but rather in the interplay of relations of opposition and complementarity with all of the other substances and other, more abstract, attributes of the differences between the sexes. For in certain societies where, contrary to the Baruya, people make love during the menstrual period so as to mingle the two substances and conjoin the features of the father with those of the mother, the woman is still regarded as dangerous, not because of her menstrual blood this time, but because of the excessive "heat" of her sex, and so on. This is not to say, however, that more or less anything can be taken to signify and justify male domination. A sign is taken as a signifier only if it is suited to such contrasts, and therefore renders the choice of signs less arbitrary. Consequently there is a need for more detailed, more extensive empirical work, and for a more searching theoretical analysis in order to discover the transformational laws (assuming that they exist) that govern systems of oppositions as they relate to the profusion of social orders encountered in history.

We might even say that it is not sexuality that fantasizes in society, but society that fantasizes in sexuality. Perhaps it is first of all – and the priority would be that of the order of reasons and structures – not sexuality that alienates individuals, but sexuality itself that is alienated, that is, instantly strange and foreign to itself as soon as it is obliged to produce, with the aid of the body, a discourse on the body that does not originate from within itself and that serves forms of alienation and social oppression for which, once again, it is not responsible. Yet the fact that this discourse is about the body means that it gathers up and imprisons all the other reasons for the existence of these forms of oppression and exploitation within sexuality. By sealing them up within the body, sexuality metamorphoses them and casts a veil over them, and it is in this sense that sexuality is not only alienated but can actually become "alienating."

In order to hear what sexuality has to say, and to explain why it invariably crops up in many different aspects of social relations, we may need to eschew a certain brand of psychoanalysis: the kind that is not concerned to seek, in the misfortunes of desire and the strata of fantasies, manifestations of subordination that are not here forms of subordination of one person to another, or even of one sex to another (regardless of sex), but of sex to social orders whose ultimate reasons mainly lie elsewhere.

I would like to raise one immediate objection to these suggestions and to my own arguments. Is there not one element in the submission of sexuality to the social order – regardless of the face of this submission and the form of the order – that makes it neither alienated nor alienating, one element common to all periods of history, namely, the ubiquitous incest taboo? This taboo affects everybody's sexuality, regardless of his or her sex, from birth till death; yet incest is surely an amputation of desire, and surely its effect is to oblige desire to direct itself toward "suitable people," that is, those regarded as suitable within a given system of kinship and social relations. Surely sexuality is alienated, and doomed forever to be so, if no society can forgo the application of some form of prohibition on incest. Yet surely all societies feel the need to strip the children's desires of their polyvalence and their polytrophism in order to channel them toward suitable people and things?

Therefore what does the incest taboo mean? Fundamentally, it is the presence, in any society, of a basic law, of a fundamental property of human existence. Unlike social animals and their cousins the chimpanzees and baboons, humans (notwithstanding sociologists or anthropologists) not only live in society but also produce society in order to live. It is this basic law that finds expression in and operates through and well beyond the incest taboo. This law was splendidly perceived and expressed by Lévi-Strauss. But how come man is not content to live in society, but feels the need to produce and change his society in order to live, unless it be some objective, incontrovertible fact that lies beyond his will, namely, the fact that he is capable of transforming nature and, in so doing, transforming his own nature? The incest taboo, which diverts the individual's desire for those who cooperated in giving him life (and not only his immediate relatives), every day and everywhere reasserts that, however great one may be, the individual is never the point of departure of society, and that no individual and no particular group can find in themselves, in isolation or in a state of self-sufficiency, all the necessary conditions for real – that is, social – existence. Is the incest taboo merely an amputation of desire, mutilating the individual, or does it represent a break that promotes his social being while at the same time laying upon him the yoke of oppression and alienation specific to his society?

We shall have to leave matters there. I would like nevertheless to add that my analysis of the way in which men dominate women in Baruya society, along with my reflection on a large number of classless societies, increasingly confirms my belief that relations between the sexes do not originate in caste and class relations, and that we cannot expect the class struggle alone to put an end to male dominance. Yet we cannot isolate struggles against forms of male oppression from the struggles against all the different forms of oppression contained in distinctions of class, caste, or of race, superior or inferior.

As I conclude this analysis of a classless society, let us imagine – and others have done so before me – that the old classless societies slowly turned into class societies when it came to be recognized that it was socially advantageous for kinship or ethnic groups to specialize in distinct functions. Yet this transformation alone could not suffice to develop class inequality. It certainly took something else for certain of these functions, namely, the religious and warrior functions, to come to be regarded as so important to the reproduction of the community that those who exercised them, being obliged to devote their entire time to them, ceased to take part in the production process. It was in these conditions that a portion of the labor that the entire classless society devotes to its reproduction thereby became surplus labor. Under what conditions did entire groups become warriors exclusively, others priests, others craftsmen, and yet others farmers, to use the distinctions that led to the emergence not of castes or classes but of great men among the Baruya (the *aoulatta,* the *koulaka,* the *tsaimaya,* the *tannaka*)? We are still unable to answer this question, but I would note in passing that castes are merely one form among others of the processes of functional division, one in which women do not circulate between groups but remain inside them, endogamy petrifying groups into so many distinct social species. For this purpose, one probably needs religions that abhor miscegenation or mixing and devote themselves to weeding out the pure from the impure.

It may be that certain readers will fail to see the point in this discussion but will assume that it must have some meaning for others, others that live far off in time and space, in a still primitive world, in a world of primitive people who will sooner or later change and become civilized. I would suggest that those readers look about themselves and observe the real place of men and women in the various contexts of our social life, and in the images, ideas, and desires that represent them and represent them to each other. If, having done so, the readers can look away and still be satisfied with being civilized, then I think we shall have to remind them of what was once said of another of racism's avatars: "If the Baruya are savages, then we are all Baruya." Let them then refrain from doing as the Baruya men, who excel at magnifying themselves in their own imagination.

Bibliography

Encyclopaedia of Papua and New Guinea, 1972. Peter Ryan, gen. ed. Melbourne, Melbourne University Press, University of Papua and New Guinea, 3 vols.

Ethnographic Bibliography of New Guinea, An, 1968. Canberra, Australian National University, Department of Anthropology and Sociology. Australian National University, 3 vols.

Allen, M. R., 1967. *Male Cults and Secret Initiations in Melanesia.* Melbourne, Melbourne University Press, 140 pp.

——— 1981. "Elders, Chiefs and Big Men: The Legitimation of Authority and Political Evolution in Melanesia," 43 pp. Typescript.

Barnes, John A., 1962. "African Models in the New Guinea Highlands," *Man* 62 (2):5–9.

Barth, F., 1975. *Ritual and Knowledge among the Baktaman of New Guinea.* New Haven, Yale University Press.

Berndt, R. M., 1971. "Political Structure in the Eastern Central Highlands of New Guinea," in *Politics in New Guinea,* ed. R. M. Berndt and P. Lawrence. Perth, University of Western Australia Press: 381–423.

Berndt, R. M. and P. Lawrence, Eds., 1971. *Politics in New Guinea.* Perth, University of Western Australia Press, 430 pp.

Bjerre, J., 1956. *The Last Cannibals.* London, Michael Joseph.

Blackwood, Beatrice, 1939a. "Life of the Upper Watut. New Guinea," *Geographical Journal* 94 (1):11–28.

——— 1939b. "Folk-Stories of a Stone Age People in New Guinea," *Folk-Lore* 50 (3):209–42.

——— 1940a. "Use of plants among the Kukukuku of Southeast-Central New Guinea." *Proceedings of the Sixth Pacific Science Congress 1939.* Berkeley, Calif., vol. 4:111–26.

——— 1940b. "Crafts of a Stone Age People in New Guinea," *Man* 40:11.

——— 1950. *The Technology of a Modern Stone Age People in New Guinea.* Oxford, Pitt Rivers Museum, University of Oxford, 60 pp. (Occasional Papers of Technology, 3).

——— 1978. *The Kukukuku of the Upper Watut,* ed. C. R. Hallpike. Oxford, Pitt Rivers Museum, University of Oxford, 204 pp.

Brown, Paula, 1963. "From Anarchy to Satrapy," *American Anthropologist* 65 (1): 1–15.

239

Bibliography

1967a. "The Chimbu Political System," *Anthropological Forum* 2:36–52.

1967b. "Kondom," *Journal of the Papua and New Guinea Society* 1 (2):61–71.

Brown, P. and G. Buchbinder, eds., 1976. *Man and Woman in the New Guinea Highlands.* Washington, American Anthropological Association, 108 pp. (Special publication of the American Anthropological Association, 8).

Bulmer, Ralph, 1960. "Political Aspects of the Moka Ceremonial Exchange System among the Kyaka People of the Western Highlands of New Guinea," *Oceania* 31 (1), September:1–13.

Chowning, Ann, 1973. *An Introduction to the Peoples and Cultures of Melanesia.* Menlo Park, Calif., Cummings Publishing Company:47–49.

1979. "Leadership in Melanesia," *Journal of Pacific History* 14 (1):66–83.

Codrington, R. M., 1891. *The Melanesian: Studies in Their Anthropology and Folklore.* Oxford, Oxford University Press (Clarendon Press), 419 pp.

Comaroff, J., ed., 1980. *The Meaning of Marriage Payments.* New York, Academic Press.

Craggs, E. M., Olga Kooptzoff, R. J. Walsh, 1958. "The Blood Groups of the Kukukuku," *Oceania* 29 (1):67–70.

Douglas, Bronwen, 1979. "Rank, Power, Authority: A Reassessment of Traditional Leadership in South Pacific Societies," *Journal of Pacific History* 14 (1):2–27.

Feil,D. K., 1978a. "Women and Men in the Enga Tee," *American Ethnologist* 5(2):263–79.

1978b. "Enga Women in the Tee Exchange," in "Trade and Exchange in Oceania and Australia," ed. J. Specht and J. P. White. *Mankind* 11 (3), Special Issue:220–30.

1981. "The Bride in Bridewealth: A Case from the New Guinea Highlands," *Ethnology* 20 (1), January:63–76.

Feldt, E., 1951. "Kukukuku Patrol," *Pacific Islands Monthly* 21 (9):58–59, 61, 87, 89.

Fetchko, P., 1972. "Anga Material Culture." master's thesis presented to George Washington University, Washington, D.C., 178 pp.

Fischer, H., 1959. "Ethnographica von der Kukukuku (Ost Neuguinea)," *Baessler-Archiv* (n.s.) 7:99–122.

1960. "Fadenspiele vom unteren Watut und Banir River (Ost Neuguinea)," *Baessler-Archiv* (n.s.) 8:171–214.

1961. "Spiele der Watut (Ost-Neuguinea)," *Veröffentlichungen des Museums für Völkerkunde zu Leipzig* 11:141–52.

1962. "Einige linguistische Indizien des Kulturwandels in Nordost–Neuguinea," *Sociologus* (n.s.) 14:18–36.

1963. "Watut. Notizen zur Kultur eines Melanesier–Stammes in Nordost–Neuguinea," *Kulturgeschichtliche Forchungen,* Braunschweig, 10 vols.

1968a. "Archäologische Funde und Beobachtungen von Tauri-Oberlauf Neuguineas," *Abhandlungen und Berichte des Staatlichen Museums für Völkerkunde,* Dresden, 28:73–81.

1968b. *Negwa, Eine Papua-Gruppe im Wandel.* Munich, Klaus Renner, 493pp.

Foucault, M., 1976. *Histoire de la sexualité. 1: La volonté de savoir.* Paris, Gallimard, 211 pp. (Bibliothèque des Histoires).

Franklin, K. J., 1970. "A Preliminary Report of a Language Survey of the Gulf District." Ukarumpa (Papua New Guinea), Summer Institute of Linguistics, 10 pp. map.

Gadjusek, D. C., 1964a. "Sex Avoidance and Pederasty with Juvenile Fellatio as Traditional Homosexuality among Bisexual Southwestern Kukukuku People in

Bibliography

New Guinea," *Program and Abstracts of the American Pediatric Society* (74th Annual Meeting, Seattle, June 16–18, abstract number 127, 137–38).

1964b. "Congenital Absence of the Penis in Muniri and Simbari Kukukuku People of New Guinea," *Program and Abstracts of the American Pediatric Society* (74th Annual Meeting, Seattle, June 16–18, abstract number 128, 138).

1971a. "Anga. Child Development among the Anga Peoples of East New Guinea (1957–1971)." Monograph, manuscript.

1971b. *The Anga Peoples of New Guinea. A Continuing Film Study of Child Growth, Development and Behavior among Warrior Peoples of an Archaic New Guinea Linguistic Family.*

1971c. "Sojourns with the Anga. Extracts from Travel Journals of Visits to the Anga Peoples of East New Guinea, 1957–1970." Monograph, limited edition (summary of extracts from the journals of D. Carleton Gadjusek).

Gillison, G., 1980. "Images of Nature in Gimi Thought," in *Nature, Culture and Gender,* ed. C. MacCormack and M. Strathern. Cambridge, Cambridge University Press:143–73.

Glasse, R. M. and M. J. Meggitt, eds., 1969. *Pigs, Pearshells and Women. Marriage in the New Guinea Highlands.* Englewood Cliffs, N.J., Prentice-Hall, 246 pp.

Glasse, R. M. and S. Lindenbaum, 1971. "South Fore Politics," in *Politics in New Guinea,* ed. R. M. Berndt and P. Lawrence. Perth, University of Western Australia Press:362–80.

Godelier, Maurice, in collaboration with J. Garanger, 1969a. "Land Tenure among the Baruya of New Guinea," *Journal of the Papua New Guinea Society* 3:17–23.

Godelier, Maurice, 1969b. "La monnaie de sel des Baruya de Nouvelle-Guinée," *L'Homme* 11 (2):5–37.

1972. "Le visible et l'invisible chez les Baruya de Nouvelle-Guinée," in *Langues et techniques. Nature et société,* ed. J. Thomas and L. Bernot. Paris, Klincksieck, 2:263–69.

1973. "Outils de pierre, outils d'acier chez les Baruya de Nouvelle-Guinée," *L'Homme* 13 (3):187–220.

1976. "Le sexe comme fondement ultime de l'ordre social et cosmique chez les Baruya de Nouvelle-Guinée," in *Sexualité et pouvoir,* ed. A. Verdiglione. Paris, Payot: 268–306.

1978. "La part idéelle du réel. Essai sur l'idéologie," *L'Homme* 18 (3–4):155–88.

1981. Temps mythique, temps historique, temps quotidien chez les Baruya de Nouvelle-Guinée," *Temps libre* 4:7–15.

1982. "Charivari chez les Baruya de Nouvelle-Guinée," in *Le Charivari,* ed. J. Le Goff and J. C. Schmidt. Paris, Ecole des Hautes Etudes en Sciences Sociales/ Mouton:347–51.

Godelier, M., C. D. Ollier, D. P. Drover, 1971. "Soil Knowledge amongst the Baruya of Wonenara, New Guinea," *Oceania* 42 (1), September:33–41.

Gregory, C. A., 1980. "Gifts to Men and Gifts to God: Gift Exchange and Capital Accumulation in Contemporary Papua," *Man* 15 (4), December:626–52.

C. J. Healey, 1978. "The Adaptive Significance of Systems of Ceremonial Exchange and Trade in the New Guinea Highlands," in *Mankind* ed. J. Specht and J. P. White, "Trade and Exchange in Oceania and Australia," 11 (3), special issue.

Herdt, G. H., 1977. "Folie, possession et chamanisme en Nouvelle-Guinée," *Journal de la Société des Océanistes* 33, special issue, ed. B. Juillerat: 153–67.

Bibliography

1981. *Guardians of the Flutes: Idioms of Masculinity.* New York, McGraw-Hill Book Company.

In Press. *Rituals of Manhood: Male Initiation in Papua New Guinea.* Berkeley, University of California Press.

Hogbin, Ian, ed., 1973. *Anthropology in Papua New Guinea.* Melbourne, Melbourne University Press, 243 pp.

Keesing, Roger, In press. "Introduction," in *Rituals of Manhood: Male Initiation in Papua New Guinea,* ed. G. Herdt. Berkeley, University of California Press.

Langness, L. L., 1967. "Sexual Antagonism in the New Guinea Highlands: A Bena Bena Example," *Oceania* 37 (3), March:161–77.

1971. "Bena Bena Political Organization," in *Politics in New Guinea.* ed. R. M. Berndt and P. Lawrence. Perth, University of Western Australia Press:298–316.

1974. "Ritual, Power and Male Dominance," *Ethos* 2 (3):184–232.

Lawrence, P. and M. J. Meggitt, eds., 1965. *Gods, Ghosts and Men in Melanesia. Some Religions of Australian New Guinea and the New Hebrides.* Oxford–Melbourne, Oxford University Press, 298 pp.

Leahy, M. and M. Crain., 1937 *The Land That Time Forgot. Adventures and Discoveries in New Guinea.* New York–London, Funk & Wagnalls Company. chap. 6: "The Fight with the Kukukukus": 106–26.

Lindenbaum, S., 1972. "Sorcerers, Ghosts and Polluting Women: An Analysis of Religious Beliefs and Population Control," *Ethnology* 11 (3):241–53.

1976. "A Wife Is the Hand of a Man," in *Man and Woman in the New Guinea Highlands,* ed. P. Brown and G. Buchbinder. American Anthropological Association (special publication, 8):54–62.

Linton, Ralph, 1955. *The Tree of Culture.* New York Knopf.

Lloyd, Joyce, 1965. *A Tentative Comparison of the Wantakia and Baruya Dialects.* Ukarumpa (Papua New Guinea), Summer Institute of Linguistics, 21 pp.

1968. *Baruya to English Dictionary.* Ukarumpa (Papua New Guinea), Summer Institute of Linguistics, 86 pp.

Lloyd, R. G., 1969. "Gender in a New Guinea Language: Baruya Nouns and Noun Phrases," in *Papers in New Guinea Linguistics* 10, ed. S. A. Wurm. Canberra, Australian National University:25–67.

1973. "The Angan Language Family," in *The Linguistic Situation in the Gulf District and Adjacent Areas, Papua New Guinea,* ed. K. Franklin. Canberra, Australian National University (Pacific Linguistics, series C, 26): 31–111.

1974. "Baruya Kith and Kin," in *Kinship Studies in Papua New Guinea,* ed. R. D. Shaw. Ukarumpa (Papua New Guinea), Summer Institute of Linguistics Press:97–114.

Lloyd, R. G. and J. Lloyd, 1963. *Notes on Baruya Grammar.* Ukarumpa (Papua New Guinea), Summer Institute of Linguistics, 51 pp.

1974. "Baruya," in *Legends from Papua New Guinea,* ed. K. A. McElhanon. Ukarumpa (Papua New Guinea), Summer Institute of Linguistics:54–68.

Lowman-Vayda, Cherry, 1968. "Maring Big Men," *Anthropological Forum* 2 (2), November: 199–243.

McCarthy, J. K., 1963. *Patrol into Yesterday. My New Guinea Years.* Melbourne, F. W. Cheshire, 252 pp.

MacCormack, C. and M. Strathern, eds., 1980. *Nature, Culture and Gender.* Cambridge, Cambridge University Press, 227 pp.

McKaughan, H., ed., 1973. *The Languages of the Eastern Family of the East New Guinea Highland Stock.* Seattle–London, University of Washington Press, vol. 1.

242

Bibliography

McElhanon, K. A., ed., 1974. *Legends from Papua New Guinea*. Ukarumpa (Papua New Guinea), Summer Institute of Linguistics.
Malinowski, Bronislaw, 1922. *Argonauts of the Western Pacific*. London, Routledge & Kegan Paul.
Mbaginta, O. I., 1971. "The Anga Initiations. Paper Presented to the Department of Sociology and Anthropology, Swarthmore College, Swarthmore, Pennsylvania," *Journal de la Société des Océanistes* 22 (32):285–94.
    1972. "Les esprits guérisseurs chez les Dunkwi Anga," *Journal de la Société des Océanistes* 28 (37):337–43.
    1976. "Medical Practices and Funeral Ceremony of the Dunkwi Anga," *Journal de la Société des Océanistes* 32 (53):299–305.
Meggitt, M. J., 1964. "Male-Female Relationships in the Highlands of Australian New Guinea," *American Anthropologist* 66:204–24 (special publication).
    1965. *The Lineage System of the Mae Enga of New Guinea*. Edinburgh–London, Oliver & Boyd.
    1967. "The Pattern of Leadership among the Mae-Enga of New Guinea," *Anthropological Forum* 2 (1), November:20–35.
    1976. "A Duplicity of Demons," in *Man and Woman in the New Guinea Highlands*, ed. P. Brown and G. Buchbinder. Washington, D.C., American Anthropologist Association (special publication, 8):63–85.
    1977. *Blood Is Their Argument*. Palo Alto, Calif., Mayfield Publishing Company.
Meigs, Anna S., 1978. "A Papuan Perspective on Pollution," *Man* 13 (2), June: 304–18.
Newman, Philip, 1965. *Knowing the Gururumba*. New York–London, Holt, Rinehart & Winston, 110 pp.
Newman, P. & D. Boyd, 1982. "The Making of Men: Ritual and Meaning in Awa Male Initiation," in *Rituals of Manhood: Male Initiation in Papua New Guinea*, ed. G. Herdt. Berkeley, University of California Press:239–85.
Oates, S. W. and L. Oates, 1961. *An Outline Pedagogical Grammar of Kapau, a Kukukuku Dialect of the Upper Watut*. Ukarumpa (Papua New Guinea), Summer Institute of Linguistics, 131 pp.
Rappaport, R. A., 1968. *Pigs for the Ancestors*. New Haven, Yale University Press, 311 pp.
Read, K. E., 1952. "Nama Cult of the Central Highlands," *Oceania* 23 (1):1–25.
    1954. "Cultures of the Central Highlands," *Southwestern Journal of Anthropology* 10:1–43.
    1959. "Leadership and Consensus in a New Guinea Society," *American Anthropologist* 61 (3):425–36.
    1965. *The High Valley*. London, Allen & Unwin.
Sahlins, Marshall D., 1963. "Poor Man, Rich Man, Big Man, Chief: Political Types in Melanesia and Polynesia," *Comparative Studies in Society and History* 5:285–303. Republished in *Cultures of the Pacific*, ed. Thomas Harding and Ben J. Wallace. New York, Free Press, 1970.
Salisbury, Richard, 1962. *From Stone to Steel. Economic Consequences of a Technological Change in New Guinea*. Melbourne, Melbourne University Press.
    1964. "Despotism and Australian Administration in the New Guinea Highlands," *American Anthropologist* 66, part 2 (4), special issue: "New Guinea: The Central Highlands":225–39.
Seligman, C. G., 1910. *The Melanesians of British New Guinea*. Cambridge, Cambridge University Press.
Sillitoe, Paul, 1978. "Big Men and War in New Guinea," *Man* 13 (2), June: 252–71.

Bibliography

1979. "Man-eating Women: Fears of Sexual Pollution in the Papua–New Guinea Highlands," *Journal of Polynesian Society* 1:77–97.

Simpson, C., 1953. *Adam with Arrows. Inside Aboriginal New Guinea.* Part 1: "The Killers in the Bark Cloaks":1–192. London–Sydney, Angus & Robertson, 239 pp.

Sinclair, J. P., 1961. "Patrolling in the Territory of Papua and New Guinea," *Australian Territories* 1 (4):26–33.

1966. *Behind the Ranges. Patrolling in New Guinea.* Melbourne, Melbourne University Press, 239 pp.

Strathern, Andrew, 1966. "Despots and Directors in the New Guinea Highlands," *Man* 1 (1):356–67.

1970a. "Male Initiation in the New Guinea Highlands Societies," *Ethnology* 9 (4):373–79.

1970b. "The Female and Male Spirit Cults in Mount Hagen," *Man* 5 (4), December:572–85.

1971. *The Rope of the Moka.* Cambridge, Cambridge University Press.

1979a. *Ongka. A Self Account by a New Guinea Big Man.* London, Duckworth.

1979. "Men's House, Women's House: The Efficacy of Opposition, Reversal and Pairing in the Malpa *Amb Kor* Cult," *Journal of Polynesian Society* 88 (1):37–51.

1980. "Bridewealth among the Melpa and the Wiru," in *The Meaning of Marriage Payments,* ed. J. Comaroff. New York, Academic Press: 49–66.

Strathern, Marylin, 1972. *Women in Between: Female Roles in a Male World.* London, Seminar Press.

1980. "No Nature, No Culture: the Hagen Case," in *Nature, Culture and Gender,* ed. C. MacCormack and M. Strathern. Cambridge, Cambridge University Press: 174–222.

Strauss, H. & H. Tischner, 1962. *Die Mi-Kultur der Hagenberg-Stämme.* Hamburg, De Gruyter.

Townsend, William, 1969. "Stone and Steel Tools in a New Guinea Society," *Ethnology* 8 (2):169–205.

Van Baal, J., 1963. "The Cult of the Bull-Roarer in Australia and Southern New Guinea," *Bijdragen Tot de Taal-, Land-, en Volkenkunde:102–214.*

Vicedom, G. F. & H. Tischner, 1943–1948. *Die Mbowamb.* Hamburg, Friederischsen–De Gruyter, 3 vols.

Watson, J. B., ed., 1964. "New Guinea: The Central Highlands," *American Anthropologist* 66, Bart 2 (4) (special issue).

1971. "Tairora: The Politics of Despotism in a Small Society," in *Politics in New Guinea,* ed. R. M. Berndt and P. Lawrence. Perth, University of Western Australia Press:224–75.

Weiner, Annette, 1976. *Women of Value, Men of Renown.* Austin, University of Texas Press: 25–60.

1977. "Trobriand Descent: Female/Male Domains," *Ethos* 5 (1):54–70.

1978. "The Reproductive Model in Trobriand Society," *Mankind* 11 (3):175–86.

West, Dorothy, 1966. "Grammar Analysis of Wajokeso Verbs." Ukarumpa (Papua New Guinea), Summer Institute of Linguistics, 8 pp. multigr.

1970. *Wajokeso Sentence, Paragraph and Discourse Analysis.* Ukarumpa (Papua New Guinea), 241 pp. multigr.

Zimmer, G. F. W., 1969. "When the Kukukuku Came from the Hills It Was to Kill," *Pacific Islands Monthly* 40 (11):85–93.

244

Index

abortion, 142
adultery, 44, 62, 197
affection, 158, 159
agriculture: division of labor and, 13–14; magic in production process and, 16–19; *tannaka* and, 107–9; taro gardens, 4, 5; women and, 141. *See also* clearing of forest; gardens
alliances, 173; female equivalence and, 25, 28; women's right to reject, 142
aoulatta (great warrior). *See* warriors *(aoulatta)*
authority: function of, 165; of *tannaka*, 109; of women, 161; over women, 153

Barnes, John, 164
Baruya: big man concept and, 215, 216–17; colonial rule and changes in, 191, 192, 194–8; economy of, 134–5; exchange and, 172–3; geographic location of, 1, 3; as government officials, 204; great warriors and history of, 103–5; history of, 3–4, 192; history of lineage of, 85–9; importance of *tannaka* to, 107–9; invasion of, 193–4; language of, 1–3, 4; population of, 1, 3; production of great men in clans of, 100–3; social division of labor and, 5–6; social organization of, 4, 10–11; submission to colonial rule by, 194; tribal affiliation of, 1; tribal solidarity of, 172; villages of, 4; warfare and, 166–7
big men societies: absence of initiation in, 180, 181; Baruya society and, 215, 216–17; basis of, 168–70; bride wealth and, 177–80; characteristics of big men and, 175; collapse of, 163; community ceremonies and, 171–2; cults and, 181–3, 184; exchange and, 163, 165, 169, 172–5, 177–8, 184–5, 187–8; faction around big men and, 163; great warrior concept and,
186; hunting and, 175–6; lineage and, 172, 173; male initiation and, 183–4; nature of society they live in, 176–7; power structure and, 162, 163–7; social conditions that give rise to, 168–70; social relations and, 170–1, 177; wealth and, 163, 164, 166, 171, 177, 184, 185
birth, 142, 209; babies at, 53; ceremony after, 38–9; huts for, 10; presents of game and, 15. *See also* reproduction of life
birthing huts, 10
bodily adornment, 5, 10; boy's initiation and, 35; cassowary hunter and, 128
bull-roarers. *See* musical instruments
Bulmer, Ralph, 167, 170, 172
burial, 39–40

cannibalism, 106
cassowary hunter *(kayareumala)*, 237; big men societies and comparison with, 168; changes and, 219; function and status of, 126–30; hierarchy and, 79–80, 97; independence and, 206; social hierarchies and, 137, 140. *See also* hunting
celibacy, 155
census, 203
ceremonial house, 81, 152; initiation of boys and, 33–4
child rearing, 14
Chowning, Ann, 166
civil service, 213–14
clairvoyance: owners of sacred objects and, 91, 92, 94; shaman and, 117, 119
class: analysis of Baruya society and, 236–7; exploitation of women and, 143–4, 146
clearing of forest, 107, 141; male magic and, 16–17; position of men and, 230–1. *See also* agriculture
climate, 4
Codrington, R. M., 162

245

Index

coffee-growing, 204–5, 211–12, 212–13, 222

colonial rule: Australian administrative expedition and, 1; changes in Baruya society and, 191, 192; dual hierarchy analysis and, 9; social consequences of, 194–8; submission of Baruya and, 194

Cook, E. A., 187

council system, 203, 204

craftsmanship, 132

Craig, Ruth, 187

crops: cash, 214, 215, 216; coffee, 204–5, 211–12, 212–13, 222; sweet potato, 5, 185; taro, 4, 5, 185

cults, 181–3, 184

culture, as women's invention, 72

dance, 44, 45, 50; cassowary hunter, 128

daughters: marriage and, 27; mother and, 154

death, 113, 152, 209; breaking of truce and, 161; burial and, 39–40; names of dead, 19; owners of sacred objects and, 93; shaman and, 117, 119; suicide and husband's, 159

debt, 173; exchange and, 179; wife, 28, women, 178

despotism, 110

diet, 5

disease. *See* illness

division of labor, 5, 142; access to means of production and, 11–13; apportioning fruits of, 15–16; between tribes, 12; colonial rule and, 192–3; independence and, 207; male domination and, 230–1; male magic and production process and, 16–19; sex differentiation and, 13–15

dogs, 62, 156, 157, 158

dominance of men. *See* male domination

dowry, 217

dreams (of cassowary hunters), 128

dress: covering buttocks of males, 152; initial initiation, 33, 84; manufacture of adornments and, 5

Dunlop, Ian, 136, 156

ecological environment, 4

economy: logic of production and, 134–5; missionaries and, 200–1; *tannaka* and warfare and, 107–9

education, 199, 202, 205, 219–20, 223

elderly (old age), 39–40

Elementary Structures of Kinship (Levi-Strauss), 185

equivalence: of females, 23–9, 172; of individuals, 187

exchange principle, 143; big men societies and, 163, 165, 169, 172–5, 177–8, 184–5, 187–8; debts and, 179; *kula*, 234; marriage and, 23–9; marriage and sisters, 20–2, 23–4, 35, 142, 153, 197; peace between tribes and, 196; salt as means of ritual exchange and, 209–10; sperm and, 52–5; women and, 155, 173, 196, 228, 230; women's milk and, 55–8

feces, 62

Feil, D. K., 179

female equivalence concept, 23–9, 172

female initiation, 36, 62; big men societies and absence of, 180, 181, 183; as different from male, 46–51; missionaries and, 202; old women in, 161; preserving of, 206, 209, 214; as puberty ceremony, 40–6. *See also* male initiation

female subordination: access to means of production and, 11–13; class exploitation and, 143–4, 146; dual hierarchy and, 9, 10; kinship system and, 19–23, 146–8; material conditions of existence and, 143–4; one woman equals one woman concept and, 23–30; production process and male magic and, 16–19; sex differentiation in labor process and, 13–15; sharing of fruits of labor and, 15–16; signs of, 9, 10; use of village paths and, 9, 10; violence toward women and, 148–9. *See also* male domination

females. *See* women

fire, 11; initiation and lighting of new, 34

flutes. *See* musical instruments

food: cassowary hunting and, 129; group activity and, 108; sharing of, 15–16

food gathering, 13

funerals, 39–40

Gahuka-Gama tribe, 187–8

gardens: division of labor and, 13–14; magic in production process and, 17–18; refusal of women to cultivate, 150; sweet potato, 5; symbolic nature of sugarcane and, 111; *tannaka* and, 107–9; taro, 4, 5. *See also* agriculture

gifts: at birth of child, 15; exchange of, 173; to mother, 154; older boys giving to younger, 53; to shaman, 123, 169. *See also* exchange principle

great horticulturist. *See* tannaka (great horticulturist)

great men. *See* big men societies; cassowary hunter (*kayareumala*); *kwaimatnie*-owners; salt maker (*tsaimaye*); shaman (*koulaka*);

246

tannaka (great horticulturist); warriors
(*aoulatta*)
great warriors. *See* warriors *(aoulatta)*
Guardians of the Flute (Herdt), 52

Halloway, Barry, 214
hallucinogenic mushrooms, 127
Herdt, Gilbert, 52
hierarchies: ability, 79–80; behavior on village paths and, 9, 10; existence of dual, 9,
10; hereditary, 79; independence and
changes in, 220; male domination and,
136–7
homosexual practices: after independence,
205; importance of sperm and, 52–5. *See
also* sperm
house building, 37–8, 75
houses: for sacred objects, 82; village family,
10–11
humor, 159
hunting, 15, 16, 71; big men society and,
175–6; women forbidden to do, 80. *See
also* cassowary hunter *(kayareumala)*

illness: medical aid and, 203, 207, 219; shamans and, 113, 114, 115, 116–18, 123,
141–2
incest, 155–8, 236
infanticide, 142, 150
inheritance, 107, 110; functions of shaman
and, 119–20; hierarchies and, 79; women
forbidden to inherit land and, 233
initiation. *See* female initiation; male initiation

joint-stock company, 216
jokes, 61

kayareumala. See cassowary hunter *(kayareumala)*
killing (murder), 152, 221; forbidden great
warrior during peacetime, 111; of husband, 150; myth of buried wife, 71; of ty-
rants, 110; of wife, 197, 223–4; women
preventing, 161
kinship, 172, 176, 177, 237; importance of
(in past), 184–5; marriage and, 20–3;
marriage and exchange and, 23–9; money
and wealth and, 212; social organization
and, 227, 230; subordination of women
and, 19–23, 146–8; violence against
women and, 153; vocabulary of, 19–20
kissing, 61
koulaka. See shaman *(koulaka)*
kwaimatnie-owners, 168; changes and, 219;
clairvoyance and, 91, 92, 94; contents of

sacred objects and, 82–3, 89; death and,
93; defined, 81–2; fabrication of sacred
objects and, 82; functions of, 96; house
for sacred objects and, 82; independence
and, 208–9; initiation cycle and, 84–5,
87, 88, 89, 90–3, 96; legitimizing of male
dominance and, 94; lineage as possession
of, 93; marriage and, 92–3; myth of origin
of most powerful, 95; name for sacred objects and, 83, 95; political significance of,
85–9; prestige and, 94; role as guardian of
sacred objects and, 83, 94–5; salt trade
and, 93; social heirarchies and, 137, 138;
status of, 89–90, 96; use of powers of, 84,
94; war and, 93, 101

labor (wage), 210–13. *See also* division of
labor
land: big men society and, 180–1; coffee
crop and, 213; marriage and Chimbu tribe
and, 217; war and redistribution of, 104;
women forbidden to own, 228, 233
land tenure, 5, 11, 12, 141
language: Baruya, 1–3, 4; English, 205;
translation of Bible and, 198
laws (tribal), 202–3
Lévi-Strauss, Claude, 185, 236
lineage: Baruya history and, 4; big men society and, 172, 173; money and wealth and,
212; owners of sacred objects and history
of, 85–9, 209; as possession of owners of
sacred objects, 93
Linton, Ralph, 167
livestock, 4
Lloyd, Richard, 2
love, 159
Lowman-Vayda, C., 186

magic: great warriors and, 106, 107; production process and male, 16–18; salt making
and, 132–3; sexuality and, 18–19; shaman
and, 113–14, 139. *See also* shaman *(koulaka)*; witchcraft
magic parcels. *See* *kwaimatnie*-owners
male domination: cassowary hunting and,
126, 127; class exploitation and women
and, 143–4, 146; components of, 228–9;
diverse nature of, 231–2; division of labor
and, 230–1; essence of, 229; female and
male bodies and, 232–6; foundations of,
29–30; girl's commandments at initiation
and, 43; idea of power and, 64–5; incest
and, 236; initiation and assertions of, 49–
50, 76, 137; initiation trials and, 74–5;
kinship system and, 19–23; marriage and,
75; modern changes and conflicts and,

Index

male domination (*cont.*)
  220–4; owners of sacred objects and, 94; power of women and, 66–74; reproduction of life and, 229–30, 234; resistance to, 30; sexuality and, 232–6; shamans and, 112, 125–6; signs of women's subordination and, 9, 10; social hierarchy and, 136–7; social relations and, 228, 231; violence and repression of females and, 65, 148–9, 151–8. *See also* female subordination
male initiation, 62, 63, 151, 152; big men society and, 183–4; big men society and absence of, 180, 181; cassowary hunters and, 130; colonial rule and, 191, 196, 197; compared to cults, 183; as different from female ceremonies, 46–51; dominance of males and, 49–50, 76, 137; film of, 136; financing of, 171, 184; great warriors and, 111; male life cycle and, 33–5; masters of, 79, 92, 93; missionaries and, 202; other tribes and, 187; owners of sacred objects and, 84–5, 87, 88, 89, 96; prediction of future and, 100–3; preserving of, 206, 209, 214; shaman and, 119–20, 121; sponsors of, 154; the sun and, 47, 53, 68, 87, 90; superiority of males and trials during, 74–5; symbolic use of weapons at, 106; trade and, 134; transformation of boy into man and, 90–3, 180. *See also* female initiation
males. *See* men
Malinowski, B., 162
Manga tribe, 187
Maring tribe, 186
marriage, 209, 224; buying of wives and, 217; colonial rule and, 197; coming of age and, 180; compensation principle and, 23, 24; "dog," 155; exchange principle and, 23–9; house building and, 37–8; kinship and, 20–3; love and, 159; as mechanism of male dominance, 75; outside of tribe, 217–18; owners of sacred objects and, 92–3; sister exchange and, 20–2, 23–4, 35, 142, 153, 197; women breaking promise of, 142
medicine, 203, 207, 219. *See also* illness
Meggitt, M. J., 165–6, 170, 172, 180
Melanesia, 162, 164, 165, 166, 170, 188
men: ceremony after child's birth and, 38–9; domination and body of, 232–6; humiliation of showing buttock of, 152; life cycle of, 31–40; prediction of future of, 100–3; purification rite (after he is with woman) and, 42; salt and, 12; secret source of power of, 123–6; self-persuasion and, 101; sexual relations and, 60–3; social evolution of young, 100–1; threshold to

men's house as "co-wife" to, 76; transformation of boys into, 90–3; use of weapons and tools by, 11–12
men's house, 10, 76
menstrual blood, 62; attitude of men toward, 58; female powers and, 63–4; initiation ceremony and, 40–2, 84; male domination and, 232–3, 235; myth of, 36; reproduction of life and, 58, 59, 60
menstrual huts, 10, 40–1, 58
menstruation: gifts at girl's first, 15; initiation and, 36; rejection of proposed husband at first, 27
milk (women's), 39; reproduction of life and, 55–8; sperm as origin of, 69
missionaries, 191, 194, 198–202, 205
money, 201; independence and, 210–13, 216–17, 221–2; sharing of, 16
moon, 149, 208; birth and, 53; a girl's initiation and, 47, 68; menstrual blood myth and, 36; sacred objects and, 82, 83, 91; shaman and eclipse of, 113
morality, 202
mothers, 197; boy's separation from, 31–3, 153–5; daughters and, 154
murder. *See* killing (murder)
mushrooms (hallucinogenic), 127
musical instruments: bull-roarers, 144–5; flutes, 145; magic and, 19; men's accumulation of power and, 144–5; myth of flutes, 70
myths: of buried murdered wife, 71; of flutes, 70; founding of cult of female spirit, 181–2; of healing power of shaman, 124–5; of incest, 156–8; of invention of bow and arrow, 65, 71; labor and, 13; of menstrual blood, 36; of origin of most powerful sacred object owner, 95; of sun and moon, 66–9; of tadpoles (how women existed before men), 70–1; of walled up sexual organs, 34, 72; women's power and dominance of men and, 66–74

names: clan, 85; of dead people, 19; flute's secret, 70; initiation of boys and, 33, 35, 48; initiation of girls and, 46; of pigs, 18; of sacred objects, 83, 95; of sun (secret), 90; *tchangitnia* ceremony and girl's, 37
National Assembly, 204, 218
nature and nurture concepts, 72
New Guinea, 162, 165, 166, 186, 187
New Hebrides, 164
nose piercing, 33, 40, 47, 84, 89, 152

old age (elderly), 39–40

Papua New Guinea, 204, 208, 214, 227
pigs, 62; names of, 18; number of wives and

248

Index

number of, 143; raising of, 174–5; selling
of, 222; slaughter and eating of, 15;
women and, 142
playfulness, 159
Polynesia, 164, 165
power: big men society and, 162, 163–67;
body language indications of, 65–6; male
dominance and female, 66–74; male and
female relations and idea of, 64–5; men
belittling of women and, 65; men's accu
mulation of, 144, 229; myth explaining
women's invention of bow and arrow and,
65, 71; myth of flutes and female, 70;
myth of sun and moon and female, 66–9;
myth of tadpoles and female, 70–1; of sacred objects owners, 84, 94; secret source
of male, 123–6; of woman's belly, 63
prostitution, 197

Quesnay, François, 143

Rappaport, R. A., 186
Read, Kenneth, 187
reciprocity. See exchange principle
reproduction of life: danger of women's sexual organs and, 59–60; infanticide and,
142, 150; male domination and, 229–30,
234; man's sperm and, 52–5; menstrual
blood and, 58, 59, 60; secrecy concerning
causes of, 51–2; tribal solidarity and, 172;
women's milk and, 55–7. See also birth
residence, kinship and, 20, 164
retail trade, 200–1, 214–16. See also trade
revenge, 103; lineage vengeance and, 152

sacred object owners. See kwaimatnie-
owners
Sahlins, Marshall D., 162, 163–4, 165, 166,
167, 170–1, 188
salt: 87; changes in production of 209–10;
male hierarchies and making of, 80; owners of sacred objects and, 93; position of
men and women and, 12; production of, 6;
as trade goods, 5, 12–13, 80, 176
salt maker (tsaimaye), 130–4, 140
school, 199, 202, 205, 219–20, 223
Seligman, C. G., 162
sex differentiation in labor process, 13–15
sexual act, dangers of, 18–19
sexual organs: danger of women's, 59–60;
myth of walled up, 34, 72; sugarcane as
representing male, 111
sexual relations, 60–3; salt making and, 132
sexual segregation, 11, 74–5
sexuality: magic and, 18–19; male domination and, 232–6
shaman (koulaka): behavior and influence of,

122; big men society and comparison
with, 168–9, 172; changes in practices of,
218–19; characteristics of, 112; clans renowned for, 102; curative sessions and,
115, 116; cures of, 116–18, 121, 122,
123; death and, 117; eclipses and, 113;
enemy spirits and, 113, 114; female, 80–
1, 112, 119, 120–2, 126, 140, 141–2;
function of, 112, 113, 123; hereditary features of, 119–20; hierarchy and, 79–80,
97–8, 137, 138–40; illness and, 113, 114,
115, 116–18, 123; independence and,
207–8; initiation and, 119–20, 121; kwalie
curative sessions and, 116; magic and,
113–14, 139; missionaries and, 201; murder and, 115, 237; myth of healing power
of, 124–5; payment to, 123, 169; process
of becoming, 118–21, 123–4; sacred objects and, 112–13; secret of male power
and, 123–6; social hierarchies and, 79–
80, 97–8, 137, 138–40; spirit standing
sentry during sleep and, 115–16; threshold
to men's house and, 76; witchcraft and,
114–15
sickness. See illness
Sinclair, James, 1, 5, 131, 192, 194
sisters: man's attitude toward, 154–5; marriage and exchange of, 20–2, 23–4, 35,
142, 153, 197
Smith, Adam, 143
social class. See class
social hierarchies. See hierarchies
social relations: Baruya tribal, 4; big men society and, 170–1, 177; hunting and male
and female, 175; male domination and,
228, 231; village social organization and,
4, 10–11
sodomy, 54
Solomon Islands, 164
songs, 44; concerning sperm, 159–60; about
great warriors, 106–7; of love, 159
sons, 197; separation from mother and, 31–
3, 153–5
sperm, 38, 39, 62, 148, 150; homosexuality
and, 52–5; initiation of girls and, 43–4;
male domination and, 232; as origin of
women's milk, 57, 69; songs concerning,
159–60; tchangitnia ceremony and, 36–7
status: ambivalent nature of female, 153; of
cassowary hunter, 120; choice in marriage
and wife's, 185; of female shaman, 122;
of great warriors, 105; initiation of boys
and, 48; ornaments in nose and, 152; of
sacred objects owners, 89–90, 96; of salt
maker, 133; of women under colonial rule,
196–7
sterility, 148

Index

Strathern, A., 178–9, 181
Strathern, M., 178–9
Strauss, H., 181
sugarcane, 111
suicide, 195; as common occurrence, 150–1;
  after death of husband, 159; during initiation, 36; taken up arms to avenge and, 34;
  of woman setting fire to ceremonial house,
  152
sun, 149, 157, 208; birth and, 53; boy's initiation and, 47, 68, 87, 90; family house
  and, 11; lighting fire with flints and, 34;
  menstrual blood myth, 36; power of shaman and, 124, 125; predicting boy's future
  and, 102; reproduction of life and, 234;
  sacred objects and, 82, 83, 91, 95, 96;
  shaman and eclipse of, 113

tannaka (great horticulturist), 107–9, 140,
  237; resemblence to big men and, 169
Tapatche tribe, 193–4
Tischner, H., 181
tools: Baruya use of, 4–5; colonial rule and
  steel, 192–3; importance of, 133; use of
  (by men and women), 11–12; women and,
  141, 221; women's work and, 15
trade: coffee-growing, 204–5, 211–12, 212–
  13, 222; salt and, 5, 12–13, 80, 93, 133,
  176. *See also* retail trade
trade stores, 200–1, 214–16
tsaimaye. See salt maker *(tsaimaye)*

Vayda, A., 186
Venus, 124, 125, 208
Vicedom, G. F., 181
villages: colonial administration and, 203;
  described, 4; independence and, 204; social organization and, 10–11; use of paths
  in, 9, 10
violence, 30, 195, 198; at boy's initiation,
  53; as customary process, 104; differentiation of sexes and, 72; protection of women
  since independence and, 221; repression of
  women and, 151–8; against women, 65,
  148–9
Virgin Woman cult, 182
Von Clausewitz, Carl, 170

wage labor, 210–13
warfare, 88, 134, 173, 186; Baruya and,
  166–7; deciding to go into, 108, 111–12;
  forbidden under colonial rule, 195–6;

great warriors and, 103–5, 107–8, 111–12;
  owners of sacred objects and, 93, 101;
  shamans and, 113; suspension of, 111;
  tannaka and, 108; trade and, 12–13
warriors *(aoulatta)*, 161, 237; Australian administration and, 9; big men society and,
  174, 186; big men society and comparison
  with, 168, 170, 172; blood enemy and,
  58–9; changes in, 218; despotism and,
  109–10; educated men taking place of,
  205; female, 80; hierarchy and, 79–80,
  97; inheritance and, 107, 110; initiation
  and, 111; land ownership and, 107; in
  1981, 10; in 1967, 9; power of, 106, 107;
  prestige of, 107; role and status of, 105; as
  single combatant, 105, 106; tadpole myth
  and, 71; tribe and, 102; warfare and, 103–
  5, 107–8, 111–12
wealth: big men society and, 163, 164, 166,
  171, 177, 184, 185; brides and, 177–80,
  217; great men concept and, 168–9; independence and, 210, 216, 217
weapons, 9, 87, 88; initiation and symbolic
  use of, 106; manufacture and use of, 11–
  12; myth of invention of bow and arrow,
  65, 71; of Sinclair's soldiers, 192
Weiner, Annette, 234
witchcraft, 114–15. *See also* magic
wives: bride wealth and, 177–80; buying of,
  217; ceremony on being separated from
  husband, 42; debt transfer and, 28; garden
  plot choice of, 17; killing of husband by,
  150; murder of, 197, 223–4; myth of buried murdered, 71; number of pigs and
  number of, 143; rancor between multiple,
  149; of shaman, 119, 123; status of, 185;
  of *tannaka*, 108, 140; threshold to men's
  house as "co-wife," 76. *See also* marriage
women: cassowary hunter choice and, 130;
  child rearing and, 14; coffee growing and,
  213; colonial rule and, 196–7; council
  and, 203; cultural changes and, 211, 213;
  danger of sexual organs of, 59–60; as dangerous individuals, 235; economic role of,
  180; eating of cassowary by, 129; forbidden to hit males and, 152; forms of resistance and, 149–51; infanticide and, 142,
  150; initiation of boys and, 34; legal protection of, 221, 222; life cycle of, 40–6;
  male domination and body of, 232–6; material conditions and, 143–4; money and,
  210, 222; powers and ambivalence of, 63–
  76; salt and, 12; segregation of, 11, 74–5;
  sexual relations and, 60–3; as shamans,
  80–1, 112, 119, 120–2, 126, 140, 141–2;

tchangitnia ceremonies and, 36–7; use of tools by, 11–12; as warriors, 80. *See also* female initiation; female subordination; male domination
women's milk. *See* milk (women's)

worianie (wretched man), 170

Yopenie tribe, 193–4
Youndouye tribe, 13, 134, 195
Yuwarrounatche tribe, 194, 215

CAMBRIDGE STUDIES IN SOCIAL ANTHROPOLOGY

Editor: Jack Goody

1   The Political Organisation of Unyamwezi
    R. G. ABRAMS
2. Buddhism and the Spirit Cults in North-East Thailand*
    S. J. TAMBIAH
3. Kalahari Village Politics: An African Democracy
    ADAM KUPER
4. The Rope of Moka: Big-Men and Ceremonial Exchange in Mount Hagen, New Guinea*
    ANDREW STRATHERN
5. The Majangir: Ecology and Society of a Southwest Ethiopian People
    JACK STAUDER
6. Buddhist Monk, Buddhist Layman: A Study of Urban Monastic Organisation in Central Thailand
    JANE BUNNAG
7. Contexts of Kinship: An Essay in the Family Sociology of the Gonja of Northern Ghana
    ESTHER N. GOODY
8. Marriage among a Matrilineal Elite: A Family Study of Ghanaian Senior Civil Servants
    CHRISTINE OPPONG
9. Elite Politics in Rural India: Political Stratification and Political Alliances in Western Maharashtra
    ANTHONY T. CARTER
10. Women and Property in Morocco: Their Changing Relation to the Process of Social Stratification in the Middle Atlas
    VANESSA MAHER
11. Rethinking Symbolism*
    DAN SPERBER, *translated by Alice L. Morton*
12. Resources and Population: A Study of the Gurungs of Nepal
    ALAN MACFARLANE
13. Mediterranean Family Structures
    Edited by J. G. PERISTIANY
14. Spirits of Protest: Spirit-Mediums and the Articulation of Consensus among the Zezuru of Southern Rhodesia (Zimbabwe)
    PETER FRY
15. World Conqueror and World Renouncer: A Study of Buddhism and Polity in Thailand against a Historical Background*
    S. J. TAMBIAH
16. Outline of a Theory of Practice*
    PIERRE BOURDIEU, *translated by Richard Nice*
17. Production and Reproduction: A Comparative Study of the Domestic Domain*
    JACK GOODY
18. Perspectives in Marxist Anthropology*
    MAURICE GODELIER, *translated by Robert Brain*

253

Cambridge Studies in Social Anthropology

19. The Fate of Shechem, or the Politics of Sex: Essays in the Anthropology of the Mediterranean
    JULIAN PITT-RIVERS
20. People of the Zongo: The Transformation of Ethnic Identities in Ghana
    ENID SCHILDKROUT
21. Casting out Anger: Religion among the Taita of Kenya
    GRACE HARRIS
22. Rituals of the Kandyan State
    H. L. SENEVIRATNE
23. Australian Kin Classification
    HAROLD W. SCHEFFLER
24. The Palm and the Pleiades: Initiation and Cosmology in Northwest Amazonia
    STEPHEN HUGH-JONES
25. Nomads of South Siberia: The Pastoral Economies of Tuva
    S. I. VAINSHTEIN, translated by Michael Colenso
26. From the Milk River: Spatial and Temporal Processes in Northwest Amazonia
    CHRISTINE HUGH-JONES
27. Day of Shining Red: An Essay on Understanding Ritual
    GILBERT LEWIS
28. Hunters, Pastoralists and Ranchers: Reindeer Economies and their Transformations
    TIM INGOLD
29. The Wood-Carvers of Hong Kong: Craft Production in the World Capitalist Periphery
    EUGENE COOPER
30. Minangkabau Social Formations: Indonesian Peasants and the World Economy
    JOEL S. KAHN
31. Patrons and Partisans: A Study of Politics in Two Southern Italian Comuni
    CAROLINE WHITE
32. Muslim Society*
    ERNEST GELLNER
33. Why Marry Her? Society and Symbolic Structures
    LUC DE HEUSCH, translated by Janet Lloyd
34. Chinese Ritual and Politics
    EMILY MARTIN AHERN
35. Parenthood and Social Reproduction: Fostering and Occupational Roles in West Africa
    ESTHER N. GOODY
36. Dravidian Kinship
    THOMAS R. TRAUTMANN
37. The Anthropological Circle: Symbol, Function, History*
    MARC AUGE, translated by Martin Thom
38. Rural Society in Southeast India
    KATHLEEN GOUGH
39. The Fish People: Linguistic Exogamy and Tukanoan Identity in Northwest Amazonia
    JEAN E. JACKSON
40. Karl Marx Collective: Economy, Society and Religion in a Siberian Collective Farm*
    CAROLINE HUMPHREY

Cambridge Studies in Social Anthropology

41. Ecology and Exchange in the Andes
   Edited by DAVID LEHMANN
42. Traders without Trade: Responses to Trade in two Dyula Communities
   ROBERT LAUNAY
43. The Political Economy of West African Agriculture*
   KEITH HART
44. Nomads and the Outside World
   A. M. KHAZANOV, *translated by Julia Crookenden*
45. Actions, Norms and Representations: Foundations of Anthropological Inquiry*
   LADISLAV HOLY *and* MILAN STUCHLIK
46. Structural Models in Anthropology*
   PER HAGE *and* FRANK HARARY
47. Servants of the Goddess: The Priests of a South Indian Temple
   C. J. FULLER
48. Oedipus and Job in West African Religion*
   MEYER FORTES *with an essay by* ROBIN HORTON
49. The Buddhist Saints of the Forest and the Cult of Amulets: A Study in Charisma, Hagiography, Sectarianism, and Millenial Buddhism
   S. J. TAMBIAH
50. Kinship and Marriage: An Anthropological Perspective†
   ROBIN FOX
51. Individual and Society in Guiana: A Comparative Study of Amerindian Social Organization*
   PETER RIVIERE
52. People and the State: An Anthropology of Planned Development*
   A. F. ROBERTSON
53. Inequality among Brothers: Class and Kinship in South China
   RUBIE S. WATSON
54. On Anthropological Knowledge*
   DAN SPERBER
55. Tales of the Yanomami: Daily Life in the Venezualan Forest
   JACQUES LIZOT, *translated by Ernest Simon*

*Also available as a paperback
†Paperback available in USA only